RESTORING
THE
BALANCE

RICHARD N. HAASS
MARTIN INDYK

STEPHEN BIDDLE
MICHAEL E. O'HANLON
KENNETH M. POLLACK

SUZANNE MALONEY
RAY TAKEYH

COUNCIL ON FOREIGN RELATIONS

SABAN CENTER FOR MIDDLE EAST POLICY
AT BROOKINGS

RESTORING
THE
BALANCE
A MIDDLE EAST STRATEGY
FOR THE NEXT PRESIDENT

BRUCE RIEDEL
GARY SAMORE

STEVEN A. COOK
SHIBLEY TELHAMI

ISOBEL COLEMAN
TAMARA COFMAN WITTES

DANIEL BYMAN
STEVEN SIMON

BROOKINGS INSTITUTION PRESS
Washington, D.C.

Library of Congress Cataloging in Publication data
Restoring the balance : a Middle East strategy for the next president / principal authors, Richard N. Haass and Martin Indyk ; contributors, Stephen Biddle ... [et al.]
    p.   cm.
  Includes bibliographical references and index.
  Summary: "Experts from the Brookings Saban Center and Council on Foreign Relations propose a new, nonpartisan strategy drawing on the lessons of past failures to address short-term and long-term challenges to U.S. interests. Issues and policy recommendations cover the Arab-Israeli conflict, counterterrorism, Iran, Iraq, political and economic development, and nuclear proliferation"—Provided by publisher.
  ISBN 978-0-8157-3869-5 (pbk. : alk. paper)
  1. United States—Foreign relations—Middle East. 2. Middle East—Foreign relations—United States. I. Haass, Richard. II. Indyk, Martin. III. Biddle, Stephen D. IV. Title.
  JZ1480.A55R47 2008
  327.73056—dc22   2008044173

9 8 7 6 5 4 3 2 1

The paper used in this publication meets minimum requirements of the American National Standard for Information Sciences—Permanence of Paper for Printed Library Materials: ANSI Z39.48-1992.

Typeset in Sabon with Frutiger display

Composition by Pete Lindeman
Arlington, Virginia

Printed by R. R. Donnelley
Harrisonburg, Virginia

Contents

Foreword

EVERY NEW PRESIDENT inherits a host of policy challenges. But the president elected in November 2008 will be confronted by a Middle East demanding his attention just as the global recession will constrain the resources and time he can devote to it. Iran's pursuit of nuclear capabilities and regional dominance, a strained U.S. military tied down in Iraq, a war that is going badly in Afghanistan, a stagnant Arab-Israeli peace process, hostility toward U.S. involvement in the region—all create a dangerous, complicated, and urgent policy environment.

Recognizing that new approaches based on in-depth research and careful consideration of alternative options would be essential, but that the new president and his team would have little time to develop them, the Saban Center at Brookings and the Council on Foreign Relations decided to join forces to tackle this problem.

Researching and debating difficult issues in a nonpartisan context and formulating policy recommendations is the central mission of both the Council on Foreign Relations and the Brookings Institution. We house leading scholars and policy experts and provide them with the ability to think independently about the greatest challenges facing the United States and develop new ideas for overcoming them. The two organizations usually do this separately from one another. However, the level of the challenges facing the next president called for a unique partnership and approach. For the first time in the history of our two institutions, we combined the talent and expertise of fifteen of our senior fellows in Middle East studies.

The Saban Center at Brookings–Council on Foreign Relations project, Toward a New U.S.–Middle East Strategy, was launched in July 2007. We divided our experts into small teams, each comprising two (and in one case three) policy researchers, and asked them to focus on the six most pressing Middle East challenges for the next president: Iran, Iraq, the Arab-Israeli conflict, proliferation, terrorism, and political and economic development. Based on each team's conclusions and recommendations, an overall strategy paper was then drafted.

We wanted to avoid the kind of reports that tend to produce lowest-common-denominator recommendations. Instead, we asked the teams to write policy planning papers that would reflect their own, independent judgments and then subjected their ideas to the scrutiny of a diverse, bipartisan board of advisors, made up of former senior government officials as well as leaders in the public and private sectors.

In addition, each team conducted in-depth field research, interviewing key Middle East policymakers and spending time in the region on fact-finding trips. The teams met on three occasions with our board of advisors, including a retreat in June 2008 at the Pocantico Conference Center of the Rockefeller Brothers Fund, to review and critique early drafts of the papers. The papers were then redrafted and scrutinized again by the board and other project members.

We would like to express our deep appreciation to the members of the board of advisors for their support of this project and for the amount of time and intellectual energy they dedicated to it. The resulting papers are much better for their detailed scrutiny and input. That said, the analysis and policy recommendations in each paper represent the views of their particular authors alone. No member of the board of advisors was asked to endorse any of the papers presented here, nor did the Rockefeller Brothers Fund take a position on them. In addition, neither the Council on Foreign Relations nor the Brookings Institution endorses the views presented in any of the papers.

Martin Indyk, director of the Saban Center, and Gary Samore, director of studies at the Council on Foreign Relations, managed the project. They depended on the unflagging efforts of Ariel Kastner at the Saban Center and Ian Mitch and Katie Ivanick at the Council on Foreign Relations, who coordinated the project and edited the manuscripts. At Brookings Institution Press, Janet Walker oversaw the editing process with much patience and guidance, and Martha Gottron and Anthony Nathe carefully copyedited the chapters. We owe them all heartfelt thanks for the time and energy they poured into it. We are grateful to those who contributed generously to the project, including the Rockefeller Brothers Fund, which also granted us use of their magnificent Pocantico Conference Center.

This book is the culmination of an eighteen-month effort. Because our goal for this project was to present a series of thoughtful recommendations for the next president—Democrat or Republican—we decided early on that we would publish the book after the U.S. presidential election, when policy, not politics, would be Washington's focus. Election Day 2008 marked the end of the longest campaign in American history, but it also marked the beginning of a short transition period. In a mere eleven weeks, the president-elect must shift from campaigning to governing, mapping out an agenda to advance American interests at home and abroad. We have tried to assist in that process by developing innovative, thoroughly researched ideas for some of the most complicated and pressing issues he will face. *Restoring the Balance: A Middle East Strategy for the Next President* is the result. We hope that its ideas and policy recommendations will provide a valuable tool for the new president and his administration as well as for Congress, the media, other governments and international organizations, and individuals in the United States and elsewhere interested in the Middle East.

RICHARD N. HAASS
President, The Council on Foreign Relations

STROBE TALBOTT
President, The Brookings Institution

RESTORING
THE
BALANCE

RICHARD N. HAASS

MARTIN INDYK

1

A Time for Diplomatic Renewal
Toward a New U.S. Strategy in the Middle East

THE FORTY-FOURTH PRESIDENT will face a series of critical, complex, and interrelated challenges in the Middle East that will demand his immediate attention: an Iran apparently intent on approaching or crossing the nuclear threshold as quickly as possible; a fragile situation in Iraq that is straining the U.S. military; weak governments in Lebanon and Palestine under challenge from stronger Hezbollah and Hamas militant organizations; a faltering Israeli-Palestinian peace process; and American influence diluted by a severely damaged reputation. The president will need to initiate multiple policies to address all these challenges but will quickly discover that time is working against him.

The next president will have to reprioritize and reorient U.S. policy toward the Middle East. For the past six years that policy has been dominated by Iraq. This need not, and should not, continue to be the case. The next president can gradually reduce the U.S. troop presence and combat role in Iraq, increasingly shifting responsibility to Iraqi forces. But because the situation is still fragile there, the drawdown should be done carefully and not so quickly or arbitrarily that it risks contributing to the undoing of progress achieved at great cost over the past two years.

Instability generated by a too rapid withdrawal could distract the next president from the other priority initiatives he will need to take and create opportunities in Iraq for Iran and al Qaeda to exploit. However, a too slow withdrawal would leave American forces tied down in Iraq and unavailable for other priority tasks, including backing his diplomacy vis-à-vis Iran in particular with the credible threat of force. He will need to strike a balance.

In no way should this call for retrenchment in Iraq be interpreted as a recommendation for a more general American pullback from the region. The greater Middle East will remain vital to the United States for decades to come given its geostrategic location, its energy and financial resources, the U.S. commitment to Israel, and the possibility both for terrorism to emanate from the region and for nuclear materials and weapons to spread there. Reduced American involvement will jeopardize all these interests.

Instead, the next president's principal focus will need to be on Iran, because the clock is ticking on its nuclear program. He should offer direct official engagement with the Iranian government, without preconditions, along with other incentives to attempt to prevent Iran from developing a capacity to produce substantial amounts of nuclear weapons-grade fuel in a short amount of time. Simultaneously, he will need to concert an international effort to impose harsher sanctions on Iran if it rejects an outcome the United States and others can accept. The objective is simple to describe but will be difficult to achieve: to generate a suspension of Iran's enrichment program before it builds the capacity to enrich enough uranium to provide it with this "breakout" capability.

Preventive military action, by either the United States or Israel, in the event that this diplomatic initiative fails, appears unattractive given its risks and costs. However, the option should be examined closely, both for what it could accomplish and given the dangers of living with a near or actual Iranian nuclear weapons capability. Because of Israel's vulnerability to an Iranian nuclear first strike, its fuse will necessarily be shorter than America's. And negotiations—as well as stepped-up sanctions—will inevitably take time to work. To increase Israel's tolerance for a more drawn-out diplomatic engagement, the next president should bolster Israel's deterrent capabilities by providing a nuclear guarantee and an enhanced antiballistic missile defense capability.

A second emphasis should be on promoting peace agreements between Israel and its Arab neighbors, in particular Syria, which is currently allied with Iran and its Hezbollah and Hamas proxies. The Syrian government is in a position to fulfill a peace agreement, and the differences between the parties appear to be bridgeable. Moreover, the potential for a strategic realignment would benefit the effort to weaken Iran's influence in the sensitive core of the region, reduce external support for both Hezbollah and Hamas, and improve prospects for stability in Lebanon. In other words, it would give the next president strategic leverage on Iran at the same time as he would be offering its leaders a constructive way out of their security dilemma.

The next president should also make a serious effort from the outset to promote progress between Israel and the Palestinians. Here, though, factors related to timing appear contradictory. There is an urgent need for a diplomatic effort to achieve a final peace agreement based on a two-state solution while it is still feasible. Yet deep divisions within the Palestinian leadership (not to mention divisions within Israel's body politic), and the Palestinian Authority's questionable ability to control territory from which Israel would withdraw, sharply reduce prospects for a sustainable peace agreement no matter what the outside effort. This dilemma does not argue for neglect, which is sure to be malign, but it does call for a devoted effort to create the conditions on the ground for more ambitious diplomacy to succeed.

What these Iranian and Arab-Israeli initiatives have in common is a renewed emphasis on diplomacy as a tool of American foreign policy—certainly more than has been the norm over the past eight years. The United States will want the backing of the world's other powers—Russia, China, and Europe—and the partnership of America's regional allies, including Israel, Egypt, Saudi Arabia, and Turkey. Consulting and concerting with all of these actors will also take time and patience.

Realities on the ground also call for a new approach to the promotion of reform in the region. Authoritarian regimes that are repressive and largely unresponsive to legitimate popular needs have set in motion a dynamic in which opposition has gathered in the mosque. Such polarization needs to be avoided. The answer is not early elections, especially not when parties with militias contest them, but rather a gradual, evolutionary process of democratization that emphasizes the building of civil society, the opening of political space, and the strengthening of independent institutions (including political parties, the media, and the judiciary). The parallel encouragement of a market economy can buttress this effort.

Finally, the next president should understand that his policy toward the greater Middle East will be severely handicapped as long as the United States remains heavily dependent on the region's hydrocarbons. U.S. consumption is helping to fuel Iran's bid to assert its influence throughout the region; U.S. dependence also leaves this country highly vulnerable to untoward developments within the region, whether it is the ability of Iraq's sects to get along or the ability of the Saudi government to maintain stability. The goal of the United States should be to sustain its involvement in the region but to reduce its vulnerability to it. Energy policy is foreign policy.

Some of these initiatives will take considerable time to ripen and bear fruit (rebuilding Palestinian capabilities, promoting political development in Arab countries, increasing energy security), whereas it may be possible or necessary to realize others relatively early on (assembling a new diplomatic offer to Iran backed by the threat of harsher sanctions, drawing down troops in Iraq, promoting Israeli-Syrian peace). At a minimum the next president will need to remain conscious of the interrelated nature of regional dynamics and try to synchronize the various branches of his Middle Eastern strategy, buying time when there is no alternative while quickly exploiting opportunities or dealing with necessities when they arise.

DIMINISHED INFLUENCE AND STATURE

Since the collapse of the Soviet Union in 1991, the United States has been the dominant power in the Middle East. But much has been done to diminish its influence there, ranging from the failure to achieve a comprehensive settlement of the Arab-Israeli conflict at the end of the Clinton administration to the Bush administration's costly war in Iraq, its unsuccessful attempt to impose democracy on Arab authoritarian regimes, and its willful disregard of the Palestinian issue for most of its two terms. For almost a decade, the United States has done little to address the region's principal conflicts and concerns and instead has opened the way for Iran to make a bid for hegemony in the Arab heartland. In the process, the United States has developed a reputation for arrogance and double standards.

This reduced regional influence is reinforced by a broader decline in the relative position of the United States in the world, as reflected in the falling value of the dollar; the shift of vast wealth to oil-exporting nations, which has emboldened Russia, Iran, and Venezuela; and the rise of China and India.[1] The net effect is an impression left by the Bush administration that the United States is unable to deliver and that when it tries, it tends to make matters worse. In so doing, the administration has raised serious doubts about American competence and intentions. Some of Washington's most important relationships have been severely strained; the Middle East is deeply unsettled.

Nevertheless, the vast majority of states in the region still look to the United States as the ultimate guarantor of their security and the power that should be most able to help them achieve their objectives. In addition, the people there still admire and identify with American values. Ironically, as the region has grown more unstable, in large part because of U.S. missteps, the need for American leadership has grown. That is particularly the case when it comes to meeting the Iranian challenge.

The Bush administration's mishandling of Iraq and Afghanistan opened the door to an Iranian bid for regional primacy by removing Tehran's most threatening enemies. Without these adversaries, Iran has been able to spread its influence into Iraq and, through its alliance with Syria, into Lebanon and the Palestinian arena as well. The Iranian challenge to the American-backed regional order is multifaceted. On one level, Arab governments see a historic replay of Persian efforts to dominate their region. Sunni regimes (particularly Saudi Arabia, Egypt, and Jordan, but also Turkey) see the threat of newly empowered Shi'i communities in Iraq and Lebanon—backed by Iran—setting an example for long-suppressed Shi'ah in other sensitive parts of the Sunni Arab world (such as Saudi Arabia and Bahrain). Similarly, moderate but weak governments in Lebanon and the West Bank—the most susceptible arenas for regional competition—find themselves under assault by extremist parties wielding Iranian-trained and equipped militias and terrorist cadres that are more powerful than the governments' own security services. In addition, Israel, Turkey, and Arab regional powers see Iran embarked on an aggressive effort to acquire a nuclear option that the international community seems powerless to stop. Iran has provided good reason for Israel in particular to fear an existential threat from an Iranian nuclear weapons capability.

Finally, in the war of ideas, Iran and its Hezbollah and Hamas proxies have been able to argue effectively that "our way works." For many frustrated Palestinians and others in the Arab world, violence, terrorism, and defiance of the United States are now seen as a better way to achieve dignity, justice, and liberation of territory than following their own leaders who, the Iranians and their proxies claim, cower under American protection and lie down with "the Zionist enemy."[2]

Iran's challenge to the existing order is so threatening that it has compelled many of the other actors in the region to begin to work together and to look to the United States to help them in countering it. That even applies to Syria, which is allied with Iran but has now launched peace negotiations with Israel in part as a way to improve its relations with Washington, and in part to avoid being stuck on the Shi'i side of the Sunni-Shi'ah divide.[3] It also applies to Saudi Arabia and Egypt, which have grown deeply disillusioned with Bush's leadership but would much prefer an effective American role. That means considerable American influence can be recouped if the next president is able to show that "America's way works," that is, that moderation, reconciliation, negotiation, political and economic reform, peaceful settlement of conflict, and the upholding of international norms can better meet the needs of the people of this troubled region than the alternative offered by Iran and its proxies.

Even though opportunity is there, some may advise the next president that the effort is not worth it, that the Bush administration paid too much attention and invested too much American blood and treasure in a ill-advised effort to transform the Middle East. They may argue that it would be better for the new president to focus on the many other priority issues on his foreign policy agenda, from global warming and strengthening the nonproliferation regime to managing relations with China, India, and Russia, not to mention the global financial crisis and the economic recession at home. The problem with this approach is that it seriously underestimates the Middle East's ability to force itself onto the president's agenda and undermine America's capacity to influence global events.

Put simply, what happens in the Middle East will not stay in the Middle East. The central reason is that the dark side of globalization, whether it is terrorism, high oil prices, or proliferation of weapons of mass destruction, finds its inspiration in the Middle East. That means the United States cannot insulate itself from the negative impact of a failure to manage the region effectively; this holds true for other global powers as well.[4] The effective management of globalization is therefore going to require the effective management of the Middle East. The good news is that other global powers have some shared interest in this endeavor.

SHAPING THE STRATEGIC CONTEXT

The president will need to put greater emphasis on diplomatic tools to take advantage of the willingness of regional and global powers to work with the United States. The return to diplomacy was already noticeable in the last years of the Bush administration when American diplomats participated in a series of multilateral efforts to engage rogue states like Iran and North Korea, rebuild trans-Atlantic relationships frayed by the Iraq War, and even promote Israeli-Palestinian peace. But for American diplomacy to be effective, the next president's diplomats will need more than the deft application of leverage and a serious commitment to working with others. A series of steps will be necessary to reshape the strategic context in a way that influences the calculations of all the actors involved in the Middle East.

Reprioritize Iraq

For the last six years, Iraq has dominated America's Middle East agenda, requiring a huge commitment of troops, funds, and presidential attention. Whatever its long-term impact, the surge—together with the willingness of Sunni and Shi'i leaders to establish order in and police their own communities—has created an opening for the next president to reduce Iraq's centrality in America's approach to the region.

The project's Iraq experts, Stephen Biddle, Michael O'Hanlon, and Kenneth Pollack, argue persuasively in the next chapter that ethnosectarian violence has been effectively suppressed and that al Qaeda in Iraq has been radically weakened. But the situation remains fragile, with a host of second-order tasks (including policing the many local cease-fires, ensuring orderly regional and national elections, overseeing the absorption of the Sons of Iraq into the government's security forces, ensuring the equitable sharing of oil revenues, and enabling the safe return of some 4.7 million internally displaced Iraqis and refugees) requiring significant U.S. combat and support forces through 2009. By mid-2010, however, they believe that the next president will be able to begin to reduce significantly overall forces, perhaps to half their levels before the surge.

This process of troop drawdown will enable the next president to make clear to Iraq's leaders and to its neighbors that he is shifting responsibility to their shoulders. At the same time, it will demonstrate to the American people that wartime involvement in Iraq is coming to an end. Implemented gradually, a U.S. drawdown should not raise questions as to American reliability in light of all the United States has done to bolster Iraq's stability over the past two years. On the political front, the highest priority will be to ensure that the reconciliation between Iraq's Sunni leaders and tribal sheiks and the Shi'i-led government is consolidated. On the diplomatic front, as this process gains traction, the next president will need to persuade Iraq's Sunni Arab neighbors to work with Baghdad's Shi'i-led government, providing it with an alternative to increased dependence on Iran as it becomes less dependent on Washington.

Focus on Iran

By the time the next president enters the Oval Office, the hands of Iran's nuclear clock will be approaching midnight. If Iran's enrichment program proceeds at the current pace, by the end of the new administration's first year, or shortly thereafter, Iran will probably have stockpiled enough low-enriched uranium to have the ability to produce within several months enough weapons-grade uranium for at least one nuclear bomb. As Bruce Riedel and Gary Samore write in their chapter on proliferation, Iran will still likely be another two to three years away from a more credible nuclear weapons capability, in terms of stockpiling enough material for several nuclear bombs. Nevertheless, once it is capable of producing large amounts of weapons-grade fuel, Iran will have for all intents and purposes reached the nuclear threshold and forced all its neighbors, as well as the United States, to rethink their security calculations.

Israel, which has maintained a nuclear monopoly in the region through preventive military strikes on Iraq and Syria, will be sorely tempted to take preventive military action again before Iran has developed a full-fledged weapons capability. That is especially so because Iran's leaders have gone out of their way to declare their intention of "wiping Israel off the map." If Israel strikes, Iranian retaliation could spark a war in Lebanon, closure of the Straits of Hormuz (through which oil tankers exit the Persian Gulf), dramatic increases in the price of oil, and attacks on American forces in Iraq and Afghanistan. If Israel does not strike, Iran and Israel will be on hair triggers, with a high potential for miscalculation. Meanwhile, Egypt, Saudi Arabia, and Turkey—the region's other powers—will likely accelerate their own nuclear programs, fueling a Middle Eastern nuclear arms race. Brandishing a nuclear deterrent, Iran may feel emboldened to step up its efforts at subversion across the region. Tehran would also have the potential to provide nuclear materials (the core of a "dirty bomb") or even a crude fission device to one of the terrorist organizations that it supports.

Rebuild an International Consensus

In this context, it will be important for the next president to attempt to reach an early understanding with the world's other leading powers about the importance of capping Iran's nuclear advance. Unfortunately, recruiting Russia has become an even greater challenge since its use of force in Georgia in August 2008. Moscow could revert to its cold war approach of backing destabilizing actors in the Middle East (such as Iran, Syria, and Hezbollah) with supplies of offensive weapons systems and diplomatic protection in the UN Security Council. Preventing Russia from playing this spoiler role may not in the end be possible, but it is at least worth testing whether Moscow is willing to join a constructive partnership in the Middle East. It may even be possible that Russia's leaders will welcome that invitation as a way of overcoming the negative repercussions of their Georgian adventure.

Russia is already a member of the Quartet that concerts policy to promote Middle Eastern peace.[5] The question is whether it will be willing to join stepped-up Western efforts to block Iran's acquisition of nuclear weapons. Russia will surely want to avoid American recourse to action outside the UN Security Council lest it find itself sidelined, as was the case in the Balkans. But Russian leaders need to know that if they do not cooperate, then they run the high risk that the United States will act with Europe against Iran and leave Russia and the Security Council behind.

Implicit in the effort to co-opt Russia is the need for it to support what the United States regards as its vital interests in the Middle East, which will inevitably generate the Russian expectation of a trade-off on issues that Moscow considers vital. The next president will need to look at the totality of the relationship and decide among competing priorities, something the Bush administration was unwilling to do. While he cannot trade away treaty commitments to eastern European states, nor sacrifice the independence of Georgia or Ukraine, the next president does have a number of incentive cards he can play to secure increased Russian buy-in on Iran: Russian accession to the World Trade Organization; ballistic missile defense installations in Europe (the need for which diminishes if an Iranian nuclear threat is neutralized through U.S.-Russian cooperation); and a number of financially lucrative arrangements for Moscow, from a Russian nuclear-fuel bank to Russian involvement in an international nuclear-fuel-enrichment consortium. The president can also adjust the pace of any Georgian and Ukrainian integration with NATO.

If the next president can succeed in recruiting Russia to a common approach toward Iran, it is likely to be easier to bring China more fully on board. Beijing will not want to be left outside an international consensus. Chinese interests in the free flow of oil from the Persian Gulf are growing alongside its energy requirements. Nevertheless, Beijing currently prefers to pursue its commercial interests with Iran rather than support the effort to increase economic pressure on it. The challenge for the United States will be to make Chinese leaders understand that a crisis with Iran will have such adverse consequences for China's economy that its political stability could be impacted.

Integrate the War on Terrorism

As Daniel Byman and Steven Simon, the project's terrorism experts, suggest in their chapter, the next president should make counterterrorism an integral part of his Middle East strategy, but it need no longer be the driver of that policy. The next president should focus his administration on strengthening local capacities to fight terrorism, preventing the reemergence of al Qaeda in Iraq, and bolstering the institutions of failing regional states. The president himself should also send a clear and consistent message to the Muslim world that the United States is not at war with Islam but rather with small groups of violent extremists who are acting against the basic tenets of their own religion.

Recalibrate the Political Reform Agenda

The Bush administration gained some traction in the Arab world—and some credit in the Arab street—with the aggressive promotion of its Freedom Agenda. But its insistence on elections in Iraq, Lebanon, and the Palestinian territories enabled Islamist parties with militias to enter the political process and then paralyze it in each place. President George W. Bush's boycott of Hamas, after it freely and fairly won the Palestinian elections, enabled America's opponents in the Arab and Muslim worlds to raise the banner of "double standards." Similarly, Bush's backing away from his public demands that the Saudi and Egyptian leadership open their political spaces undermined the credibility of the democratization enterprise.

As Isobel Coleman and Tamara Cofman Wittes explain in their chapter on economic and political development, it would be a mistake for the next president to abandon the effort entirely. Instead, he will need to strike a more sustainable balance between American interests and American values. Given the unstable nature of the region at the moment, it would be better to support a longer-term, evolutionary democratization process in which the United States emphasizes the value of strengthening civil society and reinforcing the institutions of democracy, including the rule of law, judicial independence, freedom of the press and association, women's rights, and government transparency, as well as more market-oriented economies. Above all, Coleman and Wittes argue, the United States needs to focus on supporting efforts in the region to provide a vast and rising young generation with hope for the future and reason to resist the dark visions purveyed by religious extremists.

Develop an Effective Energy Policy

High levels of oil imports and gasoline consumption render the American economy too vulnerable to the vagaries of the oil market and the Middle East's inherent volatility. Alternatives exist, and the silver lining of the dark cloud of $4-a-gallon gas prices lies in persuading the American driver to embrace these alternatives. However, as oil prices decline, the urgency to switch will also recede; the president should take the longer view and persist with the effort to promote alternatives and increase efficiencies that reduce consumption. This effort will lessen the pressure on world prices, slow the pace of climate change, and reduce the transfer of wealth to countries like Iran and Venezuela. It is more than just coincidence that when the price of oil was $10 a barrel in the 1990s, Iran's leaders were far more circumspect in their activities abroad than they are now when high oil prices allow President Mahmoud Ahmadinejad to fund foreign adventures while avoiding the domestic political consequences of his mismanagement of the Iranian economy. The lesson is clear: the next president cannot effectively reset the strategic context in the Middle East without a serious effort to reduce American oil consumption.

Regain the Moral High Ground

The United States is too powerful and influential to be loved in the Middle East, but there was a time not so long ago when it was respected for its values and commitment to peace. Regaining that respect will be important if the next president is to persuade the publics in the Arab and Muslim worlds to support their leaders in working with the United States. The new president can take two immediate symbolic steps that would do much to signal a return to a principled approach: announce that he has ordered the closure of the prison at Guantánamo Bay; and declare that resolving the Palestinian problem will be one of his priorities. These announcements should be part of an articulation of his vision of a new, more tolerant, and peaceful order for the Middle East, where governments are more accountable to the people, where young people can expect good education and productive jobs, where human dignity is respected, and where a sense of justice prevails.

TAKING THE INITIATIVE

Once the next president has reset the strategic context and articulated his vision of a changed Middle Eastern order, he will need to develop two diplomatic initiatives—one directed at modifying Iran's behavior, the other at promoting Arab-Israeli peace. The objective should be to achieve mutually reinforcing breakthroughs on both fronts within the first two years of his presidency.

The Iran Initiative

In their chapter on Iran, Suzanne Maloney and Ray Takeyh maintain that the best way to alter Iran's behavior, particularly on the nuclear issue, is to attempt to engage the Iranian government directly. Why engagement? The simple answer is that the alternatives have either been tried with no success or look too dangerous, costly, or improbable. There is no realistic prospect for toppling the regime, either through military means or through support of an internal uprising. A preventive military strike on Iran's nuclear facilities would at best delay its nuclear program a few years, while exposing Israel, and American forces in Iraq and Afghanistan, to retaliation. Containment and the application of sanctions have failed to alter Iran's behavior, partly because Russia and China have not supported effective sanctions and partly because the high price of oil makes it easier for Iran to absorb the cost of the sanctions that have been imposed. There is no assurance that an initiative aimed at engaging the Iranian government in a more constructive relationship would work any better. But a sincere attempt that failed would at least make other options more politically attractive at home and abroad.

The variety of challenges that Iran poses to American interests makes an initiative toward Iran inherently complicated. The situation is made more so by the Iranian government's simultaneous pursuit of the interests of the state and of its Islamic revolution.

The revolution views the United States as "the Great Satan," and therefore will have great difficulty coming to terms with the American devil; the state on the other hand is quite capable of recognizing a common interest and accommodating itself to it. In the past, when forced to choose, Iran's leaders have been prepared to put the state above the revolution. The best course for the next president is to find a way to address Iran's legitimate state interests while adamantly opposing its revolutionary impulses.

According to Maloney and Takeyh, an Iran initiative should aim at a direct U.S.-Iranian negotiation that would focus on bringing Iran into a new regional order, provided it is prepared to abide by established international norms:

—Strict adherence to international treaty obligations, especially the Non-Proliferation Treaty, which Iran signed and ratified

—Noninterference in the affairs of other states

—Nonviolent resolution of conflicts

—Opposition to, rather than sponsorship of, terrorism

—Acceptance of whatever peace agreements the Palestinians, Syria, and Lebanon reach with Israel.

If Iran is willing to engage with the region in a responsible way, promoting its influence by peaceful means rather than through subversion, proliferation, and confrontation, then it should be welcomed by the United States and its partners. This is, admittedly, highly unlikely. The United States will need leverage to persuade Iran to begin to change course. The carrots of normalized relations with the United States and the international community, as well as an end to sanctions, and the stick of increased sanctions (including a ban on Iranian gasoline imports, on which Iran is dependent, given its lack of refining capacity) will be important. But another effective way to get Iran's attention is through the "indirect approach" of launching an Arab-Israeli initiative at the same time as the next president holds out his hand to Iran. Substantive progress on peacemaking—especially on the Syrian track—will create concern in Tehran that, rather than dominate the region, Iran is going to be left behind by it. In the past, Iran has perceived progress in the Arab-Israeli arena to be deeply threatening to its efforts to spread its influence into the Middle East heartland and has successfully used its proxies to provoke havoc and undermine the process.[6] It will probably try to do so again. But this time the president will be opening an alternative way to the Iranian leadership, one that respects its government and seeks to accommodate its legitimate national interests should it choose to engage with the United States.

Before the next president embarks on that effort, however, he will also need to secure Arab, Israeli, and Turkish backing for his approach to Iran. The primary Arab interlocutors are Egypt, Jordan, Saudi Arabia, and the other member states of the Gulf Cooperation Council. Their lack of confidence in U.S. policy and their fear of Iran's hegemonic ambitions has led many of them to hedge their bets by reaching out to Tehran. However, they are deeply fearful that their interests will be sacrificed on the altar of a U.S.-Iran détente. The next president needs to treat them as full partners in his initiative. This includes consultations with them so that if engagement or military strikes fail to curb Iran's nuclear program, the United States would provide them with a credible nuclear guarantee in place of their own efforts to acquire nuclear weapons.

Israel is understandably nervous about the failure of the international community to head off Iran's nuclear program. Its national security establishment is quietly perturbed by the Bush administration's handling of the issue, particularly its failure to recruit Russia to support a more effective sanctions regime and its release of its National Intelligence Estimate on Iran, which undermined the efforts to achieve an international consensus at a critical moment.[7] The Israelis prefer to support an effective diplomatic effort to prevent Iran from crossing the nuclear threshold because they are well aware of the drawbacks of a preventive military strike, especially if they have to do it on their own. They too see the advantage of peacemaking, especially with Syria, as a means of acquiring leverage over Iran and seem willing to do their part.

Nevertheless, Israel's tolerance for engagement with Iran is more limited than America's because of the simple reality that the United States, with its thousands of nuclear weapons and delivery systems, has a ready fallback to a posture of nuclear deterrence while it works to curb Iran's nuclear capabilities. (To cite one example, the United States continues to tolerate a North Korean nuclear capability while it uses sanctions and diplomacy to reduce North Korea's capacities in this realm.) Israel has never been prepared to accept another nuclear power in its neighborhood, especially not one that directly threatens its existence, because a first strike of any scale would have devastating consequences for the Jewish state given its small size and concentrated population.

Therefore, at least to synchronize the American and Israeli clocks, and to give more time for a strategy of diplomatic engagement to work, the United States will want to persuade Israel not to strike Iran's nuclear facilities while U.S.-led diplomatic efforts unfold. This will require the next president to enhance Israel's deterrent and defensive capabilities by offering it a nuclear guarantee and providing it with additional layers of ballistic missile defenses and early warning systems. The United States and Israel will need to reassess their options should it become clear that diplomacy has failed.

Turkey is a regional power that is normally absent from America's calculations about Middle East strategy, except when it comes to Iraq. But Turkey is a NATO ally, and a Sunni state, that borders on Iran and Syria as well as on Iraq, and that maintains a long-standing strategic relationship with Israel. Turkey has long wanted to play a role in the Middle East but has usually been treated warily by Arab states that still recall Ottoman rule of their region. But now, its Sunni Islamist government has given it greater credibility in the Arab world. The Turkish government has taken advantage of this—and its close relationship with Israel—to step into the breach left by the Bush administration's refusal to deal with Syria, successfully brokering the resumption of indirect negotiations between Jerusalem and Damascus. Turkey, too, is deeply concerned about Iran's nuclear program and its hegemonic ambitions. It has therefore sought to remove Syria from its alliance with Iran and bring it into the circle of peacemakers. Turkey has also contributed to international forces in Lebanon and is willing to participate should international forces be required in Gaza or the West Bank. Turkey needs to be included in consultations about both presidential initiatives and about the design of a regional security framework. It might also play a useful role as a channel for messages to neighboring Iran, with which it maintains an open relationship.

The chapters on Iran deal in detail with the strategic and tactical considerations involved in an Iran initiative. The principal elements should be

—Instead of subcontracting the negotiations to U.S. allies until the Iranian government agrees to suspend its enrichment program—the approach pursued by the Bush administration—the next president should offer to have American diplomats lead U.S.-Iran negotiations in a multilateral framework. The model should be the current North Korea negotiations, in which six powers participate, providing the umbrella for a direct U.S.–North Korean engagement.

—Rather than making suspension of Iran's enrichment program a precondition for formal negotiations, suspension should be converted into a condition for progress in the negotiations. If Iran is willing to suspend enrichment, the UN should be willing to suspend sanctions that were invoked to achieve that purpose; if Iran is not willing to suspend enrichment, UN and multilateral sanctions should be ratcheted up in agreement with America's partners.

—To secure suspension of enrichment, the United States should be willing to agree to discuss what Iran, as a signatory to the Non-Proliferation Treaty, claims as its "right to enrich."[8] In the end, it may be necessary to acknowledge this right, provided that the terms of the agreement are acceptable. This would mean a sharply limited capacity under strict safeguards with inspections to deny Iran a breakout capability by which it could move rapidly to production of significant amounts of bomb-grade, highly enriched uranium. However, because Iran is acting in ways that have led the International Atomic Energy Agency to report it to the UN Security Council and to continue to express considerable concern about its activities and intentions, this right must be earned by Iran, not conceded by the United States. Otherwise, Iran will pocket it and insist on retaining its ability to develop industrial enrichment capacity, which would bring it too close to a bomb-making capability for anybody else's comfort.

—The offer of direct nuclear negotiations should be part of a broader initiative that would include parallel, bilateral negotiations on separate tracks dealing with normalization of U.S.-Iranian relations, Iraq and the Gulf, and other Middle East issues (including Iran's sponsorship of Hezbollah and Palestinian terrorist groups).

—The contents of any diplomatic initiative, with all its positive incentives if Iran decides to accept international norms, should be made public so that Iranians and Americans are aware of its contents. This transparency would require the Iranian government to defend its response at home and facilitate domestic backing in the United States and international support should more pressure be necessary.

—The United States should not insist on linking all the issues. Instead, some incentives should be tied to Iran's behavior in the nuclear realm; others could be offered contingent on its overall behavior.

—Force should never be ruled out. If the Iranian government proves unwilling to engage in direct negotiations with the United States, and suspend its uranium enrichment program in the process, the next president will be faced with a difficult decision in the first term of his administration. In advance of that moment, Ayatollah Ali Khamenei, Iran's supreme leader, will need to be apprised through private channels of the dangers he will be courting for his country and his regime if he continues down the nuclear path in defiance of the international community.

—At the same time, the next president needs to begin private discussions of security guarantees for Israel and Iran's other Middle Eastern neighbors to prevent Iran's program from triggering a regional nuclear arms race. He will also need to issue a declaratory statement that makes absolutely clear that any Iranian use or transfer of nuclear weapons or materials, regardless of the target, will have devastating consequences in Iran.

The Arab-Israeli Peace Initiatives

The next president will inherit Israeli-Syrian and Israeli-Palestinian negotiations that were put on hold by the collapse of the Olmert government. The president should aim for an early resumption of both negotiations. Once they have been relaunched, Lebanon should also be encouraged to participate in its own separate negotiations with Israel.

ISRAELI-SYRIAN NEGOTIATIONS

Syria serves as the principal conduit for Iran's influence in the Lebanese and Palestinian arenas.[9] Israeli-Syrian negotiations threaten to crimp that conduit, but an American-brokered peace between Syria and Israel is needed not only to remove Damascus from the conflict with Israel, but also to cause the breakup of the Iranian-Syrian alliance. But that could happen only if the next president decides to involve the United States in the negotiations, because Syria will not abandon its strategic relations with Iran unless it knows that normalized relations with the United States are in the offing.

Although both Israel and Syria would have preferred U.S. involvement from the outset, the Bush administration's efforts to isolate and punish the Asad regime for its efforts to subvert the neighboring Lebanese government precluded that involvement. This effort was a strategic miscalculation: the Bush administration wasted precious time and opportunities refusing to engage with rogue regimes, and America's national security interests suffered. The best way for the next president to exercise leverage over Syria (and Iran) is to join Turkey in helping to mediate the negotiations.

The Israeli-Syrian negotiations should prove less complicated than those on the Palestinian track, where Israeli claims to parts of the West Bank, as well as the Jerusalem and refugee issues, make agreement far more difficult. Unlike with the Palestinian Authority, the Israelis have little doubt that the Syrian government will be capable of fulfilling its part of the deal. Then prime minister Olmert is reported to have already offered President Bashar al-Asad a commitment to full Israeli withdrawal from the Golan Heights, and two of the leading contenders to become prime minister in some future government—Binyamin Netanyahu and Ehud Barak—both offered Asad's father full withdrawal when they were prime ministers in the 1990s. Indeed, after eight years of negotiations, most of the substantive issues between Israel and Syria were resolved by early 2000 under the Clinton administration, when all that separated the parties from an agreement was a 200-meter strip of land around the northeastern section of Lake Kinneret (Sea of Galilee).[10]

In the past Israelis sought to trade territories for peace, but that bargain was fraught because they doubted the depth of Syria's commitment to normalizing relations. Today, facing a serious threat from Iran, Israelis are more interested in the trade of the Golan Heights for what would be tantamount to Syria's strategic realignment. If President Asad proves willing to make that shift, it would deal a body blow to Iran's interference on Israel's northern and southern borders, providing a strategic dividend to replace the devalued peace dividend Israelis used to hope for.

ISRAELI-PALESTINIAN NEGOTIATIONS

Steven Cook and Shibley Telhami make the case in their paper that Palestine remains the hot-button issue for the Arab and Muslim worlds, one exploited by the Iranians to advance their otherwise implausible claim to leadership in the broader Middle East. The Bush administration's neglect of this issue cost the United States dearly in the Middle East, something that President Bush himself belatedly recognized by launching the Annapolis process.[11] Since then the process he and Secretary of State Condoleezza Rice put in place has operated on four interrelated levels that each needs to be picked up and pushed forward by the next president so that a positive synergy is created among them:

Final-status negotiations. While the gaps have been narrowed on several critical issues—borders, refugees, and Jerusalem—there will be a need for bridging formulas that the United States may have to provide.[12] Given the amount of time the parties have already spent in negotiations, these should be proposed—but not imposed—sooner rather than later. To encourage movement, it will likely be essential for the next president to outline in some detail his view of the principles of a settlement. In the meantime, he should preserve the understanding reached with the Olmert government that final-status negotiations should proceed to an agreement as quickly as possible while implementation can take place in phases.

Road map commitments to fight terror and freeze settlements. Both sides began to take steps to fulfill their commitments under the Quartet's road map for a two-state solution. The Palestinian Authority has deployed Jordanian-trained police to the West Bank cities of Nablus, Jenin, and Hebron to maintain order but still needs to act against terrorist cadres. The government of Israel reduced settlement activity beyond the security barrier, but inside the blocs and in the Jerusalem environs the Israeli government has given permission for thousands of new housing units, causing an outcry from the Palestinian and Arab leadership.

Given the importance of an effective Palestinian Security Service, the next president should secure greater congressional funding and accelerate training so that Palestinian forces have the ability to act against terrorist cadres and gangs still pursuing anti-Israeli violence. Because this process will inevitably take time, he should also prepare the ground for the deployment of international forces (preferably Arab and Muslim) as part of a peace agreement to partner with the Palestinian forces until they can police their territory on their own.

He will need to reach an understanding with the new Israeli prime minister to freeze all settlement activity for a limited period (say, six to twelve months) while the borders of the Palestinian state are finalized. Once that occurs, settlement activity could recommence in the settlement blocs that would be annexed to Israel when the other final-status issues are resolved.

Improving conditions in the West Bank. Salam Fayyad, prime minister of the Palestinian Authority, and Quartet special envoy Tony Blair have begun to make progress on local, quick-start economic projects and the removal of some strategic checkpoints. The next president should work to make sure that they are getting sufficient cooperation from Israel and funding from the Arab states.

Arab state involvement. At the initiative of Saudi Arabia's King Abdullah, the twenty-two members of the Arab League have offered to end the conflict, sign peace agreements, and normalize relations with Israel, provided that it withdraws to the pre-June 1967 borders and agrees to the creation of a Palestinian state. However, the lack of visible progress in the Israeli-Palestinian negotiations, combined with Israel's settlement activity, has soured them on the process for the time being. Renewing the involvement of the Arab states will be easier if they see that the negotiations are moving forward and settlement activity is not. They need to be pressed to fulfill their financial pledges to the Palestinian Authority (PA) and to start to engage more visibly with Israel during the process, not just at the end.

The next president will have to decide what to do about the conundrum posed by Hamas, which won the Palestinian elections in January 2006 and then took control of Gaza through a military putsch in June 2007. Hamas rejects Israel's right to exist and the agreements the Palestinians entered into with Israel. It also advocates and has been the deadliest practitioner of violence and terrorism (which it calls "resistance") against Israel. In these ways, it rules itself out of the peace process. On the other hand, given its control of Gaza and its support among at least one-third of Palestinians, a peace process that excludes it is bound to fail.

The way out of this dilemma is to shift responsibility from America's shoulders to Hamas's. As the governors of Gaza, the leaders of Hamas should have to decide between mobilizing the 1.5 million Palestinians against Israel by rocket, mortar, and terror attacks on southern towns and cities, and meeting Palestinian needs by establishing order, returning the Israeli soldier it is holding hostage, and enabling passages to be opened for goods and people. The cease-fire agreement negotiated by Egypt is holding for the moment precisely because the Hamas leadership has effectively policed it, choosing to place the needs of Gazans ahead of its interests in "resistance."

The next president should encourage that process but leave it to Egypt, Israel, and the Palestinian Authority to handle the relationship with Hamas. If the cease-fire between Israel and Hamas continues to hold, and a PA-Hamas reconciliation emerges from it, the next president should deal with the joint Palestinian leadership as well as authorize low-level contact with Hamas in Gaza. In the meantime, progress in the negotiating process will create its own dynamic in which Hamas will feel pressured by Gazans not to miss the peace train.

An early test of this dynamic may come at the beginning of the next president's term if Palestinian Authority president Abbas decides to call a presidential election when his term expires in January 2009. Hamas will likely contest those elections; its participation should be conditioned on its allowance of free and fair campaigning and voting in Gaza under international observation, and agreement to accept the outcome. It must also continue to observe a cease-fire. If elections do proceed, the Arab states will have to step up and clearly back Abbas politically and financially. He is likely to fare better (and Hamas's candidate worse) if the United States and Israel make clear before the election the extent to which diplomacy will reward Palestinian moderation. After the election, U.S. and Israeli willingness to deal with Hamas in any form should be predicated on its continued observance of a cease-fire.

Organizing for the Iran and Arab-Israeli Initiatives

If these initiatives are to succeed, the next president will need to make clear that they are a personal priority. He should avoid becoming the "desk officer" for the negotiations, but he will need to engage directly and often with the other world leaders involved in the initiatives. To build public support, the next president and his secretary of state will also need to be actively involved in making the case to the American people and the international community for what they are doing in both the Iran and Arab-Israeli arenas.

The secretary of state will necessarily have to take the lead in the diplomatic effort. But because of the many other demands on his or her time, and because the initiatives will need to be conducted simultaneously, the next president should appoint two special envoys, one responsible for the Iran initiative and the other responsible for both Arab-Israeli initiatives, each reporting to the president through the secretary of state. The relevant bureaus of the State Department should staff the two envoys. They should each be in charge of separate interagency committees to coordinate the other relevant parts of the national security bureaucracy. The "principals meetings" of the National Security Council should be the place where the two initiatives are coordinated, ensuring also that they are integrated with other aspects of U.S. foreign, defense, and energy policies.

Which initiative should have preference? The short answer is both of them. In any case, the pace of each of them will not be determined in Washington alone. The Iranian initiative needs to be launched as soon as possible because of the urgent need to suspend Iran's enrichment program before it achieves a breakout capability. Similarly, on the Palestinian track time is short because hope among Palestinians for a viable, independent state is evaporating, as Telhami and Cook show in their paper. However, the split in the Palestinian body politic, the Palestinian Authority's questionable ability to police territory from which Israel would withdraw, and the powerful opposition of Israeli settlers make an agreement difficult to reach, let alone implement. By contrast, the Israeli-Syrian negotiation is relatively straightforward, and the Syrian government has the proven ability to fulfill any commitments it might make. Moreover, the strategic importance of the Israeli-Syrian negotiations, in terms of their impact on Iran's calculus, requires prompt engagement.

As this chapter and the ones that follow make clear, renewing diplomacy in the Middle East will be a tall, complicated, and urgent order for the next president. That will especially be true because the Middle East is bound to have some unwelcome surprises in store —perhaps a coup, a terrorist attack on a U.S. embassy, a succession crisis—that will threaten to divert him from his course. Only an integrated strategy, one that anticipates the consequences of action in one arena for what the United States is trying to achieve in others, and one that is capable of staying on course despite the inevitable distractions, stands a chance of success.

NOTES

1. Richard Haass, "The Age of Nonpolarity," *Foreign Affairs* 87 (May/June 2008): 44–56.

2. In the Arab street today, Iran's Mahmoud Ahmadinejad, Syria's Bashar al-Asad, and Hezbollah's Hassan Nasrallah are far more popular than any moderate Arab leader. According to a survey of six Arab countries taken in March 2008, Nasrallah received 26 percent, Asad 16 percent, and Ahmadinejad 10 percent of support. See Shibley Telhami, "Survey of the Anwar Sadat Chair for Peace and Development at the University of Maryland (with Zogby International)," a survey conducted March 2008 in Egypt, Jordan, Lebanon, Morocco, Saudi Arabia, and the United Arab Emirates, with a sample size of 4,046 and a margin of error of ± 1.6 percent (www.brookings.edu/~/media/Files/events/2008/0414_middle_east/0414_middle_east_telhami.pdf).

3. The Asad regime is minority Alawite, which is a breakaway sect of Shi'ah Islam, but it sits atop a predominantly Sunni Arab population that is uneasy about growing Iranian influence in Syria.

4. Given its geographic proximity, Russia sees the Middle East as its soft underbelly. China and India are increasingly dependent on energy exports from the Middle East to maintain their fast-paced growth.

5. The Quartet comprises the United States, the European Union, Russia, and the United Nations.

6. In 1996, after Yitzhak Rabin's assassination brought Shimon Peres to power in Israel, Iran used Hezbollah rocket attacks into northern Israel and a Palestine Islamist Jihad (PIJ) terrorist attack in Tel Aviv to thwart Peres's efforts to achieve a quick breakthrough in negotiations with Syria before he faced Binyamin Netanyahu in an election. Iran succeeded in provoking Peres's "Grapes of Wrath" operation in southern Lebanon, which lost him the votes of Israeli Arabs and the election. The peace process stalled. Iran also used its relationship with the PIJ to prolong the subsequent Palestinian intifada that brought the Palestinian Authority to the point of collapse and facilitated Hamas's victory in Palestinian elections.

7. The National Intelligence Estimate's principal judgments were released in November 2007 at the height of the Bush administration's efforts to step up pressure on Iran. The NIE judged that Iran had stopped its efforts to develop a bomb-making capability in 2003. It went on to argue that Iran was still developing capabilities that could be used for producing nuclear weapons, but its headline created the impression that Iran was no longer seeking nuclear weapons (www.dni.gov/press_releases/20071203_release.pdf).

8. In the June 14, 2008, proposal made to Iran by China, France, Germany, the Russian Federation, the United Kingdom, the United States, and the European Union, the parties declared their readiness "to recognize Iran's right to develop research, production and use of nuclear energy for peaceful purposes in conformity with its NPT obligations." This proposal clearly opens up the possibility of accepting an Iranian enrichment program provided there is confidence in the exclusively peaceful nature of Iran's nuclear program. See Steven Erlanger and Elaine Sciolino, "Bush Says Iran Spurns New Offer on Uranium," *New York Times,* June 15, 2008 (www.nytimes.com/2008/06/15/world/middleeast/15iran.html?_r=1&scp=2&sq=Erlanger&st=nyt&oref=slogin).

9. Iran's arms and personnel flow through Syria to Hezbollah in Lebanon, and from there to Gaza. Damascus hosts the headquarters of Hamas, which is backed by Iran, and of Palestine Islamic Jihad, which is controlled by Iran.

10. See Martin Indyk, *Innocent Abroad: An Intimate Account of U.S. Diplomacy in the Middle East* (New York: Simon and Schuster, 2009), chapter 10.

11. Some American neoconservatives still argue vociferously that it is a mistake to focus on the Palestinian issue because few leaders in the region really care that much about it and solving it cannot resolve the region's more pressing problems. This argument conveniently dismisses the opinion of the people in the Arab and Muslim worlds who see the Palestinian issue as a symbol of their own humiliation and a lack of respect for their dignity. Because their leaders are not directly accountable to the people, those leaders are even more sensitive to popular views on this subject, fearing that what little legitimacy they enjoy is vulnerable to charges that they are not doing enough to promote Palestinian interests. Moreover, failure to resolve the Palestinian issue provides these leaders with an excellent excuse for diverting the attention of their people from their own shortcomings. President Bush's failure to address the Palestinian issue has been exploited by Iran to strengthen its argument that violence and terrorism is the way to liberate Palestine, which in turn undermines those Arab leaders who would work with the United States to try to resolve the problem.

12. Prime Minister Ehud Olmert is reliably reported to have offered Palestinian president Mahmoud Abbas a deal in which the territory of the Palestinian state would comprise all of Gaza, 93 percent of the West Bank, 5.5 percent of Israeli territory adjacent to Gaza as compensation, and a permanent "safe passage" between Gaza and the West Bank. See Aluf Benn, "PA Rejects Olmert's Offer to Withdraw from 93% of West Bank," *Haaretz*, August 12, 2008.

STEPHEN BIDDLE
MICHAEL E. O'HANLON
KENNETH M. POLLACK

2

The Evolution of Iraq Strategy

OVER THE PAST FIVE YEARS, Iraq has become one of the most divisive and polarizing issues in modern American history. It is now a subject on which Republicans and Democrats tend to disagree fundamentally about the past (the reasons for going to war), the present (the impact of the "surge" in American forces), and the future of American policy (how quickly, and in what way, American forces should leave Iraq). Reflecting this divide, the two presidential candidates staked out starkly opposite positions during the campaign, with much of the public debate more emotional and ideological than substantive.

With the campaign over and a new president entering office, the debate should change to one of substance over politics. Recent trends suggest that the United States may be able to reduce significantly its forces in Iraq fairly soon, premised not on the certainty of defeat, but on the likelihood of some measure of success. The past eighteen to twenty-four months have seen a remarkable series of positive developments in Iraq that offer hope that the United States may be able to ensure stability in Iraq while redeploying large numbers of American forces sooner rather than later.

The likelihood of this outcome should not be overstated. Because of the remarkable developments of recent months, it is more than just a long-shot, best-case scenario—but it is hardly a sure thing. Challenges still abound in Iraq, and their nature changes over time even as the overall risk they pose slowly abates. Thus, as a new crop of problems moves to center stage, coping with them will require the United States and its Iraqi allies to make important shifts in strategy and tactics rather than to just stick with approaches that succeeded against problems now receding in importance.

In our judgment, now that the surge is over, any further drawdowns should be gradual until after Iraq gets through two big rounds of elections of its own—provincial elections to be held perhaps in early 2009, and follow-on national elections. These have the potential either to lock in place important gains or to reopen old wounds. But starting as early as 2010, if current trends continue, the next president may be able to begin cutting back on U.S. forces in Iraq, possibly halving the total American commitment by late 2010 or 2011, without running excessive risks with the stability of Iraq and the wider Persian Gulf region.

Faster reductions would be ill-advised. But if undertaken nevertheless, it is important that they be balanced. Both combat and support functions from the United States will be necessary for years to come in Iraq; rapid drawdowns that leave an imbalanced residual force without major combat formations would be worse than rapid cuts that preserve significant combat capability.

This approach suggests another difficult year or two ahead for the brave and committed men and women of the U.S. armed forces, especially as the United States likely undertakes to increase forces in Afghanistan modestly in 2009. Although the American military is under considerable strain, most trends in recruiting, reenlistment, and other indicators of morale and resilience are relatively stable. And with the surge over, the worst of the overdeployment problem is beginning to pass. Compared with the alternative of risking defeat in a major war vital to critical American interests, concerns about the health of the military should not therefore, in our judgment, be the main determinant of future strategy.

Our suggested approach is "conditions-based" and somewhat gradual in the time horizon envisioned for reducing American forces in Iraq. But it also foresees the possibility that most (though not all) main American combat forces will come out of Iraq by 2011, and it further argues that the United States needs to continue to seek ways to gain leverage over Iraqi decisionmakers rather than assure them of an unconditional and open-ended U.S. commitment.

Although this approach matches neither of the divergent strands of American thought prevalent before the election, it thus parallels aspects of both. Similarly, it reflects important elements of Iraqi political reality if not its recent rhetoric. Iraqi prime minister Nouri al-Maliki has partisan incentives to favor rhetoric calling for rapid U.S. withdrawals, and he may overestimate his own military's ability to perform in the absence of U.S. troops. But his actual ability to secure Iraq without a significant U.S. force has serious limits, and his own commanders' awareness of this may yield an emphasis on aspirational goals for U.S. withdrawals rather than binding commitments. Implementation details always matter in Iraqi politics, and there may be more room for a continuing U.S. presence than there sometimes appears to be in the declaratory stances of Iraqi politicians

NEW PROGRESS, NEW PROBLEMS

The problems of Iraq today resemble the proverbial onion: dealing with one set of issues just reveals a deeper layer that then demands attention. As Major General Michael Jones, the chief American adviser to the Iraqi National Police put it, "Progress is *new* problems, not *no* problems." At the outer layer of the onion were a set of first-order issues that were sucking Iraq into the maelstrom of all-out civil war in 2006 and early 2007. These consisted principally of widespread sectarian conflict, a full-blown insurgency among Iraq's Sunni community (spearheaded by al Qaeda in Iraq, or AQI), and a failed state incapable of providing basic security or services such as food, medicine, clean water, electricity, and sanitation to its citizens. The change in the U.S. approach—a new counterinsurgency strategy and increased force levels (the surge)—was designed to cure these problems. Across Iraq it has had a dramatic impact, in conjunction with a range of other factors. However, even as these first-order problems abate under the influence of the surge strategy, second-order problems are emerging that demand attention lest they undermine the progress made so far. Behind them lie third- and even fourth-order problems.

Each new set of challenges is both somewhat less dangerous than its predecessors and easier to deal with. For instance, some of the most important second-order problems include factional violence within the Shi'i (and potentially Sunni and Kurdish) communities; disputed jurisdiction over key pieces of territory, most notably the oil-rich northern region of Kirkuk; the limited capacity of the Iraqi bureaucracy to administer the country, improve living standards, and reduce unemployment; the persistence of terrorism even as the insurgency recedes; the need to help more than 4 million displaced Iraqis return home or find new homes in their country; and the weak and immature political system vulnerable to paralysis, a military coup d'état, loss of power to a Hamas-like organization, or a slide into a Russian-style mafia state. These problems remain dangerous in their own right, but their greatest threat comes from the possibility that each, left unchecked, could resurrect the first-order problems and plunge Iraq into the all-out civil war that the surge strategy has so far kept in check.

It is also worth noting that the need for large American combat formations diminishes as each set of problems is addressed and the next moves to the fore, both because the lesser-order problems tend to be more political and economic in nature (and thus lend themselves less to military approaches) and because they are progressively less likely to produce the kind of catastrophic Iraqi civil war that would truly threaten American vital interests. Had it not been for the application of the full range of American resources—including the major military commitment of the surge and a new strategy focused on protecting the Iraqi population—the first-order problems would almost certainly have plunged Iraq into an all-out civil war and possibly spill over into the rest of the economically vital Persian Gulf. Many of the second-order problems probably will not require the same levels of American forces to keep them in check as the first. Third- and fourth-order problems like repairing infrastructure, rooting out corruption and organized crime, and stimulating the economy's private sector require fewer American military forces to address and are also far less likely to create the same kind of threat to America's vital national interests even if mishandled. Thus, the more that the first- and second-order problems abate, the greater the likelihood that large numbers of American combat formations can safely be withdrawn.

THE CURRENT SITUATION: FROM WORST TO BAD

Even as the situation remains fragile, Iraq is currently doing much better overall. Civilian deaths from war were down to just over 500 in May 2008, according to a count that uses both U.S. and Iraqi government sources. That is probably the lowest figure since 2003 and reflects an 80 percent reduction in violence since the surge began. Typical civilian fatality totals for 2008 ranged from 500 to 700 a month nationwide—down 75 percent from 2006–2007 and lower even than the rates in 2004–05. In addition, security force fatalities have been roughly halved since 2006–07, falling from about 70 to less than 25 a month for American personnel and from 200 to less than 100 a month for the Iraqis. This drop in violence can be attributed to a combination of factors, including waning ethnosectarian conflict, a strengthened Iraqi military, and improved state institutions.

The Waning Ethnosectarian Conflict

One of the most surprising developments over the past eighteen to twenty-four months has been the dramatic decline in ethnic and sectarian conflict across Iraq—down by more than 90 percent in 2008. Contrary to popular opinion, this drop in violence is not primarily a product of effective ethnic cleansing. Large swaths of Iraq remain heavily mixed, and relatively few areas of Iraq that started out ethnically and religiously mixed are now homogeneous. Instead, it is largely a result of the area security operations of the U.S. and Iraqi militaries, coupled with the formation of local security forces like the Sons of Iraq (SoI), that halted the progression of ethnic cleansing in those mixed areas. Today, many of these areas remain segmented by physical barriers and inundated by security forces, but because of it, they are far more secure than they once were. In important areas of Iraq, the role of American forces has shifted from crushing sectarian groups intent on causing violence to essentially policing cease-fires among the groups and reassuring ordinary Iraqis that the violence will not be allowed to resume.

Consequently, Iraq may be approaching the point where ethnosectarian violence, once the greatest problem in the entire country, has been effectively suppressed. Over time, this should enable more and more

American forces to shift over to the role of policing such cease-fires. The historical record indicates that if pressure is maintained, then there is a reasonable chance that the sectarian militant organizations that have been driven underground will lose their cohesiveness, their grip on the people, and eventually their membership, resulting in a permanent peace.

The main culprits in the ethnosectarian violence of 2006—Sunni Salafist groups, more secular Sunni insurgents, Moqtada al-Sadr's (Shi'i) Mahdi army, and the Shi'i Badr Organization—have now either stood down in cease-fires, been crippled by military defeat, or both. Sunni insurgents, for example, overwhelmingly switched sides over the course of 2007, signing onto contractual cease-fires especially through the Sons of Iraq program, which now enrolls about 100,000 participants in security roles. The most violent actors in the ethnosectarian violence—Iraq's Salafist and extreme chauvinist Sunni groups, especially al Qaeda in Iraq (AQI)—have been driven from western and central Iraq, and a series of offensives by U.S. and Iraqi forces have now largely cleared their remaining urban havens in Diyala, Salah-ad-Din, and Nineveh provinces. AQI has been dramatically weakened and may soon be driven into isolated rural hideouts at the margins of Iraqi society. It will surely continue to be able to mount occasional incidents of terrorist violence from these hideouts, but its ability to foment large-scale, low-intensity warfare may end.

Iraq's Shi'i militias, especially al-Sadr's Mahdi army, or Jaish al-Mahdi (JAM)—have been radically weakened by a combination of factors: Sunni realignment (which removed its original raison d'être), U.S. military pressure from the surge, a security presence in Baghdad since the surge, the declining popularity of the militias, and the increasing independence of splinter groups and rogue elements (which diminished the cohesiveness of their efforts and alienated the population with thuggish behavior). JAM's increasing weakness led Sadr to avoid a prospectively crippling fight with the U.S. military and instead to declare a cease-fire in late 2007. Although the mainstream JAM largely abided by this cease-fire, rogue elements did not, providing a casus belli for Iraqi government and American forces to launch a series of offensives beginning in Basra in March 2008 that have further weakened JAM and further diminished its prospects in large-scale warfare. The net result has been a virtuous spiral, in which decreasing sectarian violence weakens the hand of prospective sectarian warriors, which in turn helps reduce the scale of violence.

The Iraqi Military Comes of Age

Heading into 2008, a key question was whether the U.S.-led coalition could hold on to these gains after the five surge brigades began to return home in March 2008 (the last of these left Iraq in July 2008). Although the adoption of population-protection tactics seems to be the more decisive change in America's conduct of the war in Iraq, the additional forces were still important. The surge allowed General David Petraeus and his field commanders to take advantage of a number of important developments (including the Sunni realignment) and to secure much larger areas of the country than would otherwise have been possible, thereby denying them to AQI, JAM, and other militant groups. Recent events appear to have answered this question in the affirmative: there has not been any notable backsliding across northern Iraq, and there has been a remarkable further expansion of security into southern Iraq despite the end of the surge proper.

Major contributors to this favorable outcome have been the growth and maturation of the Iraqi security forces (ISF)—the Iraqi Army, the National Police (NP), the local Iraqi Police, the Facilities Protection Forces, and the border guards. By mid-May 2008 the total strength of the ISF had reached 559,000 personnel, reflecting growth of about 100,000 a year since the invasion, with almost 250,000 in the Iraqi Army alone. Moreover, the Iraqi security forces continue to grow, adding roughly 50,000 new troops a year to the army and a comparable number to police units. By mid-2008, some 56 percent of all Iraqi formations were in the top two readiness categories, which have been modified to require demonstrated performance on the battlefield (not just adequate equipment inventories, manpower levels, and training histories, as before).

The size of the force has allowed coalition commanders to provide ongoing protection to urban populations in the aftermath of military offensives aimed at clearing these areas of militias, insurgents, and Salafists. So many Iraqi security personnel are available (along with defensive measures like "smart fences" and berms) that Iraq's petroleum pipelines are now receiving adequate protection, with the result that attacks on the oil infrastructure are down by 80 to 90 percent since 2007. Indeed, Iraqi and American commanders now feel able to pull entire Iraqi Army battalions out of active duty one by one for advanced training that should further improve their capabilities.

In addition to the size, the quality of these units is much better than previous iterations of the Iraqi armed forces, although they are still hardly the equal of U.S. or other Western armies. Every Iraqi brigade now goes through an additional three- or four-month training process after it is created, at the end of which it is immediately paired with an American military transition team (MiTT) that aids it with combat planning, communications, fire support, and some operations.[1] In addition, many new Iraqi units are also partnered with American combat units of comparable or smaller size and typically sent to a quiet sector where the soldiers and officers can learn from their American advisers by operating in a low-threat environment. As a result, many Iraqi brigades now control their own battle space (with American formations playing an important, but supporting role), and some are good enough to be able to "clear" areas (with American fire support and other enablers), not merely "hold" those cleared by American forces.

A series of changes in the leadership and politics of the military has also been critical to the improvement of the Iraqi security forces. Major efforts have been made, especially in the last two years, to remove sectarian, corrupt, incompetent, or turncoat officers from the ISF. At the same time, a combination of aggressive recruitment of Sunnis and newly passed amnesty and de-Baathification ordinances have greatly increased both the presence of Sunnis in the security forces (especially the officer corps) and the availability of people with previous military experience.

The cooling of Iraq's underlying sectarian tensions interacts synergistically with these efforts. In an ongoing ethnosectarian war, sectarian officers can be purged but their replacements will be subject to the same pressures from above and from external forces, thus making real change difficult; with ethnosectarian violence in remission, the replacements for purged sectarians are now much more able to resist militia pressure or political interference and maintain nonsectarian policies.

The process is not complete—there are still sectarian elements in the ISF, and a renewal of ethnosectarian violence could undo much progress. But major progress has been made, especially in the leadership echelons.

A critical example of the improvement in ISF leadership has been in the Iraqi National Police. As recently as the fall of 2006, the NP was infested with Shi'i militiamen of every stripe, as well as every other form of miscreant. Police units often acted as hit squads, killing Sunnis wantonly, and they were feared by most Iraqis. Since then, a new commander, Major General Hussein al-Wadi, has fired both of the NP's division commanders, ten of its eight brigade commanders (meaning he also fired two of the replacement brigade commanders) and eighteen of its twenty-seven battalion commanders. He instituted new vetting and screening measures, made a determined effort to recruit Sunnis and Kurds into the force, and insisted on thoroughly retraining every police formation. The NP's officer corps now has roughly equal numbers of Sunnis and Shi'ah, while Sunni Arabs make up 25 percent of its rank and file, slightly higher than their percentage in the overall population. The result is a quickly growing popular trust in the police, coupled with a much-needed capability for NP units to serve as auxiliaries to American and Iraqi army units in combat zones.[2]

More broadly, there has been a deliberate, general improvement in the institutional response of the various armed services and their ministries, so that sectarianism is dealt with more quickly, more consistently, and more harshly than in the past. For instance, rules and regulations regarding the conduct of Ministry of the Interior forces (including the national and local police and the Facilities Protection Forces) now mandate harsher penalties for their personnel who commit crimes than the Iraqi law prescribes for civilians guilty of the same infractions.[3] A dedicated effort has also been made to slowly introduce personnel from other ethnic and religious groups into various Iraqi formations.[4] Consequently, coalition polling found that the number of Iraqis who did *not* believe that the Iraqi Army was sectarian jumped from 39 percent in June 2007 to 54 percent in June 2008.

If integration remains a work in progress, one notable change has been the ability of ISF formations with substantial representation by one sect to operate without significant problems in areas heavily dominated by other sects. For instance, the 26th Brigade of the 7th Infantry Division, which rushed south for the offensive in Basra in April 2008, was 80 percent Sunni, but it encountered no more difficulties with sectarian resentment in Basra than the more heavily integrated 1st Brigade—and performed far better than large elements of the heavily Shi'ah 14th Iraqi Army division (especially its 52nd brigade), which made up the government's initial attack force in the city.[5]

One of the most important residual problems for ISF units in this respect is that some formations are reluctant to operate in the specific areas from which their personnel were recruited. For some Iraqis, it is difficult, shameful, and potentially even life-threatening to have to arrest—let alone fight—old friends, distant relatives, or fellow tribesmen. As a result, there is a rule of thumb that Iraqi Army formations are generally deployed at least 100 kilometers from where they were raised. Even here, however, there are exceptions that suggest that this practice too may be a passing phase.[6]

The net effect of these improvements is that a great many Iraqi formations now conduct the full range of security operations with only American support, although that support is critically important for many of these units. While this marks a major step forward and points toward how American forces could significantly reduce their combat role (and thus presence) over time, it is not the case that the Iraqi troops are ready to stand by themselves yet. For one thing, the army is still not fully trusted by all cease-fire participants. To many Sunnis in particular, armed forces commanded by a Shi'ah-dominated government are not yet trustworthy enough to be tolerated without an American presence to provide reassurance.

But that is not the only concern. The Iraqi security forces are simply not yet able to operate effectively without Western troops to assist with planning (the original Iraqi plan for the Basra offensive was a disaster), fire support, and logistical support (in fact the "tooth-to-tail" ratio—combat troops compared with support personnel—of Iraqi Army personnel is 75:25, which is close to the reverse of the ratio in the U.S. Army). MiTT and other partnering functions are particularly critical to the performance of the Iraqi military. Across the country and across time, properly trained and partnered Iraqi formations have performed far better than similar units in similar operations that lacked such support.[7]

From Failed State to Fragile State

In 2006 Iraq had become little more than a name on a map. The government, such as it was, was barely capable enough to qualify as a kleptocracy. Despite the protestations of the Bush administration to the contrary, it was widely seen by Iraqis and foreigners alike as illegitimate, dominated by militias and organized crime, and possessing virtually no capacity except to steal oil and money from the public trust. This was as true for local and provincial governments as it was for the hollow central government.

Iraq today is not exactly Sweden, but neither is it Somalia. Slowly, Iraqi institutions are beginning to gain some degree of capacity. For instance, Ministries of Defense, Foreign Affairs, Water Resources, and a few others are finally beginning to demonstrate the ability, albeit modest, to administer their relevant sectors. Governmental capacity building, economic revival, and provision of essential services continue to lag well behind improvements in security, but they are improving.

This capacity improvement is especially evident in local and provincial governments in northern, central, and western Iraq, all regions that have enjoyed tremendous support from the U.S. government. As part of the surge strategy, a decision was made to increase such support to these provinces in the (correct) expectation that it would be easier to reform them and build their capacity to deliver essential services to the people than it would be to do the same for the central government in Baghdad. American civilian and military personnel, most deployed in new provincial reconstruction teams and embedded provincial reconstruction teams, fanned out into the countryside to help Iraqi officials build local and provincial governance structures and rebuild utilities. Training programs for civil servants from provincial governments were established in Baghdad and Irbil to complement the work of the teams in the field.

The United States made a major effort to try to jump-start Iraq's economy through targeted development efforts, providing microloans to small businesses, creating make-work programs, and reviving large Iraqi industries in an effort to create tens of thousands of desperately needed jobs as quickly as possible. Some of these efforts have started to dent the country's crippling unemployment problem. In northern Iraq, for instance, the coalition's divisional headquarters there set out to create 50,000 jobs through a community stabilization program over twelve months in 2007–08; after just nine months they had created over 60,000.[8]

Iraq has also taken some baby steps on the road toward establishing the rule of law, the foundation of any successful pluralistic society. The government has shown itself more willing to investigate and prosecute corruption and other crimes. For instance, in May the director general of the Iraqi prison system was brought up on charges of cooperating with Shi'i militias who sought to recruit Shi'ah and kill Sunnis in those prisons. Such high-level arrests are still unusual, but the hope is that when they occur, they send a signal that such activities will no longer be condoned and will incur stiff punishments.

All of these efforts are just beginning to pay off in the form of a tentative return to normality and newly reviving local economies in many places around the country. Although progress is difficult to quantify, American, Iraqi, British, and UN officials aver that there are more children in school, more markets opening up, more businesses starting or reopening, and more traffic on the roads than in the past. For instance, in an area of Iraq south of Baghdad once so violent that it was known as "the Triangle of Death," the situation has improved enough that 255 small businesses were established in the first half of 2008. In Basra property prices had started to rise and retail outlets to proliferate as little as two months after the offensive that cleared the city. Across Iraq electricity provided by the official grid is up only 10 to 20 percent from its 2003–04 levels, but the informal grid of local, private generators provides up to another 50 percent of total capacity.

This progress is limited and extremely fragile. In particular, there is a serious risk that Iraqi demand and expectations will climb faster than the improving economic and administrative performance can meet (for example, growth in electricity demand may well outstrip improving power generation as people buy more air conditioners, freezers, and other power-gobbling consumer goods). But it is a mistake to claim, as many have, that no progress has been made in economic reconstruction or the government's ability to provide essential services.

The Changing Political Landscape

The positive security and sectarian developments have had a strong impact on Iraqi politics. While the watershed of the ending of ethnosectarian violence has already had a transformative effect, it is not yet fully clear what realignments it will produce and whether these will be positive and sustained. The upcoming local and national elections may help provide answers.

Previously, the three most influential Shi'i political entities in the country—the Islamic Supreme Council of Iraq (ISCI), the Sadrist movement, and the Fadhila party—all acquired and preserved their sway by maintaining powerful militias that could provide protection for their supporters and intimidate their competitors. In the power vacuum in Iraq before the surge, those capabilities allowed them to dominate Iraq's majority Shi'i community. Today, however, these militias have largely disappeared from Iraq's streets. As noted, JAM was routed on various battlefields and its cadres driven underground or into Iran. And though they may come back, they do not have the same capability to influence the political situation. ISCI and Fadhila adopted a different path, melding nearly all of their own independent militia units into the Iraqi security forces—ISCI's Badr Organization melting into the army and the police, Fadhila's troops mostly taking jobs in the Oil Facilities Protection Force. Their approach has created a second-order problem regarding the responsiveness of the Iraqi security forces to a future government not aligned with ISCI (discussed later), but it has largely removed the first-order problem that these militias employed systematic violence to advance their political agendas beyond, and at the expense of, government control.

As noted above, an important element of ousting JAM from its previous strongholds from Baghdad to Basra was the rejection of this militia by most of the Shi'i populace. In the eyes of many Shi'ah, JAM had gone from protector to predator. JAM members were no longer considered the guardians of the oppressed Shi'ah against Sunni savagery. They had devolved into organized criminal gangs who inflicted extortion, theft, and a range of other indignities on the people of those cities, with the result that Iraqi security forces were welcomed as the legitimate, disinterested purveyors of law and order when they began to move in and push JAM out. For weeks thereafter, Sadr called for demonstrations virtually every Friday to protest the government's actions but could produce only a few thousand people, rather than the tens, or even hundreds, of thousands his call had once been able to generate.

Although this rejection of the JAM militia does not necessarily translate into a wholesale rejection of the larger Sadrist movement altogether, it does suggest that it may not be as popular as it once was, at least for now. Certainly some Iraqi Shi'ah blame the wider movement for the misbehavior of its militia. Likewise, others simply see no reason to back the Sadrist movement now that they do not feel the need to be protected by its militia from Sunni ethnic cleansing. Sadr himself remains a popular figure among Iraq's downtrodden Shi'i communities, if only because of his family ties. However, he also appears increasingly out of step with his erstwhile constituents. His long sojourn in Iran has removed him from day-to-day management of his organization and has hurt his nationalist credentials.[9] As a result, the Sadrist movement, which previously occupied a large political space in Iraqi politics (among nationalist, moderately Islamist, underprivileged Shi'ah), has been considerably weakened. However, no new group has emerged to claim its ground, which creates the potential for a comeback at some point in the future.

Prime Minister Maliki's own party, Dawa, has splintered just when he has soared to new heights of popularity. In the spring, former prime minister Ibrahim al-Jaafari split off nearly half the party after losing a vote for party leadership to Maliki. Consequently, Maliki's faction controls less than a dozen of 275 seats in the Iraqi parliament. This seems incongruous at a time when Maliki has gained tremendous stature and popularity for ordering the attacks on Basra and Sadr City that confronted JAM, as well as the Mosul operation that is seen to have neutralized AQI (at least for now). The small size of his faction may, however, help explain his interest in driving a tough, nationalistic-inspired bargain in negotiations over a Status of Forces Agreement with the United States. Even some Sunni groups in Anbar began to speak positively about Maliki after he demonstrated that he would take on JAM. But to sustain his position as prime minister, Maliki needs more than begrudging praise from Sunni leaders, he needs votes—and he needs more members of parliament from his own party to be elected in Iraq's coming elections.

The Sunnis themselves seem increasingly not only *willing* to participate in the government of Iraq as they never have in the past, but *determined* to do so. Most Sunni leaders have concluded that boycotting the 2005 elections was a mistake, one that resulted in the worst of the Shi'i militias being able to control the central and even provincial governments without any Sunni counterweight to restrain them. This time around, they are intent on participating in the provincial elections so that they will gain control over the governments of their provinces, as well as the parliamentary elections, in hope of either participating in a new government or at least preventing their rivals from depriving them of their fair share of Iraq's riches. Indeed, Sunni leaders even within the tribal community appear to be laying the foundation for cooperation with a new Shi'ah leadership—one that is no longer dominated by chauvinist militia warlords—if such a leadership emerges over the next six to twenty-four months.

The last piece in the changing kaleidoscope of Iraqi politics is the elections themselves. Now that the people are increasingly rejecting the various militias in favor of the government, the parties that serve as the political façade for the militias are scrambling to be seen as helping to improve the government's capacity to deliver security and essential services, in hope that the people will forget how badly they hindered that process before 2007. There is considerable fear among all of the established political parties that they will lose badly in the coming elections because the people will reject them for their past misbehavior and will vote for alternative parties to spur change. These incentives led to a series of compromises among Iraq's senior leadership between December 2007 and February 2008: they passed the budget, the de-Baathification law, an amnesty for former insurgents, and a Provincial Powers Act bestowing new authorities on the provincial governments as another element in the decentralization process.

All of this represents a new fluidity and hopefulness in Iraqi politics that has been absent over the past three or four years. Like much in Iraq, this promise comes with peril: elections produce winners but also losers, and it remains to be seen how the latter will respond in a country with Iraq's political history. Elections in emerging democracies can be sources of instability as well as progress. But recent changes in Iraq's underlying military and political dynamics create at least the potential to begin a very different pattern of much more positive political development and compromise, if Iraqis—supported by the United States—can realize it.

MOVING FORWARD

If the United States is going to grasp the historic opportunity created by the reduction in violence since 2007, the first step must be to see the first-order problems that threatened to drag Iraq into all-out civil war more definitively resolved. As already explained, considerable progress has been made on these issues, but the situation is hardly complete.

On the security front, important challenges remain. Across the country, the militants are down, but they are not yet out and they will almost certainly try to come back. AQI and other Salafist groups are still able to hide and operate in some areas of Iraq, and their attacks still cause casualties. Some AQI elements are using Syria as a sanctuary to regroup. JAM suffered severe setbacks in the first half of 2008, but for all its defeats, many of its cadres fled to fight another day.

Iraqi and coalition security forces have a critical advantage in that they now hold the potential battlefields, but they need to cement their control of that terrain, both through improved security measures and by convincing the local populace to remain loyal to the government. Critical to this effort is the provision of essential services. If the United States and Iraq are able to provide these basic services, it will likely be very difficult for any of these groups to insinuate themselves back into these communities; if not, it may be relatively easy. Consequently, a continued emphasis on building Iraqi capacity to provide basic services—in the central and provincial governments as well as in the private sector—must remain an American priority.

The Continuing Importance of American Combat Forces

Perhaps the most important decision the new president will make will be how and when to withdraw troops from Iraq. Some argue that the United States must withdraw, or threaten to withdraw, all major U.S. combat units to force Iraqi leaders to put their differences aside and reach a grand compromise on reconciliation. It is true that the presence of U.S. combat forces limits violence and thus reduces the stakes for Iraqi politicians. But while the threat of withdrawal might speed reconciliation efforts, it could also derail them.

Iraq's political system is factionalized, poorly institutionalized, and immature. The process of political reconciliation will require all major Iraqi factions to accept painful compromises. If any major party decides to resist rather than accept risky sacrifices for the larger good, then wary rivals who already distrust one another's motives will have great difficulty holding their own followers to the compromise—likely plunging Iraq back into open warfare. If reconciliation can be done slowly, through small steps, then each stage of compromise is likely to be tolerable, with the risk of one holdout party exploiting the others at a manageable level. In contrast, if reconciliation must be done quickly, with a grand bargain rapidly negotiated in the face of imminent U.S. withdrawal, the necessary compromise will be great—making it extremely risky for all parties. Iraqis, out of fear for their own safety, might well respond to a U.S. withdrawal threat by preparing for renewed warfare. Rather than convincing Iraqis to sacrifice and accept large risks together, a threat of withdrawal could well produce the opposite effect.

Leverage to encourage compromise is important, and the Bush administration's policy erred in rejecting conditionality for U.S. aid or for U.S. cooperation with Iraqi government preferences. But withdrawal threats are hardly the only or the best source of such leverage. Any element of U.S. policy can be made conditional as a source of bargaining leverage— from economic assistance to military aid to diplomatic or political positions, and the next president can gain leverage by offering benefits only if Iraqis deliver compromise. Withdrawal is the biggest potential threat he can use, but it is also a blunt instrument with great potential to damage both U.S. and Iraqi interests. In an environment of increasing stability, the new American president can now hope to succeed with subtler methods.

Moreover, until the first-order problems have been definitively resolved, large American military forces will remain a necessity. Indeed, they are crucial to see Iraq through a variety of ongoing processes and critical events over the next twelve to eighteen months.

Although progress on security has been maintained—even dramatically advanced—since the drawdown of the surge formations in 2008, the reduction in forces has had an impact. Some American personnel fear that further rapid reductions will make it impossible for the reconstruction teams to operate as freely as they have because they will not have the same access to security by American forces they enjoyed during the surge. The United States now has roughly 500 military and police transition teams of all kinds with Iraqi formations. Although this seems to be the maximum number that American forces in Iraq can sustain, it is still insufficient to provide for every Iraqi formation. Finally, the presence of

American forces has been an important check preventing Iraqi forces from engaging in widespread human rights abuses that might otherwise provoke further rebellion and resistance from targeted communities. For instance, the transformation of the Iraqi prison system has been a huge success story, but it was made possible only by having American advisers present at every Iraqi prison, thus dissuading the Iraqi guards from abusing their charges. Further reductions could mean the loss of such advisers, leading to recurring problems across the force.

As discussed, the upcoming elections in late 2008 or early 2009 will represent a critical moment for Iraqis. A great many Iraqis are hoping that these elections will reconcile the Sunni community, weaken militia parties, enable the emergence of moderate parties, and encourage the political system to focus on the needs of constituents. But if these expectations are not met, the fears and frustrations of millions of Iraqis will increase, possibly even driving them back in the destructive directions of 2005 and 2006. Although the Iraqi people have shown remarkable patience with the disastrous course of reconstruction over the past five years, it is just not clear how much progress on these various scores they will need to see. Many Iraqis suggest that they are very realistic about the prospects for change and will accept evolution even while hoping for revolution. But even evolution may be difficult to deliver.

Previous Iraqi elections have made the situation worse, not better, and a range of actors hope the same will be true this time around. All of the militias and current leading parties are doing what they can to buy, intimidate, and otherwise manipulate candidates and voters. In particular, Iraqi and American personnel have suggested that the infiltration of Badr cadres into the ISF could be potentially very problematic during these elections because ISF personnel will be standing guard at the various polling places. These troops could be used to intimidate voters or stuff ballot boxes, or their presence simply might open ISCI up to charges of doing so. Finally, on-the-ropes extremist groups like AQI and JAM might try to mount spectacular attacks on the election process to demonstrate their continuing influence in Iraq and to suborn the elections in hope of reigniting the sectarian conflict.

For these reasons, the elections need to be seen as reasonably fair and free, and they need to demonstrate some degree of change in all of these areas. The Sunnis need to feel, at the very least, that they have elected legitimate provincial leaders and parliamentary deputies who will truly represent their interests. The Shi'ah need to see some diminution in the dominance of the ISCI, the Sadrists, Dawa, and the other parties who did so much damage to Iraq in years past. They also need to see their representatives working to make life better for their constituents and not just treating their offices as private fiefdoms with all of the perks of corruption and patronage. For their part, the Kurds will want to see the emergence of more realistic Sunni and Shi'i parties willing to respect Kurdish aspirations and negotiate realistic settlements of their disputes. Accordingly, American forces will have a critical role to play in protecting the electoral process across Iraq; a large-scale withdrawal of forces before the elections would make that much more difficult and risky.

Finally, while the modest progress in capacity building and microeconomic revival is important, it is also far from where it needs to be. Put plainly, all Iraqis need to be able to secure the essential services necessary for their survival, either from the Iraqi government (whether at national, provincial, or local levels) or through the Iraqi economy. That is simply not yet the case. At a macroeconomic level, indicators seem better in recent months, most notably the important area of GDP growth, which has been driven up mostly by the increase in the global price of oil (Iraq's production has increased but only modestly). Inflation is also in reasonable check, and foreign investment is beginning to trickle in. But unemployment remains at 30–40 percent and essentially unmitigated by recent developments. On this front, there is still a great deal to do.

In this area in particular, the United States is still carrying too much of the burden directly. For instance, Anbar Province was receiving only about 8 percent of the fuel it needed from the central government when we visited there in the early summer of 2008. The marines took it upon themselves to begin trucking the needed oil down from the Bayji refinery while simultaneously funding the refurbishment of a local refinery at Haditha as well as the rail line from Bayji to Haditha to provide a longer-term solution. While the marines deserve praise for this effort, this is exactly the kind of problem that the Iraqi government should be fixing instead. Unfortunately, it is still too often the norm in Iraq that it falls to Americans, particularly American military personnel, to do so.

At this point, the problems on this score lie mostly within the Iraqi system itself. There is a lack of trained budgetary personnel throughout the government, and in the provincial governments a lack of trained civil servants altogether. (Under Saddam the central government did everything—badly—while the provincial governments did nothing.) Corruption still exists throughout the government, but draconian new anti-corruption regulations have so terrified many government employees that they refuse to spend any money at all. Without an electronic banking system, transferring funds from the central government to the provinces, where they can be more effectively spent, is difficult and cumbersome. Another holdover from Saddam's era is the continued over-centralization of the bureaucracy and overplanning of the economy. Iraq desperately needs to streamline its cabinet from its current bloated size (with over three dozen ministerial posts), create cabinet subcommittees to focus on critical problems like the economy, and eliminate the obsolete and crippling Ministry of Planning, which does nothing but hinder the operations of every other ministry.

Turning to the Second-Order Problems

Across Iraq, American military and civilian personnel recognize that the challenges they face are changing. At a strategic level, adapting to those changes, helping the Iraqis devise solutions to them, and doing so while helping to finish off the first-order problems, should be the principal task of the next phase of the reconstruction of Iraq. There are a great many second-order problems, but it is worth highlighting some of the most important, including terrorism and intrasectarian violence; refugees; weak political systems; Kirkuk; and the role of regional players, especially Iran.

TERRORISM AND INTERNECINE VIOLENCE

Terrorism is not as great a threat to the security of Iraq as it once was, but if left unchecked, terrorist groups could, over time, build back into full-blown insurgencies, thereby reviving the much more dangerous first-order problem. Here the incoming administration should maintain the pressure on AQI across northern Iraq.

Similarly, as the first-order problem of intersectarian conflict abates it has brought to the fore the second-order problem of intrasectarian conflict—particularly Shi'ah fighting Shi'ah. Maliki's offensives against

Basra, Sadr City, al-Qurnah, and al-Amarah dealt with that problem at least temporarily because they damaged JAM's organizational infrastructure and its hold over swaths of the Shi'i population. JAM's defeat coupled with the absorption of the Badr Organization and Fadhila's militias into the ISF have dramatically reduced the number of Shi'i militiamen on the street for the moment. However, if JAM is able to mount a comeback, the ISCI and Fadhila might be prompted to reconstitute their own discrete militias to oppose it. The solution to this problem includes a substantial, and increasingly Iraqi, troop presence to secure the population, to prevent JAM from reestablishing control, and to remove the incentive (or the ability) for the Badr Organization and Fadhila to return to militia behavior. It will also require important shifts in how these operations are conducted, focusing on activities designed to reinforce the various cease-fires among these groups and policing their interactions so that no group believes it has an incentive to break such cease-fires.

However, other problems will not be so straightforward. The stand-down of the Sunni insurgency in contractually regulated cease-fires under the Sons of Iraq program has been central to the reduction in violence. This program has not "armed the Sunnis" for the conduct of renewed warfare, as American critics have often claimed—SoIs hardly lacked weapons when they were fighting the United States and the Iraqi government and are no more militarily potent now than they were then. The potential problem is that most SoI groups want to be integrated into the government security forces (they see this as the best guarantee that a Shi'i regime will not use the ISF to tyrannize them), but the Maliki government has been dragging its feet, fearful of empowering Sunni rivals.

In fact, by late summer 2008 Maliki was even pursuing some of these Sons of Iraq and arresting them. While some are likely former AQI fighters, and many were undoubtedly shooting at American and Iraqi security forces only a couple of years ago or less, the trends are ominous. Genuine Sunni cooperation with Maliki, which has begun, will likely not continue if the Shi'ah-led government cannot bring itself to reconcile with some former enemies. It will need to make its purges of SoI limited in number, bring more of them into the security forces, and in the meantime keep paying the 100,000 SoI as it takes ownership of the program from the United States. The good news is that Maliki's efforts to bring more Sunnis, including former Baathists, into the security forces suggests a willingness to avoid sectarian bias. But Maliki's concerns about the SoI are clearly different from his worries about many other Sunnis, suggesting that an American role will remain important for gradually cajoling him into further placing Awakening Council volunteers into government jobs and ensuring that the Sons of Iraq stay on the straight and narrow until he does. This also should remind us that Maliki's interests in getting American forces out of Iraq quickly are not necessarily consistent with the interests of other major Iraqi actors—or of long-term stability.

Moreover, the cease-fires produced by the SoI movement are not inherently stable or self-enforcing. Some SoI members provide less security service than agreed in their contracts; others periodically test the waters by trying to expand their control, by challenging the ISF, or by confronting neighboring SoI groups. Such violations are to be expected in the early years of any such stand-down: a system of cease-fires implemented through more than 200 separate contractual agreements, as the SoI system is, cannot be sustained on autopilot or by its own efforts until the participants' expectations for the future change over time with the experience of peaceful coexistence.

This situation in turn creates two major challenges for the future. Some mix of security and civilian employment must be found for enough of today's SoI members to satisfy their economic needs and, more important, their security concerns vis-à-vis Iraq's Shi'i majority. And some form of ongoing enforcement of SoI contract terms is going to be essential for years to come. Until the Sons of Iraq themselves come to trust the ISF, this enforcement role will have to be played by the U.S. military. And in fact many U.S. brigades now spend much of their time in exactly such enforcement activities—this is already an important U.S. mission, and is likely to become increasingly so over time.

REFUGEES

Returning refugees are another important second-order problem. The first-order problem of the civil war is believed to have created about 4 million internally and externally displaced Iraqis. As the civil war abates, these people are just starting to return home—and many more can be expected to follow if the current positive trends continue. The problem is that they have neither jobs nor homes to come back to. In many cases, their homes are now occupied by other people who took over these properties when their own homes were destroyed. As the United States learned in the Balkans, trying to put every family back in its original home is simply impossible. But that means devising programs to resettle millions of returning refugees. If not, considerable violence could ensue—both by and against the returnees—which could help resurrect the militias, this time as champions of the dispossessed.

The next president should press the Iraqi government to set up a major voucher program to help people build new homes, perhaps in their original provinces but not necessarily in their original cities or neighborhoods. Such an effort will be needed in and around Kirkuk as well, once more disputed property claims are adjudicated (a process that will obviously produce losers as well as winners). This type of program could also help address unemployment by sparking a construction boom. The Iraqi government will have to be the major agent to devise—and fund—such a program, but the United States can help spur the process along, and U.S. troops will likely be needed to help ensure effective, safe implementation of it in the early months so that sectarian tensions are not rekindled.

POLITICAL INSTITUTIONS

Perhaps the most dangerous second-order problems are those related to the immaturity of the new Iraqi political system. Emma Sky, General Petraeus's chief political adviser, explains that while Iraq may no longer be a failed state, it is certainly a very "fragile" one. Its institutions remain underdeveloped and limited in capacity. Its political parties are unrepresentative and unfamiliar with pluralist politics. Its leaders are new to government and even new to leadership itself in many important cases. Iraq has tremendous wealth but, even with enormous help from the United States, is still not fully in control of it and is unsure about how to share that wealth. It is a new, weak political system subjected to a range of internal and external pressures any of which, in the absence of the protection provided by the United States, could cause it to collapse.

Moreover, one of the necessary solutions to the first-order problems has contributed greatly to this second-order problem: the growth in size and capability of the Iraqi security forces. Dealing with the first-order problems of the civil war and the insurgency required the creation of a large, fairly capable Iraqi military. Ironically, Iraq's military may now represent a threat to Iraq's future stability. Today, the Iraqi security forces are feeling their strength. They are proud of their capabilities and achievements, and when they look around, they see few other government institutions as capable as they are. Elsewhere in the Middle East over the past century (including repeatedly in Iraq), those conditions have often produced military coups d'état.

It is highly unlikely that the Iraqi security forces would try this while a considerable American military presence remains in the country. However, a coup is not the only problematic scenario to which the immature Iraqi political system might fall prey. Even if Iraq does not become another military dictatorship like Syria, it might become another mobocracy like Russia, with a powerful clique of politicians from the security services dominating the government, hoarding the country's vast energy wealth, and parceling out the rest of the state to organized crime. The strength of the security forces, the prevalence of organized crime, the ties between organized crime and many Iraqi political leaders, and the temptation of Iraq's oil wealth make this a very real danger. Many fear that Maliki is already headed down this path, intentionally or inadvertently. Still another possibility is a "Palestinian model"—a scenario in which the central government, despite the best efforts of the United States, fails to develop its own capacities to provide essential services but prevents provincial and local governments from filling that gap, continues to steal the country's wealth, and allows Hamas-like militias (which JAM was attempting to emulate before it was booted out by the Iraqi security forces and the Iraqi people) to move in to provide those services and so capture the support of the populace.

Perhaps the easiest threat to imagine is a reversion to the pattern in 2005–06, when chauvinistic Shi'i parties ruled the government (with the connivance of the Kurdish parties) for their own benefit and, secondarily, that of their community. Maliki's treatment of the Sons of Iraq and distrust of the Awakening Councils certainly raise fears among Sunnis about the resurgence of such majoritarian rule. This is one reason why the future of the Sons of Iraq is so important: many Sunnis see their treatment as a bellwether of Shi'i intentions, and the government's unwillingness to integrate them into the ISF will be seen as a determination to reduce the Sunni community to second-class status.

Ultimately, all of these scenarios could reignite the first-order problems that were dragging Iraq (and potentially the whole region) into civil war. For instance, a failed coup attempt could be even worse than a successful one. Any military officer making the bid could be seen by the other communities as a sectarian chauvinist trying to take over the government for his sect, which would cause them to rally together to oppose him. It could easily cause the newly formed security forces to fragment along ethnosectarian lines, as happened in Lebanon during its civil war, putting the United States and Iraqis right back where they started at the end of 2006. Likewise, if the Sunnis believed that the Shi'ah intended to rebuild majoritarian rule, they might well decide to resume their armed resistance, which could lead to a similar outcome.

KIRKUK

Another second-order problem that will demand the attention of the next president is the thorny issue of Kirkuk. Preventing Kirkuk from becoming a flashpoint will require compromises on a range of difficult issues. The city and its environs, once heavily Kurdish, were "Arabized" by Saddam in an effort to weaken the Kurdish hold on Iraq's northern oil-producing region. Many Kurds were displaced, and now, in much of the city, two different families claim every house. One solution the next president should consider promoting would involve giving most Kurds their homes back as well as creating a voucher system, described earlier, to enable those who lose out on their claim to a given disputed home (be it a Kurd or Turkoman or Arab or other) to build a new one. Ensuring that all of Iraq's major groups are comfortable with a settlement on sharing Iraq's oil revenues and oil exploration will also be critical for Kirkuk. A fair resolution on oil requires making future oil wealth a national asset to be shared equally by all Iraqis. Resolving the problem of Kirkuk is likely to take considerable time, especially since any rapid resolution might produce considerable bloodshed.

But important positive factors pertain to Kirkuk as well. So far, the Kurdish leadership has recognized the difficulties inherent in amicably resolving the Kirkuk problem and has resisted popular calls for more precipitous action. In 2008 the new UN special envoy, Staffan de Mistura of Sweden, inaugurated a process to deal with Kirkuk and other internally disputed Iraqi territories. Initially, all of the parties cheered this program; upon hearing the first recommendations for how to move forward on Kirkuk, these parties now universally condemn the program.

Taken together, both responses suggest that it is a fair and reasonable approach to the problem. Of greater importance, it is based on a gradual resolution of the problem, with both sides receiving some compensation up front to provide incentives to keep moving forward. Unless a better alternative miraculously appears, the next president should not only support this process but be prepared to put the weight of his office behind it if one party or another threatens to abandon it.

REGIONAL ACTORS

Another second-order problem the new administration must consider is the role of external actors. Iran is not the only issue in this regard, even if it is the most problematic.

Consider first the countries to Iraq's west and south. If challenges over the Sons of Iraq program, a fair sharing of oil revenue, and other issues are not well handled, significant external problems could develop. Some key Sunni-majority states in the region have finally begun to reconcile themselves to the idea of a Shi'i-majority government in Iraq, albeit grudgingly, by returning their ambassadors and encouraging investment to help the Iraqi economy. This process accelerated after Prime Minister Maliki demonstrated in the spring of 2008 that he would pursue extremist Shi'i actors (such as JAM) in addition to Sunni insurgents and terrorists. But that dynamic could end if Sunni-majority countries perceive Maliki to be reverting to Shi'i-chauvinist policies. The consequences could be numerous: no further debt forgiveness for Iraq from its neighbors, limited diplomatic contact (leaving many Iraqi leaders few alternatives to the option of currying favor with Iran regardless of the consequences), less cooperation in preventing Salafist terrorists from traveling through Sunni-majority states into Iraq, and less inclination to work together with Baghdad to bring refugees home to Iraq in an organized, nondisruptive manner.

Nonetheless Iran remains the chief regional challenge for Baghdad to contend with. In the dark days when Iraq was spinning out of control, Iranian support for various Iraqi militant groups was little more than an afterthought, another party contributing to the mayhem. However, as the ethnosectarian conflict dwindles, Iranian support looms much larger because it appears that Iran is trying to sustain (or even resurrect) conflicts that Iraqis and Americans desperately want to end. The truth, of course, is that the Iranian leadership is not entirely of one mind regarding its goals or strategies in Iraq, and the events of the past twelve to eighteen months (and particularly the setbacks to the various Shi'i militias) appear to have thrown whatever agreement they once had into considerable disarray. Moreover, while Iran is clearly doing a lot of very unhelpful things in Iraq (such as arming various insurgents and militias), it is also doing some things that are very helpful to the United States and Iraq (such as sometimes trying to restrain the Shi'i militias from fighting one another). That they are doing so to serve their own interests should not blind the United States to the fact that it is still helpful.

The key to handling Iran, in brief, is likely to lie in a joint U.S.-Iraqi effort to engage Iran in a dialogue, which the Iranians have so far refused, in hope of making Tehran more of a partner in the reconstruction effort. The new president needs to encourage Iran to do more of what is helpful and less of what is unhelpful. The best route to that is to stop trying to exclude Iran from the process altogether. That will be hard for both Americans and Iraqis (many of whom are more anti-Iranian than Americans are), but it may prove necessary. Washington and Baghdad ought to offer Tehran a permanent liaison presence in Baghdad, which the U.S. government could use to brief Iran on developments relevant to its interests and even solicit its advice on various issues. Better still would be to try to act in ways that take Iran's advice into account so that Tehran might feel that it could secure its minimal interests without having to fight either the Americans or the Iraqis for them. If nothing else, even the failure of such an attempted dialogue will underscore to Iraqis that Iran is acting nefariously in their country, leading them to further increase the political pressure they place on Tehran to stop it—and making them more willing to tolerate decisive government action against groups like JAM that are seen as being funded, armed, and even directed by Iranian agents.

Behind the first- and second-order problems lie a range of third- and even fourth-order problems such as corruption, organized crime, and Iraq's decrepit infrastructure. These are all challenges that American and Iraqi officials already confront every day, but mostly as exacerbating factors to their main problems, not as the principal problems themselves. Some day, if the United States and Iraq are able to eradicate the most crucial threats, these lesser problems will loom much larger. They are not insignificant, and the president should plan to help Iraq address them when they, in turn, come to the fore. However, they should not require large numbers of American combat troops to resolve, and they pose less inherent risk of reigniting major internal war in any event.

U.S. FORCE LEVELS AND THE COMING CHALLENGES IN IRAQ

Americans deserve some sense of how long the current strategy in Iraq may take to achieve most of its desired results. After all, Afghanistan beckons for more American troops, and other national security challenges loom as well. How much longer will a strategy centered on policing Iraqi cease-fires, strengthening national institutions, and ensuring a prudent and gradual transfer of security responsibilities to Iraqi security forces likely take?

Making precise predictions is difficult, and it is more sensible to offer a range of scenarios for war and state-building efforts as complex as those in Iraq. Some things, however, seem clear.

First, some near-term, relatively modest, drawdowns may be required to establish a sustainable posture in Iraq—especially as the United States adds troops to its presence in Afghanistan in the coming months.

Second, current trends make it possible to imagine that the next president could safely cut the U.S. troop presence in Iraq much more substantially—perhaps even by half of today's deployment—at some point during the course of late 2010–11, once the insurgency and sectarian conflicts have been further suppressed, and if the two rounds of Iraqi elections and the formation of a new Iraqi government have laid the foundations for a more positive trajectory in Iraqi politics.

One possible model for further reductions in Iraq if current trends continue is provided by the dramatic turnaround in the situation in Anbar Province. In 2007 the United States had fifteen maneuver battalions in the province; today it has only six. In 2007 American forces participated, together with Iraqi security forces and the Sons of Iraq, in most of the patrolling and hard fighting there. Now marines are included in fewer than half the total number of patrols, with an aim to go down further to only 25 percent soon. Several hundred marines remain in military transition teams (at various levels of command) with each of Anbar's two Iraqi Army divisions, and sizable numbers of Americans are also working with the Iraqi police there. These will remain necessary for some time. Border forces require further partnership with American advisers too, to secure the country's borders against smugglers and, most of all, against foreign terrorists. The United States will also have to continue to provide key "combat enablers"—aerial surveillance as well as air, artillery, and armor support—to Iraqi forces in battle. But Iraqi security forces are providing most of the infantry and policing manpower already.

Another potential measure of the necessary future size of the U.S. troop presence in Iraq is to compare it with the U.S. experience in Bosnia and Kosovo. Of course there are many differences between Iraq and the Balkans. But an important similarity is the prevalence of ethnosectarian conflict in these wars. And an important potential similarity is the ability of a system of cease-fires to underwrite sustainable stability and end the violence. A key to stability in the Balkans has been the continuing presence of outside peacekeepers to enforce the deals that ended the fighting, as U.S. forces are increasingly doing in Iraq. But the Balkan peacekeeping presence has not been static. Within four years of the cease-fires in Bosnia and Kosovo, peacekeeping forces in both countries had been reduced by about half, without a resumption of violence. Starting the Iraq clock counting in 2007, when the process of cease-fire formation culminated, this would suggest a halving of the U.S. presence around 2011, as noted.

Safe drawdowns of major elements of today's forces are becoming possible—if the United States is patient in their timing. Neither Anbar nor the Balkans involved rapid reductions to zero combat troops. Much important work remains to be done in Iraq, from policing cease-fires to supporting the ISF to stabilizing critical elections to helping refugees return safely, and more. And none of this work can be completed on demand or accelerated safely: a stable environment, for example, cannot possibly be ensured until after national elections that will not be held until late 2009 at the earliest. So eliminating American combat battalions and brigades entirely would be enormously imprudent at least in the short term. In addition, brigade headquarters provide important command, control, and liaison capabilities, suggesting that it may be prudent to keep most of them even as combat battalions are sent home. Of course, caveats abound. The northern parts of Iraq remain unsettled, Basra's newfound security is fragile, and Baghdad could again face accelerating sectarian tensions as refugees try to return home or militias try to reassert themselves. Iran may also seek to further stoke the situation, transferring even more potent weaponry to some militias. An election that proves destabilizing, a renewal of sectarian violence, a coup attempt, or some other wild card could change the situation in ways that could require a larger U.S. presence—or that could undermine the prospects for success so badly as to make any U.S. presence ineffective. The odds of such a malign future are much lower now than they were in mid-2007, and the case for hope in Iraq is correspondingly stronger. But any single projection, and any fixed schedule for withdrawal, is subject to the inherent uncertainty of a conflict as complex as Iraq's.

We thus see a combination of real promise but continuing risk. Patience could enable large, safe drawdowns in coming years, but haste or misfortune could still undermine the prospects for stability and threaten profound U.S. security interests.

This view is not uniformly shared, however. In particular, some Iraqi politicians, and especially Prime Minister Maliki, have recently appeared to favor earlier, deeper reductions in U.S. forces than we propose. More broadly, there is widespread impatience with the foreign occupation among Iraqis. Will Iraqi domestic political dynamics permit a continued presence by tens of thousands of Americans beyond 2010 or 2011?

The answer could prove to be no; foreign occupation is rarely popular, and one could certainly imagine anti-occupation sentiment among Iraqis rising to the point where all Americans are forced to leave. As a sovereign nation, Iraq has every right to ask U.S. forces to leave, and if Iraq does, the United States should comply. But this is far from preordained. Iraqi attitudes are more complex than often portrayed in the United States: for years, polls have shown that Iraqis want the United States to leave but not immediately because most Iraqis have consistently seen a need for U.S. security. This pragmatism extends even to populations that once harbored insurgents and AQI terrorists: each of us has recently walked through neighborhoods in places like Falluja where Americans would once have been shot on sight and instead we have found kids mugging for photos and Sunni parents waving from market stalls. This was not so much because Fallujans suddenly loved Americans; it was because they had come to see the security advantages of the U.S. presence and thus tolerated it. As the memory of past violence dims, this perceived need for U.S. troops will diminish, and public tolerance will likely decline with it. But, then so can the U.S. presence. In both the Anbar and the Balkan models, required troop counts fell gradually as the need for a combat presence ebbed. Managing this relationship so the U.S. posture subsides at the right rate—maintaining Iraqi public tolerance long enough to facilitate stability while drawing down safely—will be challenging. But there is no reason to assume that it is impossible.

On balance, the case for believing that a substantial U.S. drawdown can be enabled by relative success rather than mandated by failure is stronger than it has been for years. Before the surge, leaving Iraq in the midst of defeat to corkscrew into chaos and civil war would have been tremendously risky. Today there is a real possibility that persistence could enable a stable Iraq and permit major withdrawals beginning in 2010 without undermining that stability. The American people have every right to be tired of this war—indeed, the soldiers, marines, and civilians who are waging it are a lot more tired of it than the general American public. But understandable frustration with past mistakes, sorrow over lives lost, anger at resources wasted, and fatigue with a war that has at times seemed endless should not result in overlooking the positive developments that have occurred. Nothing in Iraq can ever be guaranteed. But the changes of 2007–08 have created new possibilities. If the next president is willing to build on them, the United States may yet emerge from Mesopotamia with something that may still fall well short of Eden on the Euphrates, but that averts the horrors of all-out civil war, avoids the danger of spillover to a wider regional war, and yields a stability that endures as Americans gradually come home.

NOTES

1. Advisory teams typically consist of 10–30 U.S. soldiers or marines. Each team is attached to a headquarters. Altogether, there are typically more than 100 American personnel for each Iraqi division in various MiTT teams (and a total of more than 5,000 Americans playing such roles nationwide, counting Police Transition Teams as well).

2. According to coalition polling , the number of Iraqis who did *not* believe that the Iraqi police were sectarian rose from 36 percent in June 2007 to 48 percent in 2008, while those who did not believe the police were corrupt rose from 37 to 50 percent during the same period. More anecdotally, in Mosul in the spring of 2008, throngs of people (mostly Sunni Arabs) demonstrated in protest when the government wanted to

move its local NP brigade to another sector, and in the fighting in Basra in March and April, NP personnel staunchly defended their stations against determined attacks by JAM fighters.

3. An American special forces officer who served as the commander of a MiTT team in 2007–08 noted that while the Iraqi officers he worked with might turn a blind eye toward moderate corruption and simply reprimand an officer for more extensive corruption, collaboration with one of the sectarian militant groups typically resulted in the officer's dismissal or imprisonment.

4. The most capable unit in the Iraqi Army, the 1st Brigade of the 1st Infantry Division, was formed in Anbar in 2004, but currently boasts a 60-40 Sunni-Shi'ah split. During the battle of Basra in April, Basrawi Shi'ah in the brigade were used to infiltrate into the city and gather critical targeting information on JAM leadership that helped win the fight. What is more, after the battle, the 1st Brigade's parent formation, the 1st Division, started a recruiting drive in the Hyyaniyah area of the city, formerly one of the major JAM strongholds, to try to bring more Basrawi Shi'ah into the unit. They had hoped to get about 1,000 recruits (the division had about 8,000 personnel at the time), but 3,000 volunteers stepped up on the first day of the drive.

5. Another brigade of the 1st Infantry Division, the 2nd, was committed to the fighting in heavily mixed Diyala Province, and the assessment of the American commander was that they were "pretty friggin' good" and were not encumbered by their provenance in Anbar or their predominantly Sunni composition.

6. Members of the 1st and 7th Infantry Divisions were raised in Anbar but have performed very well there—so well that the U.S. Marine commander of that sector hates losing brigades from these formations, which typically are sent to handle the toughest tasks elsewhere in the country. Likewise, as noted earlier, large numbers of soldiers and officers in the 1st Brigade were from Basra, but that did not prevent the government from deploying it there when the unit was needed.

7. For instance in Basra the best-performing formations were the 1st and 26th Brigades, which had long been partnered with U.S. Marine formations in Anbar and deployed south with their Marine MiTTs. Similarly, the three brigades of the Iraqi 14th Infantry Division, which had never received MiTT or other partnering support, performed poorly in Basra, with the new 52nd Brigade effectively collapsing in combat. Once those same formations were paired with British combat formations, they performed far better.

8. The same division's reconstruction teams also created a program to reestablish Iraq's traditional farmer-to-consumer chain to try to revive agricultural jobs, as well as creating soccer leagues to give unemployed rural youth something to do until paying jobs could be created.

9. Sadr has established offices in Lebanon and Europe, suggesting that he is more focused on becoming a leader of the world Islamic community, or *ummah*, rather than the leader of the Shi'ah of Iraq. Coalition and Iraqi intelligence officials report that captured JAM cadres evince considerable frustration with his lack of leadership and reluctance to make hard choices.

SUZANNE MALONEY

RAY TAKEYH

3

Pathway to Coexistence
A New U.S. Policy toward Iran

THE NEW AMERICAN PRESIDENT, like each of his five predecessors over the past three decades, will be confronted quickly with the need to address profound U.S. concerns about Iran, including its nuclear ambitions, its involvement in terrorism and regional instability, and its repression of its own citizenry. Thanks to events of recent years, Tehran now has acquired the means to influence all of the region's security dilemmas, and it appears unlikely that any of the Arab world's crises, from the persistent instability in Iraq and Lebanon to security of the Persian Gulf, can be resolved without Iran's acquiescence or assistance.

The new administration may be tempted to take the easy way out by offering merely new rhetoric and modest refinements to the carrot-and-stick approach that has failed its five predecessors. This would be a mistake. Today, to deal effectively with a rising Iran, the United States must embark on a far deeper reevaluation of its strategy and launch a comprehensive diplomatic initiative to attempt to engage its most enduring Middle Eastern foe.

After a consideration of the range of possible policy options, including regime change, military strikes, containment, and engagement, this chapter outlines a model of engagement that acknowledges Iran's influence while seeking to constrain and redirect it. Specifically, this approach calls for

—Implementing multitrack, delinked negotiations on each of the most critical issues at stake: the restoration of diplomatic relationships, the nuclear issue, security in the Persian Gulf and Iraq, and broader regional issues.

—Appointing a special coordinator for Iran policy, situated within the Department of State, who would coordinate the diplomatic effort.

—Normalizing low-level diplomatic relations so that the U.S. government can gain familiarity with Iranian officials and achieve a better understanding of Iranian political dynamics. American officials are currently forbidden from direct contact with their Iranian counterparts, a stipulation that further degrades the already limited capacity of the U.S. government to interpret Iran.

—Treating the Iranian state as a unitary actor rather than endeavoring to play its contending factions against one another. Iran's internal partisan skirmishes often appear ripe for creative diplomacy, but any new approach to Iran must be grounded in the recognition that no movement on the core issues of interest to the United States will be possible without the approval of Iran's supreme leader.

—Identifying effective mediators who can serve to build bridges between the administration and the inner circles of the supreme leader and the president of Iran.

—Revamping the recently established U.S. democracy initiative to mitigate the perception of American interference by focusing on programs that encourage people-to-people exchanges.

—Understanding that the process of engaging Iran will be protracted, arduous, and subject to shifts in Iran's internal dynamics and regional context. To achieve and maintain momentum, the incoming administration will have to seize openings, manage crises, and navigate carefully through both the American domestic debate as well as the interests and concerns of U.S. allies.

The proposal calls for swift early steps by the new administration to exploit the brief but crucial window of opportunity during the "honeymoon" of a new presidency and before Iran's own presidential jockeying for elections in June 2009 is in full swing.

The new paradigm of relations does not preclude tension or even conflict. In considering cases of Iran's repaired relationships with other adversaries, it is clear that rapprochement was not a magic cure-all. For the Islamic Republic, rapprochement may best be understood as a way station between conflict and normal relations. However, a new framework of relations can demonstrate to Tehran that responsibility and restraint offer greater benefits to it than does radicalism. The next president must appreciate that for the foreseeable future, Iran will remain a problem to be managed. We believe the approach detailed below provides the best option for dealing with the complexities and contradictions Iran will pose for the United States.

THE PAUCITY OF VIABLE ALTERNATIVES

Any fresh policy review will inevitably present the new president with an array of options that sounds strikingly familiar—regime change, military action, coercive and economic containment, or engagement. Washington has employed elements of each of these approaches over the past three decades, with little success. A review of each suggests that only the last option—engagement—offers a serious prospect of decisively altering the enduring antagonism between Tehran and Washington and enhancing the context for promoting and protecting American interests in the region.

Of all the possible avenues for U.S. policy, the most far-fetched is the notion that after a nearly thirty-year absence of diplomatic relations, the United States can somehow orchestrate a change in the Iranian leadership or the Islamic Republic's structure of power. Any effort to change the Iranian regime—by force, subversion, or a "velvet revolution"—offers no prospects of success, and, as the George W. Bush administration has found, even a passive embrace of the notion of regime change undermines both American diplomacy and the prospects for internal change in Iran.

On the surface, Iran seems to be a good candidate for revolutionary agitation, thanks to its disproportionately young population; restive ethnic minorities; an inefficient, distorted economy; and a regime mired in an obsolescent ideology, riven by factional feuds, and reliant on repression. But the Iranian regime retains enormous capacity for control over society and appears to be firmly entrenched in power for the foreseeable future. Despite long-term and widespread public dissatisfaction, the persistence of the Islamic Republic over three decades of considerable internal and external pressures should leave few illusions about its staying power. The Islamic Republic is unpopular at home, but revolutionary change remains unlikely.

Within Iran, deep-seated popular frustration over deteriorating economic conditions and social and political restrictions has not evolved into an organized opposition. As such, there is no coherent challenge to the system. Iranians appear trapped by revolutionary fatigue and political cynicism, the products of their historical disappointments, first in the aftermath of the 1979 revolution and more recently by the failure of the Khatami-era reform movement. In addition, the specter of instability associated with recent political transitions to their east (Afghanistan) and west (Iraq) has only further dampened Iranians' interest in revolutionary risk taking.

Moreover, even if conditions within Iran were ripe for a democratic movement, any external promotion of it would prove counterproductive. The Islamic Republic suffers from a "conspiratorial interpretation of politics" that "permeates society, the mainstream as much as the fringe, and cuts through all sectors of the political spectrum."[1] Memories of the American-backed 1953 coup that unseated Iran's democratically elected prime minister have fostered an obsessive resentment of U.S. policy and a conviction, which manifests itself even within Iran's widely pro-American population, that Washington was the root of their country's problems. For this reason, American involvement is far more likely to impair rather than advance Iran's democratic potential.

The same dire caveats apply to any effort to use force to address the threat of Iran. The United States simply does not have a viable military option available that would advance American interests across the Middle East. A military conflict with Tehran would significantly harm American security objectives in the region and would be unlikely to provide an effective solution to the nuclear program. Having learned from Israel's preventive strike on the Iraqi nuclear reactor in 1981, Iranian leaders have hardened and dispersed their nuclear installations, and several important facilities that would likely constitute targets of any strike are located in Tehran or near other population centers. Moreover, the failures of American intelligence in Iraq and the limitations on intelligence gathering in Iran leave little reason for confidence that any U.S. air campaign could conclusively or permanently incapacitate Iran's program. Even more troubling is the underlying strategic dilemma: A successful military strike will not end Iran's nuclear ambitions but instead strengthen and radicalize its leadership, likely propelling Tehran to rebuild its destroyed facilities and providing it with justification to be even less concerned about international law or opinion.

Whatever limited benefits would accrue to the United States by delaying Iran's capacity to cross the nuclear threshold for a handful of years would be offset by a wide range of negative consequences. A strike would galvanize Iran's nationalistic population and consolidate public support for an unpopular government and its nuclear ambitions. The regime's retaliatory reach, by both conventional and unconventional attacks, would be felt throughout the region, particularly by American allies such as Israel. The aftermath would almost surely doom any prospects for revitalizing the Arab-Israeli peace process or wresting a stable outcome from Iraq. The sole beneficiaries from a military conflict between Washington and Tehran would be Iranian hard-liners and the forces of radical anti-Americanism throughout the Islamic world. For this reason, many of America's closest regional partners have long viewed the consequences of an attack on Iran as more threatening than the alternative of a nuclear Iran. While they press Washington for more robust action against Iran, Persian Gulf leaders have also carefully cultivated relationships with Tehran and have consistently advocated publicly for a peaceful resolution to the nuclear dispute. Absent a more immediate Iranian provocation, there seems little evidence that Gulf states such as Qatar would readily provide the basing and support needed to undertake a sustained military campaign against Iran. Each of these caveats about the utility of military force in addressing Iran's nuclear ambitions would apply even more forcefully to the frequently discussed proposition of an Israeli strike on Iran.

In the absence of better options, Washington typically reverts to containment, the default American approach toward Tehran. American efforts to contain Iran are centered on the presumption that the systematic application of diplomatic pressure and economic sanctions can obstruct Tehran's nefarious designs and simultaneously transform Iran into a responsible and representative state. The most remarkable aspect of this conventional wisdom is its twenty-nine-year track record of failure. Containment has failed in each of its objectives: it has not isolated the Islamic Republic; it has not converted the regime to support regional peace efforts; and it has not convinced it to forgo the nuclear option. The failure of this policy can be seen in the State Department's annual documentation of terrorism, *State Sponsors of Terrorism*. The report routinely lists Iran as the most active state sponsor of terrorism and warns of Iran's advancement toward nuclear weapons capability.

Containment is actually obsolete because Iran is no longer an expansionist power. Its revolutionary mandates died on the battlefields of Iraq, as Tehran's costly war with Baghdad in the 1980s forced its leadership to realize the limits of its power and the impracticalities of its ambitions. Iran retained its universalist rhetoric as the core of its revolutionary legitimacy, while adopting a more pragmatic and highly opportunistic foreign policy. As a result, Iran today is no longer a revisionist state challenging prevailing borders or a revolutionary regime insisting that local states emulate its model of governance. Rhetoric aside, the Islamic Republic is a medium-size power seeking regional preeminence—a conundrum not terribly conducive to containment.

Beyond inapplicability, the basic problem with continuing to try to "contain" Iran is that the tools of containment have proven wholly ineffective in mitigating America's fundamental grievances with Iranian policies. The approach relies on economic sanctions as the primary instrument for influencing Iran. No capital except Washington, however, has yet been willing to curtail much beyond the most ancillary trade and investment with Tehran. The recent United Nations measures, along with newly imposed U.S. restrictions on Iranian banks and measures by like-minded states to reduce export credits and other support for trade with Iran, have clearly inflicted additional costs and inconvenience on an Iranian economy already distorted by revolution, war, and persistent mismanagement. However, more powerful measures—such as recent proposals for an embargo on Iranian imports of refined fuel products, which could pose a real crisis for a country dependent on imports for at least 40 percent of its gasoline consumption—would require a level of multilateral support for punitive economic measures that far exceeds what has been previously forthcoming. Moreover, implementing any embargo on gasoline imports would entail considerable deployment of military force that could easily escalate into armed conflict.

Ultimately, as long as Iran continues to export oil and the price of oil remains above $70 a barrel, the government will be cushioned by vast revenues—which estimates put in the range of $80 billion for Iran's most recent fiscal year. Washington can make it more costly for Iran to do business, but until and unless the United States can persuade the rest of the international community, in particular Russia and China, to impose sanctions targeting Iran's oil exports—a development that appears inconceivable at the current price or within the current political environment—the pressure will be insufficient to force Iranian capitulation on what its leadership perceives to be its vital interests.

In the past year, Iran's nuclear infractions have allowed the Bush administration to score a number of procedural triumphs, as the UN Security Council has censured Tehran and urged suspension of its nuclear program. However, such symbolic successes do not imply an inclination among the great powers to impose strenuous sanctions on Iran. This is not a product of French pusillanimity or Russian cravenness, but because the other leading powers do not share Washington's threat assessment and its sense of urgency. The conventional wisdom that Moscow and Beijing can be bullied, bribed, or cajoled into imposing strenuous sanctions on Iran disregards the manifestly clear reality that their posture toward Tehran is motivated not by greed or the inadequacies of the current U.S. administration, but by a broader strategic calculus about the immediacy of the Iranian threat and the relative utility of undermining American preeminence.

In addition to the limitations of sanctions, the prospects for effective containment are undermined by the regional context, which has shifted in ways that have profoundly benefited Iran. Although Iraq's Shi'i political society is hardly homogeneous, the parties that have come to power boast enduring ties to Tehran. The new masters of Iraq may not be wholly owned subsidiaries of Iran, but they also have no desire to alienate the Islamic Republic at American behest. A fragile Iraqi state with simmering sectarian conflicts and a dysfunctional central government has forfeited its long-standing role as the bulwark against Iranian influence and guarantor against any single regional power's dominating the critical Persian Gulf.

Regional changes have eroded both the willingness and capacity of Iran's other neighbors to participate actively in containment. The Gulf states have historically sought to balance their relations with external powers with relations with their more populous and powerful northern neighbors, Iraq and Iran. Their security alliances first with the United Kingdom and more recently the United States were intended to supplement, not substitute for, the practice of accommodating their northern rivals. Despite their deep misgivings about Iran, the Arab states of the Persian Gulf have made clear that they will not form the bulwark of an anti-Iranian coalition, even as they privately urge Washington to resolve the Iran problem without implicating or involving them directly. The chaos in Iraq has shattered their confidence in America's capabilities, and they are profoundly uninterested in jeopardizing their recent economic resurgence, which has been predicated on a trouble-free business environment and, in the case of Dubai, expatriated Iranian capital. Gulf leaders will coordinate closely with Washington and continue to host and support offshore naval forces and well-insulated bases. However, beyond this, the Gulf states will opt for accommodation rather than embracing any meaningful effort to isolate Iran. In today's Persian Gulf, there is more confidence in the limitations of Iranian ambitions than in the consequences of American intentions.

As Iran's politics have shifted in a more radical right-wing direction, the appeal of engagement—the final alternative—might seem to have diminished even to those who advocated it during the reform movement of the late 1990s. However, the best argument for engaging with Iran was never predicated on the relative palatability of America's potential interlocutors but on the seriousness of the differences and the importance of the U.S. interests at stake. The international reprobation aimed at President Mahmoud Ahmadinejad and his clique is well-earned, and yet it is ultimately an insufficient reason for rejecting the only possible option for dealing effectively with Tehran.

History suggests that engagement is an appropriate and—if undertaken judiciously—a potentially effective tool for addressing America's deep differences with Tehran. Beyond the inadequacies of the alternative policy options, engagement as a strategy has much to recommend it. In the past, the United States has succeeded in using engagement to manage adversarial relationships with opportunistic and intractable regional powers. In the late 1960s a strident China began to assert its power, confident that the American presence in its neighborhood was receding. The approach of President Richard Nixon and his national security adviser, Henry Kissinger, was to accept the reality of rising Chinese power. By opening a new relationship with China, the Nixon administration obtained its twin objectives of gaining Beijing's assistance in Vietnam and stabilizing East Asia.

Much has changed in the Middle East in the past few years and a forward-thinking American policy needs to acknowledge certain unpalatable realities—namely, the ascendance of Iran as a regional power and the endurance of its revolutionary regime with its blend of authoritarianism and populism. An attempt to engage Iran must begin with a viable assessment of the scope of its ambitions and whether they can be accommodated by the United States. Despite its incendiary rhetoric, the Islamic Republic is not Nazi Germany, a state that had limitless ambitions and saw war as the most suitable means of realizing its objectives. Rather, Iran is an opportunistic power seeking to assert predominance in its immediate Gulf neighborhood and exploit openings to expand its influence. A viable model of engagement would acknowledge Iran as a rising power, and the purpose of talks would be to craft a framework for the regulation of its influence. The central premise of such a strategy would be a willingness to coexist with Iran's influence while seeking to restrain its excesses.

The relevant question then becomes: Would Iran be a willing negotiating partner? This remains uncertain. Developments in the Middle East and Iran's own internal convulsions have placed its government at a critical crossroads. Tehran today must move either toward coexistence or toward a more dangerous mode of confrontation. The enhancement of its influence and its emergence as the most powerful regional state in the Persian Gulf make it possible for Iran to contemplate finally coming to terms with the United States. Despite prevailing perceptions and its leadership's relentless sloganeering, Iran's policies are not immutable. In response to changing internal conditions and regional circumstances, Iranian foreign policy has evolved considerably over the years, and Tehran has hammered out stable if not always harmonious détentes with several other long-time adversaries (such as the United Kingdom and Saudi Arabia). This evolution of Iran's approach to the world continues even as its internal political context has regressed—an example is the unprecedented 2006 endorsement by Iran's supreme leader of dialogue with Washington, a position that only a few years before risked a prison term when voiced by dissidents.

Finally, every American president has endeavored to deal directly with Tehran. Even the administration of George W. Bush sought to engage Iran, with the notable and unfortunate exception of a crucial three-year period after the 2003 U.S. invasion of Iraq when it froze communication. It would therefore be consistent with past policy for the incoming administration to seek to advance the prospects for direct engagement with the Iranian leadership on the key issues of U.S. concern.

The next president will have a brief but crucial window of opportunity to set a new agenda for Iran. He should take advantage of this opportunity to recast the dynamic between the United States and the Islamic Republic with a bold new initiative intended to encourage greater responsibility and responsiveness from Iran.

THE TRACK RECORD OF ENGAGEMENT

Although the United States and Iran have not had formal diplomatic relations since 1980, that should not imply an absence of any contact. Indeed, Washington and Tehran have maintained links of varying proximity and reliability, albeit without ever generating enough traction to end tensions between the two states. In fact, until recently, America's long-standing position was premised on a willingness to deal directly with authoritative representatives of the Iranian government. Notwithstanding its preconditions for direct negotiations on the nuclear issue, the Bush administration used direct diplomacy on occasion, including opening a channel between the U.S. and Iranian ambassadors in Baghdad and sending a senior diplomat to engage in nuclear negotiations. At no time in the past twenty-seven years did the United States drop its demands for significant changes to Iranian behavior. However, Washington typically expressed those demands not as preconditions for dialogue but rather as requirements for any prospective improvement in relations.

Even during moments of greatest tension and frustration in the relationship, there has been an underlying American commitment to maintaining communications with Tehran. President Jimmy Carter did not close the Iranian Embassy in Washington until a full five months into the hostage crisis. The Reagan administration pressed for the revival of direct communications even in the wake of the political damage wrought by the Iran-contra arms sales. President George H. W. Bush appealed publicly for talks with Tehran and went so far as to take a phone call from an impostor posing as Iran's president at the time, Ali Akbar Hashemi Rafsanjani. President Clinton attempted to open a private, back-channel dialogue with President Mohammad Khatami. Even President George W. Bush, who has denounced engagement with radicals as appeasement, sanctioned unconditional engagement with Iran for eighteen months following the 9/11 attacks, in what was the first sustained direct diplomacy between Washington and Tehran since the resolution of the hostage crisis.

Why then has engagement failed in the past? The answer largely lies with Iran's historic rejection of any dialogue with Washington without prior changes in U.S. policy. Ayatollah Ruhollah Khomeini's formulation—that "relations with America could be resumed if it 'behaves itself'" (*agar adam beshavad*)[2]—has been repeated over the years by senior Iranian officials from across the political spectrum. The particular preconditions typically sought by Tehran include the release of the remaining American-banked Iranian assets that were frozen by the United States after the 1979 embassy seizure, the lifting of American sanctions, and suspension of U.S. efforts to develop oil and gas transportation networks that bypass Iran.

Beginning in 2006, small cracks appeared in Iran's long-standing official aversion to direct talks with the United States. Ayatollah Ali Khamenei proclaimed in March 2006 that "there are no objections" to talks with Washington "if the Iranian officials think they can make the Americans clearly understand the issues pertaining to Iraq." He cautioned, however, that "we do not support the talks, if they provide a venue for the bullying, aggressive and deceptive side to impose its own views."[3] His announcement marked the first time since the Iranian revolution that the entire Iranian political spectrum, at the highest level, publicly endorsed negotiations with the United States. While the Baghdad talks did not get under way until May 2007 and produced little substantive outcome, the Iranians sought to expand the dialogue to other issues, a move opposed by the Bush administration for fear of undermining its diplomacy on the nuclear issue. Still, despite the limited utility of talks and the hostile regional climate, Khamenei again reiterated his willingness to countenance direct talks with Washington as recently as July 2008.

Ironically, the shift in the Iranian position toward negotiations with the United States can be credited to the conservative reconsolidation of power in recent years and at least in part to Ahmadinejad himself, whose backing from the country's conservative elites, along with his firmly established radical credentials, provides far greater room for maneuver than either of his predecessors had. As a commentary in one of the few remaining reformist Iranian newspapers explained, "If the ice of hostility between Tehran and Washington is to be broken, the likelihood of it happening at the hands of a president named Ahmadinejad is much greater than other Iranian leaders and officials."[4]

Beyond the obstacle of Iranian historical reluctance to negotiate, which the regime now seems to have overcome, U.S. efforts to engage Iran have been undermined by three primary issues: U.S. inability to judge accurately the internal dynamics of Iranian politics; difficulty in establishing an appropriate channel for dialogue; and the ongoing challenge of finding an intermediary to shepherd the engagement.

For more than three decades, U.S. officials have had only the most limited direct contact with Iranians and almost no first-hand experience inside the Islamic Republic. As a result, each U.S. administration has misinterpreted the parameters for diplomacy within Iran. The Carter administration's relationship with Iran's moderate provisional government obscured its dearth of contacts with the new regime's real power base, which was virulently anti-American. Ronald Reagan's government went astray in the Iran-contra affair, which was premised on the illusion that U.S. arms sales to Iran would empower a moderate new regime in Tehran. For its part, the Clinton administration's focus on Iran's increasing support to regional militants resulted in a failure to take advantage of overtures by then-President Rafsanjani at the peak of his power, most notably the 1995 selection of an American firm to develop two offshore oil fields in the first such contract since the revolution.[5]

The most disastrous misreading of Iran's internal dynamics took place during the George W. Bush administration. Beginning in 2002, even as U.S. and Iranian diplomats were undertaking valuable cooperation on Afghanistan, Washington began focusing on empowering the Iranian people rather than dealing with the country's leaders. The administration eventually curtailed all diplomatic contact with the regime, including the successful channel on Afghanistan. The policy reflected the impact of the administration's early successes in Iraq, which were seen as the death knell for the neighboring Iranian regime.[6] The Bush administration's misapprehensions scuttled apparent momentum within the Iranian regime for new overtures toward Washington, including talk of parliamentary exchanges, endorsements by influential conservatives, and consideration of the appointment of a high-level government committee tasked with examining engagement.[7] Fervent Bush administration calls for democratic change explicitly undermined its prospects, as well as the context for diplomacy; Khamenei declared in 2002 that "while the United States sets an official budget for anti-Iranian activities, it would be treason and stupidity to want to negotiate or talk with them."[8] In the Iranian view, Washington merely pocketed Iranian cooperation on Afghanistan as part of its broader aim to eliminate the Islamic Republic.[9]

A second flaw in previous efforts to engage the Islamic Republic relates to the difficulty in determining the appropriate channel for dialogue with Iran. Attempting to leverage differences within the regime has fatally impaired U.S. attempts at engagement, particularly the overtures launched by the Clinton administration in response to the reform movement's ascendance. Washington tried to embrace and empower Khatami through an array of gestures that included specific policy changes, an attempt at direct presidential communication, and flattering rhetoric. Rather than strengthening the embattled reform movement, the overtures merely exacerbated the conspiratorial insecurity of regime stalwarts, who took every opportunity to undermine Khatami's limited authority and his prospects for a broader Iranian détente. The Clinton experience speaks clearly to the jeopardies involved with aligning U.S. policy with a specific faction or power broker in Iran; the perception of American favoritism taints the very forces the United States hopes to use as interlocutors.

Finally, one of the most obvious lessons from the disappointing track record of U.S.-Iranian engagement is the value of an effective intermediary. Absent the crucial role of the Algerians, the 1979–81 hostage crisis might have endured even longer and its resolution might not have produced a framework that both sides have largely adhered to for nearly three decades. Algeria's mediation enabled the requisite face-saving avoidance of direct bilateral commitments and overcame a critical confidence gap by providing a third-party guarantor for synchronized recip-

rocal concessions. Similarly, the dogged diplomacy and personal credibility of UN envoys succeeded in facilitating the delicate negotiations
involved in freeing Western hostages held in Lebanon during the 1980s
and 1990s.[10] The converse holds equally true: mediators with insufficient understanding or incompatible interests of their own have compounded the inherent U.S.-Iranian dysfunctionalities. During the hostage
crisis, erstwhile intermediaries of varying nationalities, competence, and
motivation complicated Washington's efforts to decipher and deal with
Iran; some misrepresented their standing, while others helped "validate
the hostage taking and legitimize the captors' allegations."[11] Similarly,
the Iran-contra debacle was driven in large part by misinformed Israeli
intervention as well as by the self-interested efforts of a motley array of
arms dealers and Iranian expatriates.[12]

A NEW WAY FORWARD

In dealing with the challenge of Iran, it is time not just for a policy shift
but for a paradigm change. For too long, Washington has sought in vain
to develop a persuasive array of incentives and disincentives in an effort
to alter Iran's behavior. This incrementalism has produced little in the
way of identifiable improvements in Iran's policies, its rhetoric, or any
underlying commitment to a negotiating process with Washington. The
timetable on the most pressing U.S. concerns—Iran's nuclear activities
and its support for violence in Iraq—is simply too short to permit
another American president to indulge in the illusion that he can succeed with small refinements to the carrot-and-stick approach that has
failed his five predecessors. Washington needs to transform its approach
to this enduring and urgent challenge by crafting a strategy that draws
Tehran into a web of mutually reinforcing security and economic
arrangements.

Given the complex domestic politics and interests at play on both
sides, and the history of deep mistrust, reciprocal steps would inevitably
run afoul of the myriad of obstacles that have become embedded in the
relationship since 1979. Rather, progress can best be achieved by engaging with Iran in those limited arenas and on those discrete issues where
interests overlap—such as Iraq, Afghanistan, and regional security
arrangements—while generating multilateral consensus to maintain or

even intensify pressure on the key concerns of weapons of mass destruction and terrorism. Such a new approach must also incorporate a different and more nuanced array of tools, which would include using a smarter deployment of incentives alongside sanctions, and more closely coordinating American efforts with those of allies in Europe as well as Russia, China, Japan, and India to maximize U.S. leverage.

The central question in embarking on any new American diplomatic initiative concerns whether the Islamic Republic is ready to accept a new relationship with Washington, specifically one that would involve significant compromises on Iran's nuclear program and involvement with terrorist groups. Ultimately, this question is impossible to answer without testing the proposition. Although there have been innumerable missed opportunities and crossed signals from both sides, the United States has never managed to undertake a viable and sustainable diplomatic process. History demonstrates that Iranian leaders are fully capable of reversing core policies and embracing old enemies. Moreover, it is also clear that today's Iranian leaders are capable of selective, constructive dialogue with the United States and that they have cross-factional support for direct, authoritative dialogue with their American adversaries—a condition that did not exist for most of the past thirty years.

Beyond this key shift, though, Iran's domestic political environment is not particularly fortuitous at this time, and there are no guarantees of success. There is no hard evidence that Iranian leaders have ever been prepared, fully and authoritatively, to make fundamental concessions on the key areas of U.S. concern. Even more uncertain is whether Iran has had or will ever attain the level of policy coordination and institutional coherence that would enable any overarching agreement to be implemented successfully. However, the United States will only be able to gauge Iranian capacity through a direct and sustained effort at engagement.

The history and the current context should condition U.S. expectations and shape any prospective new American diplomacy. The duration of the negotiations required in analogous cases, such as Iran's rapprochements with Saudi Arabia and the United Kingdom and U.S. détente with Libya, suggests that the United States is many years away from a durable accord with Iran that settles mutual grievances and concerns, and even further away from any final resolution. An understanding of the obstacles and the effort required to surmount them should not deter diplomacy but rather spur a proportionate American bureaucratic and political investment in it. Within this strategy of engagement, the following are key tactical decisions the next president should consider.

Move Quickly

A key variable with respect to constructing a successful diplomatic initiative toward Tehran involves timing. Any new administration will inevitably undertake a thorough policy review, and as the chapter on nonproliferation policy notes, the urgency of the Iranian nuclear issue may be less immediate than an often overheated media debate would suggest. Iran remains at least several years away from crossing the nuclear threshold, which should give the new administration sufficient opportunity to consult with allies and formulate its diplomatic strategy. Significant delays in clearly articulating a new approach would be unfortunate, however. First, precedent indicates that the new president's opening posture and signals will have a disproportionate impact on his ability to deal effectively with Tehran. As both the Clinton and George W. Bush administrations experienced, revising or reversing Iran policy midcourse in an effective manner can be exceptionally difficult, both because of path dependencies inherent in American bureaucratic politics and because for Iranians, first impressions tend to be lasting ones. Whatever tone the new president adopts toward Iran at the beginning of his term will shape his options for the ensuing four years at least. The uniquely intractable nature of the Iranian challenge warrants an effort by the new administration to seize the limited prospect for progress that is most manifest in its earliest months.

Tehran has demonstrated a pattern of reaching out to new U.S. presidents, albeit not always in the most coherent fashion. For example, consider the 1980 hostage release, Rafsanjani's 1989 offer to help in Lebanon, and a variety of signals sent in 1993 and again in 2001–02. Iran is very likely to repeat this pattern in 2009, particularly because the advent of a new American administration precedes Iran's presidential elections by a mere five months, and the past two such ballots have featured considerable forward-leaning debate on the question of future rapprochement. Delay in formulating the U.S. approach could sacrifice this possible window of opportunity.

Some, such as *New York Times* columnist Thomas Friedman, argue that "talking with Iran today would be tantamount to appeasement . . . because the Bush team has so squandered U.S. power and credibility in the Middle East, and has failed to put in place any effective energy policy, that negotiating with Iran could only end up with us on the short end." Friedman argues that "when you have leverage, talk. When you don't have leverage, get some. Then talk."[13] This logic mirrors that of the Bush administration, which first embraced a chimerical notion of the regime's vulnerability and later boxed itself into a corner by insisting that nothing could be achieved so long as the Iranians perceived momentum to be on their side.[14]

The quest for optimal leverage is a red herring. The ideal opportunity for dealing with Tehran will never come; the objective of American policy must be to create the grounds for progress with Iran even if the Iranian internal environment remains hostile or the regional context continues to present challenges. And though a new president will certainly experience a diplomatic honeymoon, it is highly unlikely that a new U.S. administration will be able to achieve newly effective leverage over Iran. Seemingly insatiable Asian demand for energy will maintain high oil prices and dissuade fence-sitters from more strenuous sanctions on Iran. Moreover, waiting until American leverage appears sufficient will inevitably only reverse the equation; even Iranian reformists were averse to negotiating when they perceived Washington to be "in a position of strength," because "they are threatening us, and if we negotiate we will be in a weak situation."[15] Timing matters in negotiations, and the concern about the impact of regional dynamics is justifiable, but to avoid diplomatic interface because of a perceived power imbalance is effectively to consign the countries to permanent antagonism.

Others have highlighted Iran's June 2009 presidential election as a rationale for deferring any initiative toward Tehran. Ahmadinejad is a profoundly problematic leader, and the prospect that U.S. diplomacy might inadvertently boost his standing is cause for concern. Tying any overture to the election results, however, risks the perception that the United States is linking an opening to a change in Iran's leadership, a perception that will likely weaken any candidate that Washington might prefer. Any successor to Ahmadinejad will likely have very limited room for independent maneuver and would be quickly painted as an American stooge if he were to embrace a new overture from Washington. In any case, despite widespread unhappiness with Iran's economic conditions, the prospect that Ahmadinejad could use the prerogatives of his position to manipulate another four-year mandate is not inconceivable. He enjoys the full-throated support of the supreme leader and the security bureaucracy and has cultivated a significant base of support outside the major cities through his provincial tours and giddy distribution of oil largesse. Since the real address for American diplomacy is the office of the supreme leader, Iran's presidential election should not dictate Washington's timetable.

Create a Framework for Negotiations

Devising an effective formula for engaging Tehran and maintaining momentum will be critical tasks for the incoming administration. The ultimate objective must be clearly understood by both sides from the outset: a comprehensive effort to address all the issues and produce a framework for eventual normalization of relations. Washington should develop the outlines of this process but incorporate sufficient latitude and time to integrate Iranian input and buy-in. The operational aspect of such diplomacy should entail four separate negotiating tracks—diplomatic relations, the nuclear issue, security in the Persian Gulf, and the broader regional issues, including the Arab-Israeli peace process. These tracks should be distinct and noncontingent, so that logjams in one arena would not preclude progress in another. Only a multifaceted process that tackles the broad host of issues at stake between the two governments will generate both the versatility and credibility to make real progress on the hardest issues. Indeed, as the Bush administration's diplomatic difficulties demonstrated, making progress on the most urgent issues is difficult if they are addressed in isolation. A broad effort to resolve the underlying political and strategic divergences between the United States and Iran will be essential for constructing a durable nuclear accord.

The first track should deal with a timetable for a resumed diplomatic relationship, outlining the reciprocal steps and obligations needed for incrementally phasing out U.S. sanctions and returning Iran's frozen assets. This track would likely move at the slowest pace, but its very existence would provide Tehran with both the presumption of reciprocity and a demonstrable American commitment to diplomacy rather than regime change. This track would hold out the prospect of meaningful incentives for the regime that might facilitate productive discussions on more contentious issues, such as the broader regional questions and the peace process, and would likely enhance goodwill toward the United States among the general Iranian public. Since it would likely accomplish very little of actual substance in the near or medium term, this track should be constructed to provide both sides with a mechanism for communication as well as an opportunity for the perception of early achievement—for example, the drafting of a statement of principles to outline the shared objectives and govern the ongoing interaction between the two sides, along the lines of the Shanghai Communiqué that was issued by the United States and China in 1972 and that called for normalization of relations.

Discussions on the nuclear issue, the second track, should be opened by setting aside the failed proceduralism of the past two years, specifically the P5-plus-one package of incentives intended to draw Iran to the negotiating table as well as its corresponding precondition, suspension of uranium enrichment. This track should retain the existing multilateral approach involving the five permanent members of the UN Security Council, plus Germany, with the multilateral process providing an umbrella—like the North Korean case—for the integral bilateral exchanges between Washington and Tehran. Building on the Bush administration's implicit concession in authorizing a senior State Department official to join the July 2008 nuclear talks, the new president should indicate his administration's readiness to participate in multilateral nuclear talks without prior conditions but also remove any specific assurances to Tehran for its cooperation. Negotiators would have a clean slate to develop a fresh array of confidence-building measures and a rigorous inspection regime to ensure that Iran's nuclear program is not being diverted for military purposes. These negotiations cannot be open-ended, a format that would reward Iran's proclivity for opportunistic stalling; rather, a firm deadline should be set early on for arriving at an accord that satisfies both parties.

While the ultimate objective of this track must be a full and durable suspension of uranium enrichment, any serious U.S. negotiating strategy should incorporate contingency plans for moving beyond the prolonged impasse of recent years over Iran's intransigence on the question of enrichment. Persuading the Islamic Republic to accede fully to the international community's demands and accept a long-term moratorium on enrichment activities represents the ideal outcome of any diplomatic initiative. Such an arrangement might involve incentives along the lines of those proffered in 2006 and again in 2008, sweetened by more credible measures to ensure Iranian access to fuel supplies for its civilian nuclear power plants. However, the experience of the international community since 2005 suggests that absent some dramatically negative shift in the strategic realities facing Iran's current leadership, predicating negotiations on achieving an enduring suspension will not succeed. Iranian officials maintain that their enrichment activities are consistent with the provisions of the Nuclear Non-Proliferation Treaty, although this argument is contested by much of the international community. Perhaps more important, Iran's ongoing enrichment is the objective reality in the continuing absence of negotiations. For this reason, U.S. negotiators—in cooperation with American allies—should develop a fallback position, as outlined in the chapter on nonproliferation, that permits a limited Iranian enrichment capability in exchange for rigorous safeguards, such as snap inspections, permanent presence of International Atomic Energy Agency personnel, and full transparency on its previous activities. Iran's motivations for its nuclear program may well be production of weapons; however, an exacting verification process backed by the authority of the international community can play a vital role in obstructing the ambitions of determined proliferators. This outcome would not represent an ideal conclusion to negotiations, but any interim steps that impede Iran's advancement toward nuclear self-sufficiency would represent a substantial short-term improvement over the unchecked progress that has transpired since its 2005 decision to end a voluntary suspension, pledged two years earlier as part of negotiations with Britain, France, and Germany, and resume enrichment.

On a third and separate track, negotiations should focus on Iran's immediate neighborhood—Iraq and the Persian Gulf. Since the toppling of Saddam Hussein, Washington has worked hard to limit Iran's influence in Iraq. Although Iran has been busy buttressing the fortunes of its Shi'i allies and arming their militias, beneath the veneer of recriminations and accusations the two powers actually share many common interests. Tehran, like Washington, is interested in defusing the existing civil war and sustaining Iraq as a unitary state. Moreover, the clerical regime appreciates that the best means of realizing its objectives in Iraq is not through violence but through the democratic process, which will inevitably empower Iraq's Shi'i community. For Iran, a functioning and legitimate Iraqi state would be in a position to neutralize the insurgency, sap Baathists of their remaining power, and incorporate moderate Sunnis into an inclusive but Shi'ah-dominated governing order.

In dealing with Iran's actions inside Iraq, the new administration should recognize that long-standing personal, cultural, and religious ties give Tehran enormous capacity to influence the future of Iraq. Washington should endeavor to pressure and persuade Tehran to channel its power in a constructive direction. Key U.S. objectives in these discussions would include tempering the Shi'i push for regional autonomy, eliminating arms supplies to militias and insurgents, supporting efforts at political reconciliation, and reining in recalcitrant actors such as Moqtada al-Sadr. The new administration should also use a dialogue to maximize the benefits from those constructive elements of Iran's involvement in Iraq. As one of Iraq's largest trading partners, Iran could also play a useful role in funneling investment and building infrastructure in Iraq's historically underdeveloped Shi'i regions and cities, including Basra and Sadr City.

Although suspicions are deep on both sides, and Iran's responsibility for the death of American soldiers naturally invokes great sensitivity within the U.S. political context, surprisingly the Iraq track could provide an avenue for achieving small-scale progress relatively quickly. First, the evolving context—including both Iraq's internal political environment and changing regional dynamics—provides new incentives for Tehran to relinquish some of the more dangerous dimensions of its activities inside Iraq, particularly its involvement with militias and "special groups." Baghdad's recent assertiveness vis-à-vis Tehran as well as Washington represents a constructive step forward in achieving a competent central government empowered to act in Iraq's independent interests, and future provincial elections could reinforce this trend. New cooperation and assistance from the Arab Sunni world in the form of debt forgiveness and diplomatic presence may also influence Iran's shifting internal debate over its Iraq policy in a more positive direction.

In addition, the existence of many mutual interests could facilitate greater scope for satisfying both sides' needs than is commonly assumed. A range of largely peripheral issues within the Persian Gulf region, including naval protocols on smuggling and preventing incidents at sea, could offer opportunities to mitigate potential bilateral flash points while also serving as the building blocks for a broader regional dialogue on Gulf security some time in the future. Similarly, a serious effort to devise an acceptable framework for the permanent demobilization of the Iraqi-based Mujahideen-e Khalq—an Iranian opposition group considered a terrorist organization by the United States—could serve as a first step for securing Iranian cooperation on related issues, including the long-standing U.S. interest in obtaining access to Saad bin Laden and other senior al Qaeda leaders reputed to be under some form of house arrest in Iran.

The fourth and final track should deal with what is by far the most entrenched of Iran's problematic positions: its violent opposition to Israel and the Arab-Israeli peace process and its related support for regional and international terrorist networks. Iran's antagonism toward Israel is rooted in its revolutionary ideology and buttressed by the strategic influence that its antipathy produces within the region. Tehran has long perceived that the advantages it gains from such a posture are worth the price of U.S. sanctions and criticism. At a time when Hezbollah has emerged triumphant from its 2006 conflict with Israel and is a source of much popular acclaim in the Arab world, Iran's resolve is further stiffened. To change Iran's policy, Washington must alter that calculus by making clear that should Iran contemplate a constructive relationship with the United States, then its bellicosity toward Israel will lead to a potential loss of tangible benefits.

A careful look at Iran's international relations reveals that its attachment to terrorism is not necessarily immutable; its abandonment of terrorism in Europe and the Persian Gulf demonstrates the importance of incentives. The 1997 conviction of Iranian officials by a German court in the 1992 murders in Berlin of Kurdish dissidents led the European Union to impose restrictions on trade and to recall their emissaries from Tehran. Given the costs, the Islamic Republic quickly abandoned the practice of targeting exiled dissidents. In a similar vein, as a precondition for normalizing relations with Iran in the 1990s, Saudi Arabia and the Gulf states demanded Iran's cessation of support for radical elements within these states. Once more, the strategic advantages of such a détente compelled Iran to pay the price. Both episodes reveal the value of diplomatic and economic inducements as a lever on Iran's behavior.

As the United States and Iran attempt to resolve their differences, self-interest and negotiating momentum can begin to move the theocratic state away from its reliance on terrorism and anti-Israeli demagoguery. It is unrealistic to expect that the Islamic Republic will ever reconcile formally with Israel or wholly abandon Hezbollah, but a persistent effort to engage Iran's leaders can persuade them of the utility of restraining their rhetoric and facilitating the evolution of their semiautonomous Lebanese proxy into a "normal" political party.

Appoint an Envoy

To coordinate this daunting diplomatic effort, marshal the internal bureaucratic resources needed, and ensure appropriate coordination with key allies, the incoming president should create a new locus of responsibility and authority through the appointment of a special envoy. Ideally, this envoy, the special coordinator for Iran policy, would be situated at the State Department operating under the authority and direction of the secretary of state. The justification for such a post is clear—Iran touches upon a range of vital U.S. interests that cannot be adequately managed on a part-time or an ad hoc basis.

The responsibility of the special coordinator during the prenegotiations period would be to shepherd the internal U.S. bureaucratic process, including a standing interagency policy coordination committee that would report to a regular principals meeting on Iran. In addition, the Iran coordinator would be responsible for developing an in-depth strategy for the negotiating process that would include mapping the players, positions, and possible Iranian actions and reactions. While the United States has long-standing and clearly enumerated concerns and objections to Iranian policies and conduct, Washington has never developed a negotiating strategy or even detailed positions on what it would seek at each interval of an extended dialogue with Tehran on any individual issue.

Once a dialogue is under way, the Iran coordinator would serve as the primary U.S. representative for each negotiating track, directing the process, setting priorities, managing agendas, and ensuring that the diplomatic strategy is closely synchronized with relevant American initiatives in Iraq and on the peace process. The very establishment of the post should help to mitigate any tendency toward policy freelancing within the U.S. government, as well as provide an early signal to the Iranians that the new administration is serious about embarking upon a new approach. Should a diplomatic initiative categorically fail, the Iran coordinator would offer a focal point for alternative strategy development, particularly the mobilization of a tightly coordinated international campaign of economic pressure and sanctions.

Unilaterally "Normalize" Low-Level Diplomatic Relations

The absence of normal diplomatic contacts is a far greater impediment to policymaking than is generally understood or acknowledged. Without eyes and ears on the ground, the U.S. government is deprived of basic understandings that an embassy and its staff usually provide: the sense of political dynamics; the historical knowledge; the routine business that provides irreplaceable insights. Currently all American officials are prohibited from any direct contact with their Iranian counterparts except in narrowly defined, exceptional circumstances. As a result, relatively few U.S. diplomats have had any personal experience with or exposure to the official thinking of Iran. This is a grievous deficiency in our own diplomacy.

The George W. Bush administration began to mitigate some of these deficiencies with the establishment of a specially tasked Iran office within the State Department's Bureau of Near Eastern Affairs, the creation of a dozen overseas listening posts, and an Iran-focused office based in Dubai where hundreds of thousands of Iranians live and do business. The administration also moved closer to reopening a U.S.-staffed interests section in Tehran. These efforts—a few new working-level posts—will not overcome the inadequacies inherent in a three-decade estrangement, however. Therefore the incoming administration should quickly request the establishment of a new U.S. presence post in Tehran, rebrand the Dubai office as a "shadow embassy" led by a senior diplomat, and authorize a much wider array of ordinary diplomatic contacts between the two countries, including permitting routine interaction between American diplomats and their Iranian counterparts.[16] These channels will give the United States additional avenues of information and communication, enabling the government to begin to get to know Iranian interlocutors who may one day be in positions of influence. The next administration should also initiate direct engagement with Iranian media outlets, particularly the state broadcasting network, and permit representatives of the Iranian media to report from Washington. While the imperfections of Iran's officially sanctioned news sources are myriad, they remain the primary source of information for most Iranians and thus an important outlet for U.S. policymakers.

Know the Address

As detailed above, previous attempts at engaging Iran were derailed by U.S. efforts to exploit factional divides within the regime. In the end, the historical track record makes clear that the only path toward resolving American differences with Tehran is one that deals directly with the ultimate power center—the supreme leader. This office does not hold a monopoly on authority but remains the crucial locus of decisionmaking, particularly on issues of ideological sensitivity, namely, those often of greatest concern to the United States. In 1981 it was Ayatollah Khomeini who finally relented and approved the release of the U.S. hostages, just as he was the one who later authorized the arms sales during Iran-contra and took public responsibility for the decision to accept a cease-fire in the 1980–88 war with Iraq. Despite the public rhetoric of then-president Rafsanjani, it appears to have been Khamenei who, once he had consolidated his authority as Khomeini's successor, forced Hezbollah to release Western hostages held in Lebanon during the 1980s and 1990s.[17] Khamenei also bears responsibility for the factional stalemate and sabotage that obstructed progress during the uniquely fortuitous conditions of a reformist Iranian presidency and a receptive Clinton administration.

Understanding that Khamenei is the appropriate starting point for any American engagement clarifies the task but also underscores the challenges. Although Khamenei has condoned talks with Washington in recent years, his writings and public rhetoric since 1979 contain nothing that would suggest he harbors any positive sentiments toward Washington. Furthermore, his vast power base within Iran is little known or understood outside the country. As a result, the U.S. government has no real capacity for influencing Iran's ultimate decisionmaker in a direct fashion. Still, by addressing the Iranian state as a unitary actor and by acknowledging Khamenei as its head of state, Washington may avoid some of the pitfalls that have undermined previous U.S. efforts at engagement.

Identify Credible, Effective Mediators

The role of a good international mediator will be critical to the incoming administration's attempts at engaging Iran. Although Khamenei and his inner circle should be the focal point for American efforts, any negotiating process with Tehran will also have to win the support of President Ahmadinejad and his inner circle. Both these groups are intensely distrustful of the United States, and neither has had meaningful direct exposure to Washington. In addition to addressing Khamenei, a new U.S. initiative will need to find a way to co-opt, contain, or circumvent Ahmadinejad's nefarious tendencies, unlikely to prove an easy task with a populist president who has surrounded himself with devoted, like-minded advisers who have little international experience.

Given our long estrangement, reaching out to these individuals and building trust will prove exceptionally difficult, and it is unlikely that most of the United States' traditional European partners will be substantially better equipped to assist. The president will have to seek out alternatives in the Islamic and developing worlds—India, Indonesia, Turkey, and South Africa may be potential candidates, as well as traditional Gulf interlocutors—that have had greater informal contacts with the insular elites of the Islamic Republic. The Russians may also be able to play a special role here, based on existing relationships with the old guard surrounding Khamenei. The United States might also use third parties as informal partners in a cooperative multilateral effort to help us interpret Iranian behavior and tactics as well as reinforce our messages with Tehran.

Retool Democracy Initiative

Any serious effort to initiate a new negotiating track with Tehran will have to reconsider some of the post-9/11 ideological verities, including the issue of democracy promotion. It is understandable that the precedents of American assistance to fledgling movements in Georgia, Serbia, Ukraine, and other emerging democracies have prompted an interest in replicating these successes (even if there is a tendency to overstate the American role and to disregard subsequent regressions in several cases). However, policy measures must be judged on their utility, as well as their prospective damage to other priorities, and with respect to Iran it is clear that U.S. democracy programming is highly detrimental.

The incoming administration should understand that it will have almost no chance of making a positive impact on Iran's embattled civil society. After a thirty-year absence and with only the most hazy sense of the day-to-day dynamics of the Islamic Republic, Washington is unlikely to succeed in stirring up an opposition or orchestrating political mobilization from afar. Unlike Eastern Europe of the 1980s, Iran does not have a cohesive opposition movement willing to take direction and funding from the United States. Wasted resources is hardly the worst-case outcome here; the publicity surrounding American democracy programs in the region has already helped spark a crackdown on Iranian dissidents and activists, harming the very civil society the United States had hoped to support. Even among the most ardent opponents of the Islamic regime, accepting support from an external government remains taboo because it contravenes one of the enduring and still largely accepted tenets of the revolution—Iran's struggle for independence from the machinations of foreign powers.

The United States' misplaced idealism constrains not just Iranian democracy but U.S. diplomacy as well. Washington's rhetorical fulminations and its provision of aid to nonexistent democratic forces have paradoxically succeeded in convincing Iran's suspicious hard-liners that U.S. negotiations represent a ruse to undermine the regime. Thus any efforts by Iran's more moderate actors to engage the United States are perceived and portrayed as acceding to the "Great Satan's" subversive ploys. Washington needs to accept that Iran will change but only on its own terms and at its own pace. A more subtle strategy of attempting to integrate Iran into the global economy and international society would do far more to accelerate the process of democratic transformation than America's discursive diplomacy of calling for talks with a regime whose demise it pledges with regularity. The substantial funds that Congress has appropriated under the Bush administration for democracy program-ming could be far more effective if directed toward depoliticized efforts to intensify people-to-people contacts through exchanges, scholarships, and programs that bring the world to Iran and Iran into the rest of the world. The new administration should shift this effort explicitly, and announce the change publicly, as a means of signaling to Iranians that regime change is no longer an implicit part of the American agenda.

This does not imply forsaking the United States' vocal commitment to criticizing Tehran's abuses of its citizens' rights. The United States can and should speak out in favor of greater social, political, and economic liberalization in Iran, and it should press vigorously against the regime's repression of dissidents, activists, and students.

Mitigate Surprises, Set Expectations, and Insulate the Process

For any diplomatic process to gain momentum, it will be critical to establish a realistic understanding of the challenge ahead—including the likelihood that any progress will be extremely protracted, erratic, and fragile. Negotiating with Iran will not be pleasant or easy, nor will it pro-vide the most important potential payoffs quickly. Even during the hey-day of the reform movement, Washington's concerted attempts to engage Tehran in a direct and ongoing dialogue found little success. Engagement can be a powerful tool for dealing with Iran, but the United States should not embark on this course with illusions about the simplicity of the task at hand. The new administration should strive to maintain realistic expectations of what negotiations with Iran will entail, and what is at stake, in both its internal deliberations and its dealings with Congress and the American public.

In other cases where the Iranians have managed to negotiate a détente with former adversaries—in particular, Britain and Saudi Arabia—one of the critical elements of the diplomatic process was the ability and willing-ness of Iran's adversaries to accept a considerable degree of ambiguity in Iran's undertakings and to provide significant scope for face-saving rhet-oric and actions. Negotiations between the United States and Iran are unlikely to spark a wholesale transformation of the Islamic regime and its ideology, so the next president needs to consider what kind of strategic bargain he is willing to accept, as previous presidents have done with a range of other states, including China and Pakistan.

History has shown that the region will not remain static as the United States strives to develop a viable mechanism for dialogue with Iran. Developments may realign Iranian interests in a more pragmatic fashion, as did the 1990 Iraqi invasion of Kuwait, the fall in oil prices thereafter, and the 9/11 attacks. It is equally likely, however, that destabilization in some related arena—Lebanon, Afghanistan, or the Arab-Israeli peace process, for example—could torpedo an incipient negotiating process. The next president's advisers need to plan in advance for these almost inevitable shocks. The new administration will also have to manage Israel's intensifying concerns carefully to ensure that the Israelis see no temptation or acquiescence to take independent military action, which would only generate an even more disastrous payoff than the downsides of a U.S. military attack. Maintaining or even expanding the already routine communication and cooperation between American and Israeli policymakers on Iran will be essential to ensuring a conducive international context for pursuing engagement.

Seen through the prism of our often overheated tendency to attribute all the region's woes to Tehran, American policy toward Iran is inevitably freighted with the burden of resolving a multitude of regional crises. The next administration needs to be clear in both its strategy and its communications that dealing with Iran will not provide an adequate substitute for a more sensible policy in other arenas. Iran has a malign influence over any effort to promote a lasting solution to the Arab-Israeli conflict, but in and of itself Tehran is not the principal roadblock to resolving that festering wound. The only effective way to curtail Iran's ability to inspire and support anti-Israeli sentiment and violence is to devote sufficient leadership to ensuring a settlement that provides security and dignity for both sides. For this and many other reasons, the peace process should be accorded a high priority by the incoming administration.

At the outset, the next president will have to take pains to "overcommunicate" in an attempt to bring the Iranians along as much as possible. This includes shifting his rhetoric to make it more appropriate to a policy intended to foster reconciliation. Washington cannot denounce Iran as an "outpost of tyranny" and then anticipate Iranian support for serious negotiations. Iran's leaders, as with all revolutionaries, insist that the international community not just recognize their interests but also legitimize their power. Such gestures are not unique to Iran's theocrats; consider, for example, decades of Soviet demands that the United States officially acknowledge postwar demarcations of Eastern Europe.

The incoming administration should dial back the propensity to depict Tehran as the nefarious mastermind of all the region's woes, which conflates discrete crises and sorely overstates Iran's influence as well as antagonizes its leadership. At the same time, after such a long estrangement, the United States will have to educate patiently our Iranian interlocutors about the realities of American political culture, including the autonomy of a Congress that will remain vocal on Iran policy. While the administration should continue voicing opposition to Iranian abuses of its citizens' rights, it will also have to accept the likely continuation or even intensification of Iran's problematic rhetoric.

CONCLUSION

As the next president enters office and considers how to deal with Tehran, he will face the same dilemmas as his predecessors did following the Iranian revolution—identifying Iranians who might constitute the most effective interlocutors for Washington; ascertaining the combination of pressure and persuasion that could move Tehran in a positive direction; and determining whether the Iranian leadership is capable of crafting and implementing a durable bargain with what its leaders still regard as the Great Satan. These three central uncertainties posed immediate relevance during the hostage crisis and have continued to frustrate U.S policy for much of the subsequent three decades.

The unknowns persist for a variety of reasons, but ultimately they are the legacy of the lengthy estrangement and absence of direct contact or first-hand experience within Iran. Washington knows so little about the shape and nature of power in Iran today that State Department officials were forced to rely on a Google search to identify potential subjects for United Nations sanctions in 2006.[18] Presence does not always imply prescience, as the failure of Washington to anticipate the revolution itself might suggest, but American capacity to undertake effective policy toward Tehran must recognize the severe restrictions under which Washington operates, at least some of which are self-imposed. The only viable means for resolving these quandaries and enhancing our ability to influence Tehran is to deal directly with Iran itself.

NOTES

1. Ervand Abrahamian, *Khomeinism: Essays on the Islamic Republic* (London: I. B. Tauris & Co., 1993), 112.

2. R. K. Ramazani, *Revolutionary Iran: Challenge and Response in the Middle East* (Johns Hopkins University Press, 1986), 237.

3. Speech delivered by Ayatollah Ali Khamenei in Mashhad, March 21, 2006, broadcast by the Vision of the Islamic Republic of Iran Network 1.

4. Sadeq Zibakalam, "Ahmadinejad and Breaking the Taboo of Discussions with America," *Etemaad-e Melli,* July 19, 2008, p. 16 (www.roozna.com/Images/Pdf/16_29_4_1387.Pdf).

5. Washington perceived this as another Iranian ploy to undermine the American push for sanctions; from Rafsanjani's perspective, "this was a message to the United States that was not properly understood." Elaine Sciolino, "Iranian Leader Says U.S. Move on Oil Deal Wrecked Chance to Improve Ties," *New York Times,* May 16, 1995 (query.nytimes.com/gst/fullpage.html?res=990CE1DF1731F935A25756C0A963958260&scp=2&sq=rafsanjani+conoco&st=nyt).

6. This presumption that Iraqi democracy would have a positive ripple effect on its neighbors continued to hold sway with the Bush administration even as violence in Iraq escalated. In January 2006 Secretary of State Condoleezza Rice said that "I might note that the specter of Iraqis in exile in Iran—displaced people in Iran voting for a free election in Iraq from the territory of Iran and the specter of Afghans earlier than that voting from the territory of Iran for free elections in Afghanistan, there's a deep irony in that, that Iranians have got to take notice of. And the neighborhood is changing; it's changing quite dramatically. . . . And that, in the final analysis, has got to be threatening to an Iranian regime that relies on coercion and relies on control of its population, not on the consent of its population." On-the-Record Briefing by Secretary Rice, January 12, 2006 (www.state.gov/secretary/rm/2006/59083.htm).

7. "American Congress Replies to the Letter Sent by the Association of Veteran Majlis Deputies," *Iran,* June 27, 2001 (www.iran-newspaper.com/1380/800406/html/politic.htm#PoliticCol2). Conservative editor Taha Hashemi, who was closely associated with Ayatollah Khamenei, argued during the 2001 U.S. presidential campaign that Khamenei could be persuaded to support a new relationship: "If the scenario is planned and prepared wisely and he becomes confident that this relationship won't hurt our national pride and won't make the Islamic Republic passive, I believe he would not be far from accepting." See "'Islamic New Thinker' Sees Formula for Iran-U.S. Ties," Reuters, May 29, 2001.

8. "Ban on US Talks Revives Leftist-Rightist Tensions," Agence France-Presse, May 26, 2002.

9. "America has shown that it has always followed its own interests without taking the interests of the other side into consideration; and it has never been bound to the

mutual agreements," complained Emad Afruq, then a conservative member of the Iranian parliament and one of Ahmadinejad's most vocal critics. "We will not forget the story of Afghanistan, how the Americans misused our cooperation; and unfortunately, Afghanistan was turned into a bargaining chip." "Investigation of the Issue of the Breaking Off of Relations between Iran and America: 'America Is Not Bound to the Agreements,'" *Hezbollah*, April 15, 2007 (accessed through World News Connection).

10. As Warren Christopher has attested, "The Algerians served an indispensable function in interpreting two widely disparate cultures and reasoning processes to each other. . . . This unique role was possible because the Algerian diplomats involved had and kept the full confidence of both sides." Similarly, the dogged diplomacy and personal credibility of both UN Secretary General Javier Perez de Cuellar and his special envoy Giandomenico Picco succeeded in facilitating the delicate negotiations involved with freeing Western hostages held in Lebanon during the 1980s and 1990s. Warren Christopher, "Introduction," in *American Hostages in Iran: The Conduct of a Crisis,* edited by Christopher and others (Yale University Press, 1985), p. 9.

11. Mark Bowden, *Guests of the Ayatollah: The First Battle in America's War with Militant Islam* (New York: Atlantic Monthly Press, 2006), p. 330.

12. To Israel's enduring expectations of rapprochement, it is worthwhile to note then-Defense Minister Yitzhak Rabin's words at a 1987 press conference: "Iran is Israel's best friend and we do not intend to change our position in relation to Tehran, because Khomeini's regime will not last forever." Trita Parsi, *Treacherous Alliance: The Secret Dealings of Israel, Iran, and the United States* (Yale University Press, 2007), p. 128.

13. Thomas L. Friedman, "It's All about Leverage," *New York Times*, June 1, 2008 (www.nytimes.com/2008/06/01/opinion/01friedman.html?_r=1&scp=1&sq=iran+friedman&st=nyt&oref=slogin).

14. Secretary Rice brushed off congressional queries about dialogue with Iran over Iraq in January 2007, saying that approaching Tehran while neighboring Iraq was still in turmoil would be counterproductive. "[If] we go to the Iranians and as supplicants say to the Iranians, help us to secure Iraq, do we really believe that the Iranians are going to treat Iraq over here and not demand that we do something to alleviate the pressure that we're now bringing on their nuclear program and their nuclear ambitions? I don't think it's going to happen" Secretary of State Condoleezza Rice, "Iraq: A New Way Forward," Testimony before the House Foreign Affairs Committee, January 11, 2007 (www.state.gov/secretary/rm/2007/78640.htm).

15. Quote attributed to reformist Mohsen Armin, then a member of Iran's parliament. "Majlis Discloses 'Contacts' with United States," Agence France-Presse, March 14, 2002.

16. The sorry spectacle of our self-imposed limitations, which included rebuking a senior official for sitting across the podium from Iranian influence brokers and banning government employees from attending a public speech by a former Iranian president, should be a thing of the past. In February 2008 Zalmay Khalilzad, the U.S. ambassador to the United Nations, was reportedly reprimanded for appearing on a panel at the World Economic Forum in Davos with two senior Iranian officials, without having sought or received prior authorization to do so. "Rice Chastises Ambas-

sador over Iran Talk," Reuters, February 6, 2008. In 2006 the State Department announced internally that no U.S. government employees were permitted to attend a speech by former president Khatami at the National Cathedral in Washington.

17. Elaine Sciolino, "Tea in Tehran: How Hostage Deal Was Born," *New York Times*, December 6, 1991, p. 1.

18. Dafna Linzer, "Seeking Iran Intelligence, U.S. Tries Google; Internet Search Yields Names Cited in U.N. Draft Resolution," *Washington Post*, December 11, 2006, p. A1.

BRUCE RIEDEL

GARY SAMORE

4

Managing Nuclear Proliferation in the Middle East

CURRENT U.S. EFFORTS to stop Iran's nuclear program have failed. Fortunately, however, because of technical limits, Iran appears to be two to three years away from building an enrichment facility capable of producing sufficient weapons-grade uranium quickly enough to support a credible nuclear weapons option. As a consequence, the incoming U.S. administration will likely have some breathing space to develop a new diplomatic approach to prevent Iran from acquiring a nuclear weapons capability. Part of this new approach should involve direct and unconditional talks between the United States and Iran on a range of bilateral issues, as well as formal nuclear negotiations between Iran and the EU-3 plus 3 (France, Germany, and the United Kingdom, plus China, Russia, and the United States). To make these negotiations effective, the new administration should seek agreement among the EU-3 plus 3 to support stronger political and economic sanctions if Iran rejects an offer to resolve the nuclear issue and improve bilateral relations with the United States. Faced with more attractive inducements and the prospect of more serious sanctions, the Iranian regime might be persuaded to limit its nuclear activities below the threshold of a nuclear breakout capability.

If this new diplomatic effort fails to stop Iran from achieving completion of a nuclear breakout capability (that is, the ability to produce significant amounts of weapons-grade uranium), the United States will face a difficult choice: It could accept Iran as a nuclear-capable state with a breakout option and try to build firebreaks to prevent Iran from actually producing such material (and building nuclear weapons). If that fails, the United States could attempt to contain and deter a nuclear-armed Iran, while seeking to discourage others in the region from developing nuclear weapons. Or the United States could decide to attack Iran's nuclear facilities in an attempt to damage and set back Iran's breakout capability. But that choice has uncertain prospects for success and very high likelihood of wider conflict and instability. Complicating this dilemma is Israel, which faces a perceived existential threat and could decide to take matters into its own hands even before the United States has decided that the course of diplomacy has been exhausted. Neither an American nor an Israeli military option is likely to produce sufficient gain to be worth the potential costs, but, paradoxically, without a credible military threat, Iran is much less likely to make nuclear concessions that meet U.S. requirements. Therefore, the next U.S. administration will want Iran to believe that it is prepared to use force if Iran rejects a diplomatic solution.

To prepare for dealing with these difficult choices—and mitigating the downsides of whatever decision is taken—the next U.S. administration will need early on to begin a quiet discussion with countries, especially Israel and the Arab Gulf states, which will be most directly affected by a nuclear-armed Iran. Iran is already a dangerous adversary and a nuclear-capable or -armed Iran would be more dangerous. If Iran acquires nuclear weapons, it is likely to behave like other nuclear weapons states, trying to intimidate its foes, but not recklessly using its weapons, nor giving them to terrorists, if faced with a credible threat of retaliation by the United States. While a nuclear Iran will prompt a regional nuclear arms race—indeed it already has begun—none of the Arab states has a capability to develop an indigenous weapons program for at least a decade.[1] American diplomacy will have an opportunity to shape the regional reaction to a nuclear Iran but will also be constrained by the universal perception of inconsistency in its handling of the Israeli nuclear arsenal. If diplomacy or force fails to prevent Iran from acquiring nuclear weapons, a declared U.S. nuclear umbrella for the region or parts of it should be a key mechanism for deterring Iran, reassuring Israel, and incorporating our other allies into an effective regional balance.

BACKGROUND AND DIPLOMATIC STATE OF PLAY

The Middle East has been a hotbed of nuclear proliferation for five decades. Driven by security fears, regional ambitions, and nationalism, at least seven Middle Eastern states have sought to acquire a nuclear weapons capability. Israel was the first and so far the only successful claimant and has demonstrated repeatedly its determination to maintain its monopoly on nuclear weapons in the region, by force if necessary. Israel has also threatened the use of its nuclear arsenal against its enemies at least once.[2] Most estimates suggest Israel has a substantial number of sophisticated nuclear weapons that can be delivered by aircraft (F-15Is), missiles (Jericho), and perhaps submarine-launched cruise missiles. In September 1986 an Israeli technician, Mordechai Vananu, revealed that the Dimona facility, where he worked, had already produced enough plutonium to construct a large number of nuclear weapons and possessed the technology for sophisticated, high-yield nuclear weapons.

Egypt, Iraq, Algeria, and Libya all made unsuccessful nuclear attempts in the past. President Gamal Abdel Nasser of Egypt sought to match Israel in the early 1960s, but his efforts were stymied by technical difficulties, Israeli sabotage, and the refusal of his Soviet patrons to provide assistance. President Anwar Sadat finally abandoned the Egyptian program after the October 1973 War, as part of a larger political strategy of peace with Israel and alliance with the United States. The demise of Iraq's nuclear effort was more violent. Launched by Saddam Hussein under the guise of a civilian nuclear program in the mid-1970s, Iraq's main French-supplied nuclear research reactor was destroyed by an Israeli raid in 1981. Iraq's subsequent secret enrichment program was largely destroyed by U.S. bombs during the 1991 Gulf War and—we now know—completely dismantled by UN inspectors and sanctions following that war. The U.S. invasion of 2003 has extinguished Iraq's ability to revive its nuclear program for the foreseeable future.

In North Africa Algeria secretly acquired a heavy-water research reactor from China in the mid-1980s but joined the Non-Proliferation Treaty

(NPT) and accepted International Atomic Energy Agency (IAEA) inspections under pressure from the United States, France, and other countries when the project was revealed in 1991. It has apparently abandoned any efforts to develop nuclear weapons. Libyan leader Colonel Muammar Qaddafi quixotically pursued nuclear weapons on and off starting in the early 1970s, most recently giving up a nascent centrifuge enrichment program (based on black-market technology from Pakistani scientist A. Q. Khan) in a December 2003 deal with the United States and the United Kingdom to lift political and economic sanctions.

Most recently, Syria's efforts to build a secret research reactor with North Korean assistance—as a counter to Israel's nuclear capabilities—were abruptly terminated by an Israeli air raid in September 2007. Even though a number of Arab states have announced plans to revive or initiate nuclear power programs, none of these states has the scientific and industrial infrastructure or the skilled human capital to advance quickly, even with a crash program. Moreover, none of the established nuclear suppliers is prepared to export fuel-cycle technology or facilities to the region. In these circumstances, the only near-term option for an Arab country is to seek to purchase nuclear material or weapons from another state. At least one state probably has already set the diplomatic basis for doing so: Saudi Arabia with Pakistan.

With the destruction of the Syrian reactor, the only Middle Eastern country aside from Israel within reach of developing a nuclear weapons capability is Iran. Like others in the region, Iran's historical interest in nuclear weapons is deeply rooted. As part of his ambition to secure Iran's dominance in the Persian Gulf, the shah Mohammad Reza Pahlavi began an extensive nuclear power program in the mid-1970s, which included plans to develop civilian fuel-cycle facilities (both enrichment and reprocessing) that would have created a latent nuclear weapons option. The 1979 revolution shattered the program, as scientists fled the country and sources of external assistance dried up. Even though Supreme Leader Ayatollah Ruhollah Khomeini was religiously suspicious of nuclear technology, the program slowly reformed in the mid-1980s, as Iran began small-scale research on centrifuge enrichment technology that it had secretly acquired from Pakistan. After Khomeini's death in 1989, the new supreme leader, Ayatollah Ali Khamenei, and President Ali Akbar Hashemi Rafsanjani expanded the covert enrichment program and pursued nuclear reactor deals with Russia and China. Although U.S. diplomatic pressure limited official nuclear assistance from Moscow and Beijing, Iran was able to purchase design technology for the production of heavy water and heavy-water research reactors from Russian scientists and nuclear institutes. This Russian technology allowed Iran to begin a secret plutonium production program to complement the existing secret enrichment program.

Iran's secret enrichment and heavy-water reactor programs were publicly exposed in August 2002 by an Iranian dissident group.[3] After the U.S. invasion of Iraq in March 2003, Washington spurned an overture from Tehran to begin bilateral discussions on nuclear and other issues. Iran turned to France, Germany, and the United Kingdom (the EU-3), which agreed to negotiate with Iran and block U.S. efforts to refer Iran to the UN Security Council, where it would be subject to sanctions for violating the NPT. The EU-3's condition was that Iran suspend its enrichment and reprocessing activities and cooperate with the IAEA to clear up questions about its past nuclear violations. Between the beginning of EU-3 negotiations with Iran in October 2003 and their collapse in August 2005, Iran did suspend some critical aspects of its enrichment program, but the stormy negotiations never came close to resolving the central issues. The EU-3 demanded that Iran accept a permanent, or ten-year, moratorium on its enrichment and reprocessing programs, whereas Iran insisted on its right to develop a commercial-scale enrichment facility. As a concession, Iran offered to provide additional political commitments and transparency arrangements to strengthen confidence that it would not divert the facility for military uses. The EU-3 experience illustrates that the current leadership in Iran, though deeply committed to acquiring a nuclear weapons capability, may be willing to accept tactical delays and limits if confronted with sufficient pressures and risks.

After the election of President Mahmoud Ahmadinejad in August 2005, Iran resumed its enrichment activities, apparently calculating that the mounting turmoil in Iraq weakened American options to punish or attack Iran. The IAEA board of governors responded by referring the Iranian nuclear file to the UN Security Council. In New York, the EU-3, joined by China, Russia, and the United States, supported a series of UN Security Council resolutions that imposed targeted sanctions on Iran and sought to pressure the Islamic Republic to again suspend its enrichment and reprocessing activities. In return, the EU-3 plus 3 offered to suspend the UN sanctions while negotiations took place. With the pain of sanctions blunted by high oil prices and broad economic sanctions blocked by divisions among the big powers, Iran said it was prepared to negotiate with the EU-3 plus 3 but rejected suspension as a condition for any talks.

In an effort to find a compromise, the European Union's foreign policy chief, Javier Solana, proposed a two-step solution in 2007. First, there would be a "double freeze," in which Iran would refrain from installing additional centrifuge machines (while continuing to operate the existing machines) and the EU-3 plus 3 would refrain from imposing additional Security Council sanctions (while the existing sanctions would continue in force). In exchange for the double freeze, Iran would begin talks with the EU-3 plus 3 (minus the United States) at the level of political directors. After six weeks, in the Solana scenario, both sides would move to a full double suspension (that is, Iran would suspend operation of existing centrifuges, and the Security Council would suspend existing sanctions), and the United States would join the negotiations.

In July 2008, amid hints that Iran might be interested in elements of the Solana proposal, the Bush administration decided to send Undersecretary of State William Burns to join the EU-3 plus 3 "prenegotiations" between Solana and Iranian nuclear negotiator Saeed Jalili over the terms and conditions for holding formal nuclear negotiations. The U.S. decision reflected an important tactical adjustment—ending the U.S. administration's previous refusal to enter nuclear talks with Iran until suspension was in place—but it did not change the objective of achieving suspension during formal nuclear negotiations. In fact, the decision to send Burns was intended to bolster the EU-3 plus 3 demand for suspension and to deflect any Iranian effort to accept a freeze without committing to full suspension within a short period. In this scenario, Washington feared that Iran would use the freeze to exploit differences among the EU-3 plus 3, reducing the risk of additional sanctions or military attack while it continued to work on resolving technical problems with its existing centrifuges. Iran, however, refused to accept even temporary limitations on its enrichment activities, and the most recent UN Security Council resolution, passed in September 2008, adds nothing to existing sanctions.

Aside from the disagreement on conditions to begin formal negotiations, the two sides remained far apart on the core nuclear issue. In a May 2008 proposal to the UN, Iran's foreign minister offered to accept an "enrichment and nuclear fuel production consortium" in Iran, as well as "improved supervision by the IAEA" to provide assurances that the facility would not be used for military purposes.[4] Drawing on the earlier EU-3 proposals, the EU-3 plus 3 offered to provide technical and financial assistance to Iran's civil nuclear program if Iran would accept a ten-year moratorium on its enrichment and reprocessing (that is, the heavy-water research reactor) programs. The proposal offered Iran access to modern, European-designed, light-water power and research reactors and legally binding assurances of fuel supply.

Iran, however, has rejected reliance on foreign-supplied fuel and insists that it needs its own plant to produce low-enriched uranium (LEU) for power reactor fuel. Iran's planned industrial-scale enrichment plant at Natanz is designed to produce roughly enough LEU every year to meet the annual fuel requirements for the Russian-supplied Bushehr nuclear power plant, Iran's only nuclear power facility. Although Russia has contracted to provide fuel for the lifetime of the Bushehr facility (and to dispose of the spent fuel in Russia), Iran argues that the Natanz enrichment plant is necessary as a backup in case Russia cuts off fuel supplies. Even if Iran produced its own LEU, however, it does not have the technology to fabricate fuel elements for the Bushehr reactor, a fact that reinforces suspicions that the real purpose of Iran's enrichment effort is military rather than civilian.

Progress at the IAEA also seems frozen. Although the IAEA has resolved most questions about Iran's past secret enrichment and reprocessing activities, the agency and Iran are locked in a standoff over Iran's nuclear weaponization program. In its May 2008 report, the IAEA offered extensive documentation (provided by the United States and other countries) of past Iranian weaponization research efforts, including efforts to design a nuclear warhead for the medium-range Shahab-3 missile. Iran claims that these documents are "forgeries"—an explanation that the IAEA does not accept. Until the weaponization issue is resolved, the IAEA cannot officially close the nuclear file, and Iran will remain in "noncompliance" with its NPT commitments, a situation that the EU-3 plus 3 believes provides the legal basis for the UN Security Council demand that Iran suspend its enrichment and reprocessing programs until "international confidence" is restored in Iran's nuclear intentions.[5] In the meantime, the IAEA reports that Iran continues to deny the agency's inspectors full access to facilities and activities, including facilities for the production of centrifuge parts and equipment. Under the circumstances, it seems likely that Iran has stockpiled some of these parts and equipment in a secure location, creating options to build a covert enrichment facility or to rebuild in the aftermath of an attack on its IAEA-safeguarded facilities.

TECHNICAL STATUS OF IRAN'S PROGRAM

Although diplomatic efforts to stop Iran's nuclear program have so far failed, Iran still appears to be at least two to three years away from acquiring a nuclear breakout capability (sufficient to use civilian nuclear facilities and safeguarded nuclear materials to produce enough weapons-grade material for a few nuclear weapons within a few months of achieving the capability).[6] The inherent difficulty in detecting and monitoring a weaponization program means the most reliable measure of Iran's nuclear weapons capacity is its ability to produce fissile material, the most challenging technical barrier to developing nuclear weapons.

According to the most recent IAEA report, of September 2008, Iran has completed a 3,000-centrifuge machine unit at the Natanz enrichment plant and about one-third of a second 3,000-machine unit. A total of 16 such units are planned for the facility. As of September 2008, Iran has produced about 480 kilograms of low-enriched uranium hexafluoride (UF6) and is producing about 2 kilograms of low-enriched UF6 every day. According to IAEA, Iran has steadily overcome early technical problems with its P-1 centrifuge machines and appears to operating the machines at more than 75 percent of their design output. The P-1 machine is an older design developed in Europe in the 1960s and has a number of features that make it difficult to manufacture and operate. The P-1 is also considered very inefficient compared to more modern centrifuge machines.

In addition to the P-1, Iran is developing two new types of machines (dubbed the IR-2 and IR-3), which are based on the more advanced P-2 centrifuge, a machine developed in Europe in the 1970s that is about

twice as powerful as the P-1. These new machines display clever technical innovations that illustrate Iran's growing mastery of centrifuge technology, but they are still at an early stage of development and are
deployed only in very small numbers at Natanz. Moreover, Iran is apparently still dependent on foreign suppliers for some of the essential materials and components for the IR-2 and IR-3 machines.[7] As a consequence, concerted export controls and interdiction efforts can delay
Iran's acquisition of a substantial enrichment capacity based on these
more advanced machines.

The timeline for Iran's acquisition of a nuclear breakout capability
depends on how quickly it can master centrifuge technology and install
significant numbers of centrifuge machines and produce a large stockpile
of low-enriched uranium, which, in turn, can be used as feed material to
produce weapons-grade or highly enriched uranium (HEU). The most
recent U.S. National Intelligence Estimate (NIE), released in December
2007, predicts with "moderate confidence" that "Iran probably would
be technically capable of producing enough HEU for a weapon sometime
during the 2010 and 2015 time frame." At its current production rates,
Iran is likely to accumulate a sufficient stockpile of LEU to support production of a weapon's worth of HEU by late 2009. Very roughly, about
1,000 kilograms of low-enriched $UF6$ is sufficient to produce enough
HEU for a single simple nuclear weapon.[8]

Being able to produce enough highly enriched uranium for a single
weapon, however, may not make for a practical nuclear weapons option.
For example, assuming it was operating at maximum efficiency, the existing pilot-scale facility of P-1 machines would need to operate for nearly
a full year (starting with natural uranium) or several months (starting
with LEU) to produce enough HEU for a single weapon. Even a pilot-
scale facility with the more efficient centrifuge machines based on P-2
technology would likely take a few months of continuous operation to
produce its first bomb's worth of HEU. Since the IAEA would quickly
detect the shift in production from low- to highly enriched uranium,
these pilot-scale facilities would be vulnerable to military preemption
during the time required to produce a weapon's worth of HEU.

To reduce the risk of preemptive action, Iran might wait until it has
installed a much larger number of centrifuge machines and accumulated
a larger stockpile of LEU, which would allow it to produce a large

amount of HEU before effective preemptive action could be taken. For example, the industrial-scale enrichment facility planned by Iran (designed for 54,000 thousand machines) would be capable of producing enough HEU for a handful of nuclear weapons within a few months or even weeks, once a political decision was made to break out and use the facility for military production.[9] Building a large-scale enrichment facility is likely to take at least several more years and could be delayed even further if international efforts successfully restrict Iranian access to essential materials and equipment.

In other words, defining Iran's breakout options is based on political strategy as well as technical capacity.[10] In the worst-case scenario, Iran might choose to break out once it has a minimum capacity, that is, a sufficient stockpile of LEU and enough centrifuges to produce enough HEU for a single bomb within a few months. Alternatively, rather than build a single nuclear weapon as quickly as possible, Iran might choose to install the enrichment capability necessary for building a small arsenal of weapons before making a political decision whether or not to break out. These different scenarios mean there are different definitions of what constitutes the so-called point of no return. Israel, whose very existence could be threatened by a single Iranian bomb, is inclined to adopt a worst-case assessment and therefore conclude that the time remaining for diplomacy is limited.

In contrast to its uranium enrichment program, Iran's program to develop a plutonium production capability is clearly several years away from fruition. Construction of a 40 megawatt heavy-water research reactor at Arak began in the mid-1990s, and Iran says the reactor is planned to be operational by 2014, although delays seem likely. Operating at maximum capacity, the Arak reactor is theoretically capable of producing enough plutonium for one or two nuclear weapons annually. However, Iran has announced that it does not intend to build a reprocessing plant, which would be necessary to separate plutonium from the reactor's spent fuel. In the past, Iran has carried out secret reprocessing experiments involving very small quantities of plutonium, but design and construction of an industrial-scale reprocessing plant would be a significant technical hurdle and relatively difficult to hide.

The status of Iran's ability to design and fabricate a deliverable nuclear weapon is uncertain. According to the 2007 NIE, Iran halted its nuclear weaponization efforts in 2003, as part of a broader decision to allow international inspections of its previously secret enrichment and heavy-water research reactor programs. At that time, the U.S. intelligence community believed that Iran was experiencing serious technical difficulties perfecting an implosion weapon that could be delivered by the Shahab-3 intermediate range missile, capable of striking Israel. The NIE acknowledged, however, that the United States has only "moderate confidence" that Iran has not resumed its weaponization program since 2003, and other intelligence agencies (such as those in Israel, France, and the United Kingdom) believe that Iran has most likely reconstituted weaponization research and may have made significant advances in developing a nuclear warhead for missile delivery. Given the inherent difficulty in detecting and monitoring a weaponization program, which involves relatively small numbers of personnel and easily hidden facilities, it is probably not possible to have much confidence either way.

Complicating any technical assessment and evaluation of breakout scenarios is uncertainty about possible covert nuclear activities and facilities. Even if Iran does not currently possess significant covert fissile material production facilities, which the NIE assumed to be the case in December 2007, it seems very plausible that Iran would favor this route in the future if it decides to build nuclear weapons. If undetected, a covert enrichment facility would allow Iran to produce nuclear weapons with little or no warning, and without the risk that it could be destroyed before the first batch of weapons-grade material could be produced. For Tehran, *sneak out* is better than *break out*. From its past behavior, the Islamic Republic does not feel obligated to respect its international nuclear treaty commitments, and it seems prudent to assume that any nuclear deal with Iran would be vulnerable to cheating, if Iran thinks it can get away with it.

PROPOSING A NEW WAY FORWARD

Barring a breakthrough, the next U.S. president will need to develop an approach to overcome the current diplomatic stalemate and get international nuclear negotiations started. Assuming he is successful, the new president will also need to decide on a negotiating strategy: what kind of limits to seek on Iran's nuclear activities and what kind of concessions (both nuclear and non-nuclear) to make in return; how a nuclear deal intersects with other U.S.-Iranian issues; and, finally, how to respond if an acceptable deal cannot be negotiated. Fortunately, the new administration will not be operating under desperate time constraints. As already explained, technical problems and export controls have appeared to slow the pace of Iran's nuclear development, and the new president should have time to put his team together, consider options, and build international support for his new approach. Many elements of the next administration's diplomatic approach can be built on the existing strategy, but we recommend several additional features to enhance prospects for success.

Getting to the Table

The immediate diplomatic issue facing the new administration will be whether to propose dropping the EU-3 plus 3 demand that Iran suspend its enrichment and reprocessing activities as a precondition for formal international nuclear negotiations.[11] We recommend proceeding cautiously. The United States should drop or modify this demand only as part of a broader negotiating strategy agreed upon by the EU-3 plus 3, including the incentives to be offered to Iran and the actions the EU-3 plus 3 are prepared to take if Iran rejects this offer. Developing this negotiating strategy will require high-level bilateral and multilateral consultations with the EU-3 plus 3 governments, as well as with governments in the region, during the opening months of the new administration.

In the meantime, as discussed in chapter 3, we recommend that the new administration offer to resume direct bilateral talks with Iran (preferably with a representative of the supreme leader) on a range of issues, including the nuclear issue, U.S.-Iranian relations, Iraq, and the Israeli-Palestinian peace process, without requiring Iran to suspend its enrichment and reprocessing activities as a precondition for such talks. The Bush administration has already authorized bilateral talks on Iraqi security and has allowed Ambassador Burns to participate in the EU-3 plus 3 meetings with Iran to negotiate terms for achieving suspension, but it has continued to insist that Iran suspend enrichment and reprocessing activities before holding broader, bilateral discussions at more senior levels.

While seeking to engage Iran directly, the new administration should not abandon the EU-3 plus 3 framework for nuclear negotiations. Like any multilateral group, the EU-3 plus 3 can be ungainly, and the parties differ significantly in their perceptions of the Iranian nuclear threat and how to deal with it. Nonetheless, a multilateral approach supported by the major powers is likely to be more effective in influencing Iran's behavior than a purely bilateral negotiation between the United States and Iran. At the same time, opening a bilateral channel with Iran may help to invigorate the multilateral process. In particular, Washington can bolster the existing EU-3 plus 3 package by offering to add improvements in U.S.-Iranian relations to an overall solution to the nuclear issue.

As direct U.S.-Iranian talks and consultations with the EU-3 plus 3 proceed, the new administration can consider its position on the suspension issue. In response to the new administration's offer to hold bilateral talks and the perception that a new administration may be able to muster stronger international pressure, Iran may agree to a freeze or suspension, perhaps for some limited period. Alternatively, the United States, in consultation with the other EU-3 plus 3 countries, may agree to relax the requirement that Iran freeze or suspend enrichment and reprocessing as a condition for beginning formal nuclear negotiations with the EU-3 plus 3, as part of an agreement on a new package of carrots and sticks. Clearly, however, if the EU-3 plus 3 agrees to drop the precondition, it must also agree that the talks cannot proceed endlessly while Iran continues to enrich uranium and build its heavy-water research reactor. Once formal negotiations have begun, the United States (and the other parties) should make clear to Iran that the negotiations are not sustainable unless Iran agrees to suspend its enrichment and reprocessing activities as long as the negotiations are taking place. Otherwise, Iran will have every incentive to drag out the talks while it continues to develop its nuclear capabilities.

Terms of a Nuclear Deal

Assuming that nuclear negotiations between the EU-3 plus 3 and Iran begin, the primary nonproliferation objective of the next president should be to limit as much as possible Iran's acquisition of fuel-cycle facilities capable of producing fissile material, that is, enriched uranium and separated plutonium. Given Iran's propensity for violating its nuclear commitments, any agreement must include strong verification mechanisms.

On the enrichment side, the new administration should endorse the basic elements of the existing EU-3 plus 3 proposal to assist Iran's civilian nuclear power program, including giving Iran access to advanced power reactors and fuel guarantees in exchange for a ten-year moratorium on Iran's enrichment activities. To make this existing offer more attractive to Tehran, the administration should endorse the position already taken by the other EU-3 plus 3 governments that Iran has a "right" under the NPT to develop enrichment capabilities for its civil nuclear program, once Iran has resolved questions about its past nuclear actions and once "confidence" is restored in Iran's nuclear intentions.[12] Such a concession would provide Tehran a face-saving argument that the moratorium is not a permanent sacrifice of its national rights and pride.

In addition, the EU-3 plus 3 should consider making its offer of legally binding fuel guarantees more concrete by agreeing to provide a repository of Russian LEU fuel for Iran's Bushehr power reactor at a facility in Iran under IAEA safeguards. Such an offer would undercut Iran's argument that it needs to build the Natanz enrichment plant as a backup to provide fuel for Bushehr if the Russians renege on their contract to provide lifetime fuel services to the reactor. A fuel repository in Iran does carry some risks. Even though the LEU fuel is not directly usable in nuclear weapons, Iran could seize and convert the fuel into feed material for a clandestine enrichment facility. In practical terms, however, it would be time-consuming for Iran to move the fuel assemblies to the Esfahan nuclear center, where their metal cladding would have to be removed to recover the low-enriched uranium dioxide and then the uranium dioxide would have to be converted to uranium hexafluoride before it could be used as feed material for enrichment. Since IAEA inspectors would know of the fuel seizure very quickly, the EU-3 plus 3 would have time to take action before Iran could convert the material for use in a nuclear weapons effort. Thus, while a stockpile of LEU fuel represents a potential nuclear risk, it is far less risky than allowing Iran to continue to develop its own enrichment capacity.

From a nonproliferation standpoint, a total moratorium on enrichment facilities is far superior to various possible arrangements to limit or circumscribe Iran's enrichment program. Even a limited enrichment program would provide additional options for Iran to resume its efforts to develop a large-scale enrichment capability if it decides to renege or tries to cheat on the agreement. Moreover, a limited enrichment program is more likely to contribute to pressure on others in the region to pursue their own nuclear hedge, and it sets a dangerous precedent that a country caught seeking to develop a nuclear weapons option under the guise of a civilian program is allowed to benefit from its violations of the NPT. Concession on this point carries a very heavy potential price in terms of the long-term viability of the international nonproliferation regime.

The "zero option"—a multiple-year moratorium on Iran's enrichment activities—may not be achievable, however. From the beginning of its nuclear negotiations in 2003, Iran has rejected demands to suspend its enrichment program for a long period, and the United States and other countries may not be able to force Iran to roll back its program now that Iran has achieved a rudimentary enrichment capacity. Therefore, in the end game of the negotiation, the United States may need to consider an ultimate fallback that allows Iran to maintain a limited enrichment capacity under strong international supervision and inspection if that is necessary to obtain a long-term moratorium on the construction of a large facility.

If it becomes necessary to accept an enrichment option, the administration should focus on limiting the size of the facility (that is, the number of a given type of centrifuge machines), for size determines how quickly Iran could theoretically use the facility to produce highly enriched uranium for nuclear weapons. For example, Iran could maintain a research and development program on new centrifuge types in exchange for deferring a decision for ten years or more on whether to build a commercial-scale enrichment facility. In addition, any low-enriched uranium produced in Iran could be exported to Russia for fabrication into fuel elements for the Bushehr nuclear power reactor, which would prevent Iran from building up a stockpile of LEU that it could use to produce weapons-grade uranium. Such arrangements would seek to keep Iran as far away as possible from nuclear breakout at the allowed facility. To reduce the risk of breakout, the United States could seek a Security Council resolution declaring that any violation of IAEA safeguards at the allowed facility would constitute a "threat to peace and security," thereby authorizing members to take any actions necessary to prevent Iran from using the facility to produce nuclear weapons.

If a final agreement allows Iran to maintain a limited enrichment program, it is critical that monitoring and verification measures be enhanced beyond the existing IAEA safeguards system to guard against the threat that Iran will seek to circumvent the agreement by building clandestine enrichment facilities. In general, intelligence agencies and international inspectors would find it easier to detect covert enrichment activities if no overt activities are permitted. Aside from requiring that Iran implement the IAEA Additional Protocol, which gives the agency some added tools to detect clandestine nuclear activities, the United States could insist that the standard IAEA inspection protocol for enrichment facilities be bolstered by additional real-time monitoring devices installed in the facility and by the continuous presence of international inspectors. In any event, the United States and other countries will need to maintain an independent intelligence effort to detect Iranian efforts to cheat on the agreement. This intelligence mission should be a high priority for the next administration, as it has been for recent administrations.

Even if the United States decides to accept some limited enrichment activity in Iran, the administration should not agree to negotiate on the basis of Iran's proposal for locating an international "enrichment and nuclear fuel production consortium" in Iran.[13] Under such an arrangement, an enrichment facility in Iran would include some international ownership and operation including the presence of foreign managers and technicians at the facility. Depending on the details, such a multilateral facility would impose some constraints on Iran's nuclear weapons option, but it has two inherent drawbacks. First, once such a facility is operational, Iran could "nationalize" it and quickly produce a large quantity of highly enriched uranium—within a few months or weeks, depending on different scenarios. Second, a large-scale enrichment program would provide ample cover for a smaller covert facility. To build, operate, and maintain a commercial-scale facility, Iran would need to train a large number of technicians and operators and establish an extensive infrastructure of support facilities to produce centrifuge components, activities that would make it harder to detect an Iranian effort to divert personnel and equipment for a smaller clandestine facility. Finally, if the United States agrees to participate in or accept a multilateral enrichment facility in Iran, it will be difficult to reject similar requests from other states in the region demanding equal treatment.

On the plutonium side, the United States should also require that Iran suspend work on its heavy-water research reactor or redesign the reactor so that it is capable only of low-power operations and therefore incapable of producing significant amounts of plutonium. Other measures could include arrangements to remove all spent fuel from the heavy-water reactor (as Iran has already agreed to do in the case of fuel from the Bushehr nuclear power plant, which will be shipped to Russia) as well as Iranian political commitments not to develop reprocessing technology. The Additional Protocol also gives the IAEA rights to environmental sampling, which can help detect clandestine reprocessing operations.

Any new U.S. proposal, however, should not be limited to a strictly "nuclear for nuclear" deal because Iran's interest in acquiring a nuclear weapons breakout capability far outweighs its interest in obtaining external assistance for its nuclear power program. Although the Bush administration has been willing to support the nuclear carrots offered by the EU-3 plus 3, such as legally binding fuel assurances, it has not been willing to offer improved U.S.-Iran bilateral relations as part of a nuclear deal, arguing that these inducements need to be saved for resolving other issues, such as Iran's support for terrorist groups, opposition to the Israeli-Palestinian and Israeli-Syrian peace processes, and efforts to destabilize Iraq. Given the importance of the nuclear issue—and the potential threat a nuclear-armed Iran would pose to U.S. interests and the security of its allies—we recommend that the new administration be prepared to offer some of these bilateral inducements if Iran meets U.S. nuclear demands. Such inducements could include normalization of bilateral political relations, lifting of U.S. economic sanctions, assurances against attempting regime change, and "respect" for Iran's status in the region. As a negotiating tactic, it makes sense to see whether these inducements are sufficiently attractive to obtain Iranian nuclear concessions before considering compromises in the essential U.S. nuclear demand for a long-term moratorium of Iran's enrichment and reprocessing activities.

Increasing the Pressure

Bigger carrots alone are unlikely to produce a satisfactory solution, unless Iran believes that the consequences of rejecting the new EU-3 plus 3 and bilateral American offers will be severe. Iran's ruling elite, including the increasingly influential Iranian Revolutionary Guard and, most important, Supreme Leader Khamenei, appears confident that Iran's star is on the rise and U.S. power is on the wane. Any U.S. overture suggesting that the United States is prepared to relax conditions and terms of a nuclear deal is bound to reinforce Iran's perception that it does not need to compromise on its nuclear ambitions. The biggest challenge for the new president will be to convince Iran's leadership that rejecting a more generous offer will mean significantly greater cost and risk in terms of political isolation, economic punishment, and potential military action.

Therefore, any new U.S. proposal for a more attractive offer to resolve the nuclear issue must be matched by prior agreement on the steps the EU-3 plus 3 is prepared to take to increase pressure if Iran were to stall or reject a new offer or table an unacceptable counteroffer. The administration should work to build support for broader sanctions that go beyond the targeted sanctions already passed by the Security Council. These broader sanctions could include a comprehensive arms embargo, limits on investment and technology transfers to Iran's oil and gas industries, and even restrictions on the import of refined petroleum products. If Iran believed these types of sanctions were imminent, it would be more likely to make concessions to delay or limit its nuclear program. In addition to working through the Security Council, the United States and its allies should also continue efforts to increase "informal" economic sanctions against Iran by persuading private businesses and other governments to limit exports and investments in Iran. With support from the United Kingdom and France, the European Union and some other individual European states already have taken some significant steps to limit financial transactions and oil and gas investment in Iran. As the new U.S. administration moves to improve trans-Atlantic relations across the board, it should be in a stronger position to overcome the reluctance of some European states to impose even stronger informal sanctions against Iran.

More effective UN sanctions require cooperation by Russia and China. Although both countries have supported sanctions targeted against entities and individuals directly associated with Iran's nuclear and missile programs and have limited their own assistance to these programs, they have not been willing to support broader economic sanctions that would hurt their core bilateral relationships with Tehran. These differences over sanctions reflect and reinforce a deeper disagreement over the Iranian nuclear issue. Compared with the Western powers, Russia and China are extremely skeptical that sanctions can force Iran to give up its enrichment program, and they fear that an escalating UN Security Council confrontation with Iran will pave the way for a military attack by the United States or Israel. Moreover, they seem to be more willing to accept and tolerate Iran as a nuclear-capable country with a large safeguarded enrichment capacity that will not actually build nuclear weapons. Even if Iran eventually builds nuclear weapons, Russian and Chinese officials argue that Iran will act as a responsible nuclear power, susceptible to being managed through the usual tools of deterrence and containment.

As a result, Russia and China are likely to resist making firm commitments to support stronger sanctions in exchange for a more generous offer to Iran from the United States. Furthermore, if the EU-3 plus 3 negotiations actually get under way, Russia and China would certainly be reluctant to declare the talks a failure and return to the Security Council. Nonetheless, both would prefer that Iran not acquire a nuclear weapons capability because of the threat this capability would pose to their interests in the Middle East, and neither wants its overall relationship with Washington and Europe to be damaged because of a fundamental disagreement over Iran.

Therefore, the new U.S. president will need to make Iran a central issue in Washington's bilateral relationship with Moscow and Beijing and enlist the support of European and Japanese leaders to place the same emphasis in their own relations with the Russians and Chinese. With Moscow, the Iranian issue has become entangled with a range of contentious bilateral U.S.-Russian issues, such as missile defense in Europe and NATO expansion to Georgia and Ukraine. In particular, the short war between Russia and Georgia in August 2008 has raised serious questions about how likely Moscow will be to provide any further support for the international effort to stop Iran's nuclear weapons program. Russia has reacted harshly to the nearly universal criticism of its operations in Georgia, suspended its participation in NATO–Russia Council activities, and made clear it will link the Georgia issue to other global issues. Iran has been careful not to criticize Russia's operations in Georgia, undoubtedly hoping a quiet posture will be repaid by Russian opposition to any new Security Council sanctions on Iran. Trying to keep these issues unlinked will be an important challenge for the next administration. As long as Russia and the Western powers remain opposed over Georgia and related issues, a common approach toward Iran will be more difficult to coordinate. On the other hand, progress on addressing disputes with Moscow over the countries on its borders may facilitate cooperation toward Iran.

The new president will need to decide how to prioritize these various issues and whether to propose trade-offs with Moscow. The president and European leaders will need to weigh the value of pressing ahead with EU and NATO membership for Georgia and Ukraine against the risk that Moscow will retaliate by withdrawing support for pressing Iran. One option for the president is to defer development of missile defenses in Europe (which are primarily directed against the Iranian missile threat) if Russia agrees to cooperate with a new U.S. diplomatic strategy to prevent Iran from acquiring a nuclear weapons capability. The president would make clear to Moscow that if the EU-3 plus 3 negotiators fail to agree on an effective approach, then the United States would have to proceed with missile defense in Europe. Another carrot to Moscow for its cooperation on Iran could be the expansion of U.S.-Russian nuclear cooperation, including support for the planned Angarsk international enrichment center in Siberia, which could provide an alternative to Iranian enrichment and help Russia provide expanded enrichment services to nuclear power facilities worldwide.

Unlike Russia, the Chinese view toward Iran has not become entangled with broader geostrategic issues and big-power rivalry with the United States but is largely driven by China's growing dependence on Iranian oil and gas. Moreover, China, unlike Russia, has a strong incentive to avoid a crisis that could lead to price spikes and supply disruptions. This reliance on oil from the Middle East has made Beijing extremely reluctant to risk damaging its bilateral relationship with Tehran. However, the next administration has a clear path to affecting China's behavior: Beijing has typically not been willing to use its veto to block actions that the other permanent members of the Security Council support. If the United States and its European allies are able to reach agreement with Russia on a new diplomatic strategy—including the threat of broader economic sanctions if Iran rejects a more generous offer—then China is less likely to block consensus by using its veto in the Security Council.

Consult with Allies in the Region

In addition to reaching agreement on a new strategy with the EU-3 plus 3, the president will need to coordinate with America's Middle Eastern allies who feel directly threatened by Iran's nuclear program and its rising regional influence. The most important of these is Israel. There is a strong consensus in Israel that Iran cannot be allowed to acquire a nuclear weapons capability given the oft-repeated threats by President Ahmadinejad to wipe Israel off the map. From left to right on the political spectrum, Israelis see an existential threat to their survival from a nuclear Iran. Israeli leaders are determined to maintain Israel's regional monopoly on nuclear weapons. Israel's leaders fear Israel's strategic room for maneuver in the region would be constrained by an Iranian nuclear deterrent. Outgoing prime minister Ehud Olmert, for example, declared that Israel will not tolerate a nuclear Iran. The success of the Iranian-backed terrorist groups Hezbollah and Hamas in the last few years adds to the Israeli concern.

From discussions with Israeli military and intelligence officials at the November 2007 Saban Forum in Jerusalem, it is clear that Israel has been planning for some time for a military operation to prevent Iran from acquiring nuclear weapons. Israelis say the mission is not an "impossible" one. Given the distances involved and the number of potential nuclear targets, Israelis concede that they have limited capabilities to destroy Iran's nuclear program, but they claim an Israeli attack could set Iran's program back a few years and help galvanize international diplomatic efforts to address the issue. The 2007 attack on the Syrian reactor is widely believed in Israel to have been in part a message to Tehran, and the success of the raid and lack of international repercussions may have given Israeli leaders more confidence that a similar feat could be achieved in Iran.

The next president will have to make a decision about a potential Israeli military attack against Iranian nuclear facilities. He will have three options:

—The president could give Israel a green light, allowing Israel to transit American-controlled airspace over Iraq. The benefit of this option would be that the United States could coordinate with Israel before the strike on options to manage the consequences of an attack.

—The president could avoid making a clear decision, which Israel is likely to see as an amber light, namely, U.S. passive acceptance of an Israeli strike. The drawback of this option is that it will entail many of the costs of the first one without any of the benefits.

—The president could decide on a red light, actively discouraging an Israeli attack, either because he has concluded that the United States can carry out the attack more effectively and with fewer political complications on its own or because he decides that the likely costs of an Israeli or American military attack outweigh the potential benefits.

Whatever policy the United States chooses, an Israeli attack on Iran's nuclear installations would almost certainly be seen by Iran (and the rest of the world) as American-approved if not inspired. The aircraft in any strike would be American-produced, -supplied, and -funded F-15s and F-16s, and most of the ordnance would be from American stocks. As a result, Iran would likely choose to retaliate against both Israeli and American targets. To demonstrate its retaliatory prowess, Iran has fired salvos of missiles (some of which are capable of striking Israel), and Iranian leaders have warned they would respond to an attack by either Israel or the United States with attacks against Tel Aviv, U.S. ships in the Persian Gulf, and other targets. Even if Iran chooses to retaliate in less risky ways, it could respond indirectly by encouraging Hezbollah attacks against Israel and Shi'i militia attacks against U.S. forces in Iraq, as well as terrorist attacks against U.S. and Israeli targets in the Middle East and beyond. The Israelis are already aware of the risks of an attack, especially the possible cost in American lives and the implications for U.S.-Israeli relations should there be American casualties after an Israeli attack. Given these risks, Jerusalem may be willing to give diplomacy a chance in the near term, but the Israelis will feel compelled to act if they judge that the new administration's diplomatic push has failed.

An Israeli attack on Iran would adversely affect key strategic American interests, and it is not likely to be a long-term solution because Iran would seek to rebuild its nuclear program after an attack. In addition to Iranian retaliation against both U.S. and Israeli targets, short-term oil prices would skyrocket and long-term prices would rise if the resulting conflict affected shipping and oil production in the Gulf. As a result, the president would still need to implement a strategy to deal with the basic problem within a more complicated diplomatic environment. Specifically, Iran could argue it was the victim of aggression, could withdraw from the NPT, and could then attempt to rapidly rebuild its nuclear program without international inspection.

Moreover, an Israeli air strike on Iran most likely would transit airspace under the control of the United States in Iraq. The most direct route from Israel to Natanz is roughly 1,750 kilometers across Jordan and Iraq. As the occupying power, the United States is responsible for defending Iraq's airspace. The alternatives via Turkish airspace (over 2,200 kilometers) or via Saudi airspace (over 2,400 kilometers) would also put the attack force into the skies of American allies equipped with American fighter aircraft. In Turkey's case it would be a NATO ally that the United States has a commitment to defend and in which it has a large airbase.[14] The United States could expect severe diplomatic problems at a minimum if these routes were used by Israel without the consent of the states involved (a certainty) and if America were seen to be complicit in the Israeli attack. If Iran were to retaliate against the overflown state, the United States would be called on to defend it.

The United States at least once before persuaded Israel not to use force against a military threat. In the 1991 Gulf War, President George H. W. Bush pressed Prime Minister Yitzhak Shamir not to attack Iraqi Scud missile launchers that were attacking Israel. Most important, the president refused to give the Israelis the Identification Friend or Foe (IFF) codes or approval to enter Iraqi airspace, thus indicating that Israeli aircraft would be flying in harm's way. Israel's preferred option of a limited ground-force incursion into western Iraq was also turned down. In turn, the United States committed to stepping up its own attacks on Iraqi Scuds, with little or no immediate effect on Scud launches, although the rapid success of the U.S.-led military attack on Iraqi forces in Kuwait ended the Scud threat in short order. In this sense, it was easier for Washington to persuade Jerusalem to stand down while the United States was mounting its own military operation; it would be much more difficult to convince Israel to refrain if the United States itself were not willing to act.

Whatever decision the new administration takes, it should engage Israel in a discussion on how to ensure that Iran does not threaten Israel with nuclear weapons if diplomatic actions ultimately fail to prevent Iran from acquiring those weapons. At the end of the day, the United States is probably not going to be willing or able to prevent Israel from carrying out an attack against Iranian nuclear facilities if Israel decides that it can execute an attack successfully and believes that it has no other choice. If Israeli leaders are uncertain about the effectiveness and consequences of a military raid, however, joint planning with the United States on how to contain and deter a nuclear-armed Iran could influence their decision. For example, if Israel were confident that a formal U.S. assurance that a nuclear attack on Israel would be met by a U.S. nuclear attack on Iran, Jerusalem might be more inclined to calculate that the risks of living with a nuclear-capable Iran were manageable. Therefore, the new administration should begin a quiet policy-planning exercise with Israel to consider options if diplomacy fails.

Specifically, the next president should consider extending an American nuclear guarantee to Israel. At the Camp David summit in 2000, Ehud Barak, Israel's prime minister at the time, requested that a U.S.-Israeli mutual defense treaty be signed to provide Israel with a nuclear guarantee against Iran. The idea died when the Israeli-Palestinian peace process collapsed, but it is an idea worth revisiting. Although Israel has adequate nuclear resources to retaliate massively against an Iranian nuclear attack, we reiterate that a guarantee of U.S. retaliation against Iran would provide important psychological and political reassurance to the Israeli public and strengthen deterrence against Iran.

In addition to Israel, the Sunni Arab regimes—Egypt, Jordan, Saudi Arabia, and the smaller Gulf states—feel directly threatened by the Iranian nuclear program. These states cannot be counted on to make a substantial contribution to U.S. diplomatic efforts, however, primarily because they are too weak and too frightened of Iran to take an exposed position. While Arab leaders may quietly urge the United States to take care of the Iranian nuclear threat, including through military attacks if necessary, or make noises about turning to China, France, or Russia for arms and security assurances, they are not ready to reduce ties with Washington (especially with a new president), nor are they willing to incur Iran's hostility. In addition, these states will not align publicly with the United States because of a deep popular resentment of U.S. nonproliferation policy in the region. Within the Arab world, the failure of any Arab country to develop nuclear weapons is deeply frustrating and humiliating, and the United States is blamed for "allowing" Israel to have nuclear weapons. Washington has never seriously pressed Israel to sign the Non-Proliferation Treaty or to give up its nuclear program, arguing instead that a stable peace between Israel and its neighbors must be achieved before Israel should consider changing its policy on the NPT.

Nonetheless, U.S. consultations with the Arab states will be important for managing the consequences if diplomacy fails and the United States decides to live with or attack Iran's nuclear facilities. Because of this, the next administration should begin quiet discussions with major Arab states. Most important, the next administration should reach out to Riyadh because Pakistan may already have given a commitment to Saudi Arabia to provide it with a nuclear deterrent in the event that Iran or any other country threatens the kingdom.[15]

Since no Arab state has the technical or industrial capacity to build its own bomb in the next decade or more, the United States should focus its concerns on the possibility that one or more of the super-rich Gulf states might try to buy one. If Saudi Arabia already has such an arrangement with Pakistan, it is conceivable that other wealthy Gulf states—most notably, the United Arab Emirates—might do the same. To reduce this risk, the next administration will have a variety of options. One would be to extend any nuclear umbrella and security guarantees offered to Israel to the Saudis and other Gulf states. Such a formal commitment would reduce the incentive for the Saudis to get a weapon from Pakistan and would make clear to the Iranians that the United States will not tolerate nuclear blackmail in the Persian Gulf. The issue of Israel will again complicate the issue. The Arabs will ask why they must forgo their own nuclear weapons program but Israel does not, and the United States must articulate that any nuclear umbrella does not include U.S. protection for Israel should it initiate conflict against these Gulf states. Of course, the United States already has such a nuclear commitment to Turkey through the NATO alliance. Unlike the Arab states, Turkey has a well-developed industrial and scientific infrastructure, but it has not invested resources in the development of its nuclear sector beyond small-scale scientific research. Therefore Turkey does not have the technical capability to build its own bomb in the near term. Moreover, in our discussions with Turkish officials and experts, we did not detect a strong motivation to acquire nuclear weapons to counter Iran. The Turks see Iran as a "peer competitor," and they believe that Iran's nuclear program is an element of Iran's effort to strengthen its influence in the region, but they do not generally see Iran as a military threat that would justify the expense and risk of acquiring nuclear weapons, especially since Turkey already has U.S. nuclear assurances under NATO.

Another option is for the president to make a declaration that the United States would respond with overwhelming force were Iran to use its nuclear arsenal in any capacity. This would be a unilateral American commitment to react not tied to a specific country or set of countries. As such, it would provide more ambiguity and require less "buy-in" from the Arabs, who could simply take advantage of the declaration without having to endorse it. Of course, they would not have any concomitant commitment to refrain from pursuing their own nuclear programs either indigenously or through Pakistan. Therefore, the more informal an American security commitment is, the less credibility it will have both for Iran and the Arabs.

A final option would be to combine elements of the first two in a hybrid: Israel might want a formal treaty commitment; the Arabs may prefer a declaratory commitment.

Understand the Feasibility of Deterrence

If diplomatic efforts fail, the president will have to confront the difficult choice of living with a nuclear-capable, even a nuclear-armed, Iran or undertaking military action. As noted, some have argued that once Iran gets nuclear weapons, it will not behave according to the rules of other states. The history of the Islamic Republic suggests otherwise, however.

We believe that Iran would be likely to behave like a "normal" nuclear weapons state. It will try to use its nuclear status for political advantage and to intimidate other states, which already fear Iran's power and influence. If Iran acquires nuclear weapons, it will appear impervious to American pressure and threats, and the weak Arab states of the Gulf are more likely to accommodate Iranian interests on a range of issues from setting oil prices and production levels to allowing American forces and bases in the region. At the same time, Iran is likely to avoid conflicts that could escalate into a nuclear exchange with another nuclear power because Iranian leaders recognize that a nuclear war would be devastating for the Iranian nation and culture. Similarly, Iran is not likely to transfer nuclear weapons to a terrorist organization, even Hezbollah, because of the risk that it would be held accountable if Hezbollah were to use its weapon. The United States can reduce the risk that Iran would transfer nuclear weapons to Hezbollah by strengthening American technical capabilities to trace the origins of nuclear materials back to Iran and by making clear in public and private statements that it would retaliate if Iran engages in such transfers. Throughout its history, the Islamic Republic has behaved like a very disagreeable state, but it has been careful to avoid taking actions that would lead to catastrophic consequences for itself.[16]

As such, Iran will be subject to the same deterrence system that other nuclear weapons states have accommodated themselves to since 1945. Nonetheless, even rational states can find themselves faced with the possibility of nuclear use, as happened with the United States and the Soviet Union during the Cuban missile crisis and with India and Pakistan during the Kargil crisis. There is a danger that a future Israeli-Hezbollah war in southern Lebanon, for example, could escalate to a nuclear confrontation. In such a scenario, a nuclear-armed Iran could threaten to attack Israel to prevent it from destroying Hezbollah, and Israel could feel compelled to preemptively attack Iranian nuclear forces before they could be fully mobilized or used. As in the cold war logic of "crisis instability," both Israeli and Iranian nuclear forces and societies are likely to be vulnerable to preemption, which tends to drive leaders toward early use of nuclear weapons. In addition, if Iran acquires nuclear weapons, there would be some risk of accidental or unauthorized use or loss of control if Iranian nuclear security were breached. It is impossible to evaluate how serious this potential risk would be because no one knows what mechanism for nuclear command and control and security a nuclear Iran would put into place.

Build a Credible Threat of Force, but Be Wary of Using It

Is there an effective military option that could damage Iran's program significantly for an extended period of years at a cost that would be acceptable? The United States might decide to use military force against Iran's nuclear facilities under three distinct scenarios:

—A *preventive scenario,* in which the United States attacks Iran's overt, safeguarded nuclear facilities to prevent Iran from using these facilities in the future to produce fissile material for nuclear weapons.

—A *preemptive scenario,* in which the United States attacks Iran's nuclear facilities after Iran has begun to execute nuclear breakout (for example, by expelling inspectors from the facilities) but before Iran has been able to produce enough weapons-grade uranium or separated plutonium for a bomb.

—A *Syrian scenario,* in which the United States detects and destroys a secret nuclear facility in Iran before it is operational.

From a political standpoint, the second and third scenarios would be easier for the president to justify and defend domestically and internationally. Even the first scenario might have some acceptance if it appeared that Iran had ignored generous offers by the United States to resolve the nuclear dispute diplomatically. In all cases, however, the decision to use force should be based primarily on the expected utility of the attack versus the expected risk. Although Iran's nuclear facilities are dispersed and some, such as the main production hall at Natanz, have been hardened against attack, the United States has the resources to destroy or heavily damage known nuclear targets in Iran and nearby air defenses. Iran's conventional military forces are still relatively weak and its air force is still heavily reliant on old U.S. equipment. U.S. intelligence is unlikely to have a complete picture of all the installations in the Iranian program, however, and Iran has almost certainly taken the precaution of hiding some key equipment, materials, and components in secure locations. As a result, some parts of the nuclear program would likely survive an American strike.

Given these unknowns, the utility of an attack is uncertain at best. The U.S. intelligence community is unlikely to be able to give the next president a clear assessment of the consequences of an attack on Iran's nuclear program. More likely, he will be told that an attack would probably set

back Iran's program by some range, such as two to ten years or five to fifteen years, depending on certain assumptions and uncertainties. Intelligence assessments will likely be more certain about the short-term impact
of one to two years than about the longer-term impact. Intelligence will
also be uncertain about the ability of the United States to detect and
attack rebuilt facilities, especially if Iran leaves the NPT and ends the
presence of international inspectors.

A U.S. military attack on Iran has potentially dangerous ramifications. In an optimistic scenario, Iran would respond cautiously, perhaps limiting its retaliation to indirect attacks through proxies and terrorist operations, to avoid the risk of a broader conflict with the United
States. In this scenario, Iran would play the victim, seeking to mobilize
regional and international condemnation of the United States. Alternatively, Iran may carry out its threats to attack Tel Aviv and U.S. ships in
the Persian Gulf, actions that would almost certainly lead to a broader
conflict. A war with Iran may be similar to the 2006 war between Israel
and Hezbollah in Lebanon, in which there were hundreds of clashes,
dozens of air strikes, and extended salvos of missiles and rockets—close
to 4,000—into cities. A war with Iran would not be fought in the relatively small space of the Galilee, however; it could spread across the
whole of the Middle East from Lebanon to the Khyber Pass and include
attacks on U.S. targets.

The regional political consequences of an attack are difficult to predict. As noted earlier, quiet satisfaction might emanate from Arab
palaces, but the reaction in the Arab and Islamic street would be vio-
lently negative. An early casualty of military confrontation could be the
government of Prime Minister Nouri al-Maliki in Iraq. The Shi'i population and the Shi'i warlords in Iraq would align themselves with Iran,
whereas the Kurds would be in a precarious situation, torn between the
United States and Iran. In addition, President Hamid Karzai's government in Kabul would face dangerous challenges, and given its growing
weakness, could collapse. As a result, the United States would find the
twin insurgencies in Iraq and Afghanistan burning more intensely while
it struggled to destroy targets deep inside Iran. Of course, the potential
ramifications of an attack on the domestic politics of Iraq and
Afghanistan will depend on the circumstances at that time. For example,
the more that the Iraqi government is able to take over internal security

responsibilities and address domestic political issues, the more able it will be to weather the reaction to an American attack on Iran.

Any future conflict in the Gulf could also have an enormous impact on the world energy market at a time when oil prices are already at unprecedented highs. In the short term, nervous oil markets are certain to increase prices in the aftermath of an attack, but the consequences would be even more severe and enduring if the conflict escalates. Although Iran is likely to be reluctant to escalate by attacking oil tankers and Arab oil installations—actions that would invite a major U.S. retaliation—Iran could carry out desperate measures should it conclude the United States was seeking to disable Iran's air and naval forces or attempting regime change in the conflict. Once started, a war may be difficult to contain.

We assess the military option to be unappealing. In deciding whether to use military force, the president will be faced with irresolvable uncertainties, both about the effectiveness of an attack, in terms of its impact on Iran's nuclear program, and about the risks of an attack, in terms of triggering a broader conflict with Iran and implications for regional politics and oil prices. In short, launching an attack would be a gamble not worth taking except as a last resort when and if diplomacy has indisputably failed to prevent Iran from developing a nuclear breakout option. Moreover, it is clear that a military strike is not likely to terminate Iran's nuclear efforts. If anything, Tehran would likely emerge even more determined to acquire nuclear weapons. At the same time, the credible threat of force—the perception in Tehran that the United States might be prepared to use force—is an essential element of a successful diplomatic strategy. Therefore, whether or not the United States is ultimately prepared to use military force, the next administration must convince Iran that it is willing and able to attack if Tehran does not agree to a diplomatic resolution acceptable to Washington. In any event, force needs to be retained as an option if Iran attempts a nuclear breakout or if the United States detects a secret nuclear facility in Iran.

CONCLUSION

Preventing further nuclear proliferation in the Middle East will be a vexing problem for the next president. Iran is the heart of the problem but not all of it. The U.S.-U.K. invasion of Iraq and the Israeli bombing of

Syria have sent strong signals to Iran and others: if you do not have a nuclear deterrent you can be attacked by stronger powers. Moreover, Iran has historical aspirations to assert its regional primacy, and its nuclear program has become intertwined with national pride and ambition. Iran's current pursuit of a nuclear deterrent would almost certainly be the policy of any regime in Tehran. Had the shah not been overthrown and were his son on the throne today, for example, Iran would probably have a nuclear deterrent by now. The Islamic Republic regime is particularly difficult and dangerous, and acquisition of a nuclear weapons capability will make it even more so. Fortunately, technical problems and export controls have delayed Iran's acquisition of a nuclear weapons breakout capability. The next president will not be at the eleventh hour on assuming office, but he may be there by the end of his first term.

The existence of Israel's nuclear arsenal has undermined the legitimacy of U.S. efforts to promote nonproliferation in the region and strengthened pressures on Arab countries to seek their own nuclear capabilities. The nearly universal perception in the region and elsewhere that the United States pursues an inconsistent policy on nuclear proliferation in the Middle East—which effectively protects Israel's nuclear monopoly—makes the diplomatic challenge to pressure Iran even more complex because it makes it more difficult to rally Arab pressure against Iran. This problem has no obvious solution, because Israel is not prepared to abandon or limit its nuclear weapons program as part of a diplomatic effort to address the Iranian nuclear issue, and even if Israel were prepared to sign the NPT, that would not change Iran's plan to develop an enrichment capacity under the NPT. However, the EU-3 plus 3 countries will have to portray any diplomatic agreement with Iran as a step toward achieving the ultimate objective of a Middle East free of nuclear weapons, and the U.S. president should be prepared to reaffirm U.S. support for this ultimate objective.

The next president will need to authorize tough and direct diplomacy with Tehran, going beyond the limited steps that the current administration has authorized. The new administration should return to the formula of Presidents George H. W. Bush and Bill Clinton and be open to direct, authoritative negotiations with Iran on the full agenda of issues. These bilateral talks should be well prepared and well coordinated with our allies in the region and around the world. As discussed in chapter 3, soon after taking office, the new administration should seek a direct channel to an authorized representative of Iran's supreme leader to discuss a broad range of issues, including the nuclear dispute. The substance of the discussions should remain confidential and the level of diplomacy decided as the talks progress. The administration should be open to engagement on the presidential level, if that is necessary to secure U.S. interests.

Even as the administration seeks to restore a bilateral channel with Iran, the next president and his team should develop a new package of inducements and pressures, in close coordination with our allies, to prepare for international nuclear negotiations with Iran and the EU-3 plus 3. The new U.S. administration should preserve the existing EU-3 plus 3 framework for nuclear negotiations because a coalition of big powers is more likely to be effective in influencing Iranian behavior than unilateral U.S. efforts would be. An early decision for the new administration and the EU-3 plus 3 is whether to maintain their current demand that Iran suspend its enrichment and reprocessing activities as a condition for beginning formal negotiations. If this objective proves unobtainable, the United States should be prepared to agree with the other EU-3 plus 3 countries to relax the demand as a condition for beginning talks, provided that the other powers agree to press Iran to accept suspension as a basis for keeping the talks going. Otherwise, Iran will be content to let the talks spin out while it spins centrifuges.

In these negotiations, the United States should support the current EU-3 plus 3 offer to provide assistance to Iran's civil nuclear power program, including guarantees of fuel supply, if Iran agrees to a multiple-year moratorium of its enrichment and reprocessing programs. From a nonproliferation standpoint, a complete moratorium is far and away the best outcome. If a complete moratorium is not possible, however, the United States should consider arrangements that would sharply limit Iranian breakout capabilities, such as limiting the number of centrifuges that Iran is allowed to operate. Enhanced international monitoring and verification of Iran's nuclear activities must be part of the package because of the high danger that Iran will renege or cheat on any agreement that constrains its nuclear program in meaningful ways.

This new package should also go beyond the nuclear dimension to try to achieve a more fundamental and enduring security understanding with Tehran. At a minimum, it should include explicit commitments by the United States renouncing regime change, but the United States should also be prepared to lift economic sanctions and normalize political relations if Iran meets American nuclear demands. Although these incentives are of little appeal to the hard-line elements of the regime, they may strengthen the argument of some factions within the Iranian elite.

Bigger carrots alone, however, will not be effective. As long as Iran perceives the United States as being on the defensive in the region, it is not likely to accommodate U.S. demands. American nuclear nonproliferation strategy needs to be buttressed by effective policies that reverse our weakness in the region and put new pressures on Iran. Agreement on tougher sanctions in the United Nations, as well as informal sanctions imposed by private industry and nongovernmental organizations, will be necessary to persuade Iran to accept a long-term moratorium on its enrichment and reprocessing programs. Such an agreement will require focused diplomacy with Moscow and Beijing, especially to achieve a set of UN sanctions if Iran rejects a more generous offer from the EU-3 plus 3 and an American side offer to improve bilateral relations with Iran as part of a nuclear deal. In addition, the more Iran believes that its nuclear program risks triggering a military attack, the more likely Tehran will be to accept a diplomatic solution that limits or delays its nuclear ambitions.

Even the toughest diplomacy and sanctions may not be sufficient to keep Iran from crossing the nuclear threshold. This is even more the case because Tehran is seeking an ambiguous crossing—it wants to acquire a latent capability to produce weapons-grade fissile material without actually producing such material and building nuclear weapons, at least for some period of time. The next administration will want to study carefully its military options and have a serious military contingency available. The use of force is an unappealing option with high risks and limited gains, but the next administration needs to convince Iran that is a serious threat, if diplomacy is going to be successful.

The next administration should also engage in a serious and discrete dialogue with Israel on its military plans. History demonstrates Israel will use force to protect its monopoly on nuclear weapons in the region.

Israel views a nuclear-capable Iran as an existential threat and is prepared to run high risks in exchange for inflicting even limited damage on Iran's nuclear program. The next president may not be able to dissuade Israel from attacking Iran, but he should not leave Jerusalem uncertain as to the United States' views. Most important, if the next president rejects an American military option, he should make clear to Israel as privately as possible that the United States opposes an Israeli attack. At the same time, the administration should offer Israel a credible security alternative based on deterrence and missile defenses and backed by formal commitments.

If diplomacy fails and military force is not used, the next administration will have to develop a strategy to contain and deter a nuclear-capable Iran. In the first instance, this means building firebreaks—including the threat of sanctions and force—to dissuade Iran from using overt nuclear facilities or building covert facilities to produce weapons-usable fissile material. The president must recognize, however, that preventing Iran from crossing the nuclear threshold will grow more difficult, the closer Iran comes to the threshold. If Iran builds a nuclear bomb, the danger of a nuclear arms race in the region is real but not immediate. No other state is technically capable of developing a weapons capability on its own for at least a decade. The real immediate danger is an arrangement like the one that may exist between Saudi Arabia and Pakistan: a bomb on demand in return for financial assistance over a prolonged period of time.

If Iran acquires nuclear weapons, it is likely to behave like a "normal" nuclear weapons state, not recklessly using the bomb or giving it to terrorists, but trying to extract maximum leverage from its nuclear deterrent to increase its influence and defend itself from external threats. This behavior will include trying to intimidate other states, especially the small Gulf states, and perhaps providing a nuclear umbrella to Iranian allies, such as Hezbollah in Lebanon or, less likely, the Hamas state in Gaza. Under these circumstances, the danger of nuclear use arises not from recklessness or fanaticism, but from possible escalation of conventional conflicts, plus the possibility of accidental or unauthorized use or loss of control. The next administration should not be sanguine about the difficulties of managing these risks.

Thus, the next president should consider extending America's nuclear umbrella and security arrangements to both Israel and U.S. allies in the Persian Gulf (Turkey already has one through NATO). The goals of such an approach would be to discourage Iranian adventurism, reassure allies, and encourage nuclear restraint. Such an extension of the American nuclear umbrella should be done through treaty and be subject to the consent of the Senate. Promising American defense to other countries—either by treaty or by public declaration—is not a trivial matter and must be fully debated by the public and Congress. It is not too soon to begin such a debate.

The first order of business for the next president, however, will be to muster stronger commitments from the existing international coalition (primarily the EU-3 plus 3 plus Japan and the other EU countries) to confront Iran with a clear choice. To muster this support, especially from reluctant partners like Russia and China, the new administration will need to make Iran a central issue in overall relations with those countries. Faced with the threat of serious international sanctions and political pressure (and the implicit threat of force), Tehran may feel forced to accept delays and limits on its nuclear program. This would not represent a fundamental shift in Iran's nuclear ambitions but rather a tactical adjustment to avoid risks and penalties. To make this tactical adjustment more likely (and to play on internal divisions within Iran), the United States should be prepared to offer a fundamental improvement in bilateral relations if Iran makes nuclear concessions.

NOTES

1. For example, see the International Institute of Strategic Studies report, *Nuclear Programmes in the Middle East: In the Shadow of Iran* (London: 2008), which comes to the same conclusion.

2. In 1991 Israel warned Iraq that it would use nuclear weapons to respond to any chemical or biological attack on Israel. Jordan's King Hussein passed the message to Baghdad, according to a new biography by Avi Shlaim, *The Lion of Jordan: The Life of King Hussein in War and Peace* (London: Penguin, 2008).

3. The Iranian dissidents got the information from Israeli intelligence, who fed it to them through a cutout, according to former Israeli Defense Forces chief of staff Moshe Ya'alon; see Adrian Levy and Catherine Scott-Clark, *Deception: Pakistan, the United States and the Secret Trade in Nuclear Weapons* (New York: Walker, 2007), p. 525.

4. "Iran Says Ready to Start 'Serious, Targeted' Negotiations," Agence France-Presse, May 21, 2008.

5. The NPT does not restrict the development of any nuclear activities for peaceful purposes. Hence an NPT party is allowed to develop enrichment capabilities for civil nuclear purposes, a right that Iran claims. The counter legal argument is that the NPT does not allow a country to pursue a military option under the guise of a peaceful nuclear program, and there are sufficient grounds to doubt that Iran's nuclear intentions are truly peaceful, including persistent violations of its NPT obligations and evidence of secret nuclear weapons research and development.

6. For most simple nuclear weapons, approximately twenty to twenty-five kilograms of highly enriched uranium—uranium enriched to about 90 percent U-235—would be required for each weapon, while approximately six to eight kilograms of separated plutonium-239 would be required for each plutonium-based bomb.

7. In contrast, Iran reportedly has sufficient components and materials on hand to make thousands of the older and less reliable P-1 machines.

8. Assuming perfect efficiency, about 27 to 29 kilograms of 3.5 percent LEU are required to produce 1 kilogram of 90 percent HEU. Therefore, a stockpile of about 540 to 725 kilograms of LEU would be needed to produce 20 to 25 kilograms of HEU. Note that these figures are given as amounts of uranium contained in uranium hexafluoride (UF6), not amounts of total UF6. The comparable numbers for UF6 are about 700 to 900 kilograms of low-enriched UF6. Assuming some inefficiencies and losses, 1,000 kilograms of low-enriched UF6 is a rough estimate of the amount required to produce enough HEU for a single bomb, although the actual amount required could be higher if inefficiencies are greater.

9. The exact time required for nuclear breakout is difficult to calculate because it includes both the time required to reconfigure the plant from the production of LEU to production of HEU as well as the actual operating time to produce the first bomb's worth of HEU. In general, the more time that is taken to reconfigure the plant, the more efficient the plant operation and therefore the less operating time would be required. Conversely, the less time taken to reconfigure the plant, the less efficient the operation and therefore the more operating time required to produce a given quantity of HEU.

10. For further discussion of Iran's breakout options, see International Institute for Strategic Studies, *Iran's Strategic Weapons Programmes: A Net Assessment* (London: 2005).

11. The various Security Council resolutions on Iran do not specifically mandate suspension as a condition for nuclear negotiations, but the EU-3 plus 3 has made this demand in public statements and in private meetings with Iranian officials. For example, the June 12, 2008, letter from EU-3 plus 3 foreign ministers to Iran says, "Formal negotiations can start as soon as Iran's enrichment-related and reprocessing activities are suspended."

12. The current U.S. position offers to reaffirm Iran's right to "nuclear energy for exclusively peaceful purposes" but does not explicitly acknowledge enrichment as one of those rights.

13. Iran has not provided details on its proposal, but some nongovernmental experts in the United States and Europe have developed their own ideas for such a multilateral enrichment facility. For example, see William Luers, Thomas R. Pickering, and

Jim Walsh, "A Solution for the US-Iran Nuclear Standoff," *New York Review of Books* 55, no. 4 (March 20, 2008).

14. See Whitney Raas and Austin Long, "Osirak Redux? Assessing Israeli Military Capabilities to Destroy Iranian Nuclear Facilities," *International Security* 3, no. 4 (Spring 2007).

15. Shortly after Pakistan tested its nuclear weapons in 1998, Saudi defense minister Prince Sultan bin Abdul Aziz toured Pakistan's nuclear and missile facilities outside Islamabad. Pakistan's famous A. Q. Khan provided some of the color commentary for these unprecedented tours. At the time, U.S. officials expressed concern that the Pakistanis might have promised to provide a nuclear weapon to the kingdom. Sultan had been defense minister since 1962 and today is also crown prince. After Pervez Musharraf took control of Pakistan in a coup in 1999, the nuclear relationship continued and matured. In October 2003 then–crown prince Abdullah bin Abdul Aziz visited Pakistan for a state visit. Several experts reported after the trip that a secret agreement was concluded that committed Pakistan to provide Saudi Arabia with a Pakistani nuclear weapon deterrent to be deployed to the kingdom if Saudi Arabia felt threatened by a third-party nuclear program in the future. Both countries, of course, denied the stories. See, for example, Arnaud de Borchgrave, "Pakistan and Saudi Arabia in Secret Nuke Deal," *Washington Times,* October 22, 2003; and Amir Mir, "Where Terror and the Bomb Could Meet," *Asia Times,* July 7, 2005.

16. In the defining event of modern U.S.-Iran relations, the hostage crisis of 1979–81, Iran took actions that were in clear violation of international law, but when it perceived that an action would provoke a massive violent American response, it desisted from that course. In the summer of 1980 Iranian leaders repeatedly threatened to put the American hostages on trial for espionage. President Jimmy Carter made clear that any trials would produce a military response and Iran retreated. In the 1988 undeclared naval war in the Persian Gulf between the United States and Iran over reflagged Kuwaiti tankers, Iran attacked U.S. Navy ships but was careful to keep the conflict from escalating into a full-scale war. When the USS *Vincennes* inadvertently shot down an Iran Air civilian airliner, Ayatollah Khomeini sensed the conflict was getting out of control and agreed to a cease-fire with Iraq and the United States. Similarly, throughout the Iran-Iraq war, Iraq was the first to use chemical weapons on the battlefield, not Iran, and it was Iraq that first used missiles against Iranian cities. In the mid-1990s when the United States determined that Iran was behind the terrorist attack on the U.S. Air Force barracks at Khobar, Saudi Arabia, and warned that any further attacks would prompt a military retaliation, Iran desisted from targeting American military facilities in the Gulf and elsewhere. Today, Iran is careful to limit its support of anti-American insurgents in Iraq and Afghanistan to low-intensity conflict and asymmetric warfare to preclude a major American military response. The Iranian decision in 2003 to cease development of its nuclear weaponization program and to acknowledge publicly its secret efforts to develop fissile material production facilities probably reflected its calculus of the risks involved in provoking the United States in the aftermath of the invasion of Iraq and the toppling of Saddam Hussein.

STEVEN A. COOK

SHIBLEY TELHAMI

5

Addressing the Arab-Israeli Conflict

AFTER SEVEN YEARS ON the back burner of American foreign policy, Arab-Israeli peacemaking needs to become a priority for the next president. Recent trends in Israel and the Palestinian territories have created a situation in which the option of a two-state solution may soon no longer be possible. Failure to forge an agreement will present serious complications for other American policies in the Middle East because the Arab-Israeli conflict remains central not only to Israel and its neighbors but also to the way most Arabs view the United States. Failure will also inevitably pose new strategic and moral challenges for American foreign policy. The need for active and sustained American peace diplomacy is therefore urgent.

The new administration's agenda in the Middle East will be crowded: the Iraq war, Iran's nuclear program, the war on al Qaeda, and the supply and cost of energy. These immediate issues make it harder to emphasize Arab-Israeli peacemaking since many of the costs of ignoring it are not directly visible (such as the impact on Arab public opinion) or are long term, such as the consequences of the collapse of the two-state solution. While Arab-Israeli diplomacy should be an important goal of the new administration, it can succeed only as part of a regional initiative that frames the Arab-Israeli issue in the context of other American priorities.

131

Because the way an administration frames its foreign policy objectives is highly consequential for the direction and effectiveness of any particular initiative, very early in the administration, the president should announce a multitrack "framework for security and peace in the Middle East" that connects the Arab-Israeli conflict to the regional and global agenda.

Resolving this conflict is an important American interest. This is not to suggest that settling the Arab-Israeli conflict can resolve all the other challenges Washington confronts in the region. Nevertheless, it is a mistake to underestimate the importance of the conflict, even beyond its psychological role in the political identity of most Arabs: it is certainly central to Israel, the Palestinians, Syria, and Lebanon. It remains important to both Jordan and Egypt, the only two Arab states at peace with Israel, who could be drawn further into the conflict if the two-state solution collapses. The conflict remains the prism through which many Arabs view the United States and the source of much of the Arab public's anger with American foreign policy. It is a primary source of militancy, and it is a source of influence for Iran in the Arab world. Pro-American governments in the region face internal public pressures whenever the conflict escalates. While Arab authoritarians have withstood this pressure through repression and co-optation, the gap between publics and governments in the region is wide. This has been a constant source of empowerment for militant groups posing threats to the regional order and to American interests. The American commitment to Israel and American interests in the Arab world ensure that when conflict escalates, the United States is affected or drawn into the conflict. As the United States seeks to end the Iraq war while minimizing its detrimental consequences, regional cooperation in that effort becomes more likely when the Arab-Israeli conflict is reduced. Arab-Israeli peace could change the regional environment for American foreign policy, open new alliance options, and turn public opinion against al Qaeda, much of whose support appears to be based on the logic of the "enemy of my enemy" rather than on an embrace of its agenda. In designing a broad framework for security and peace in the Middle East, the new administration should learn from the failures and successes of previous American diplomatic efforts. Of particular note are the lessons drawn in a recent report by a study group of the United States Institute of Peace (of which one of us was a member).[1]

Specifically, the new administration should undertake a number of steps on the Arab-Israeli front:

—Begin by recognizing that an effective diplomatic initiative aimed at a lasting peace cannot be attained so long as the Palestinians are organizationally divided and without an enforced cease-fire with Israel. These divisions could become even wider if Palestinian presidential elections are not held in January 2009 and Hamas (the Islamic Resistance Movement) no longer recognizes the legitimacy of the presidency. Thus, American diplomacy must begin with the twin aims of encouraging an effective cease-fire and supporting a Palestinian unity government. A unity government negotiating with Israel is not sustainable so long as Hamas carries out violent attacks against its Palestinian competitors and Israel. A central feature of Washington's diplomacy must be to work with its regional allies to induce Hamas into an effective cease-fire coupled with sustained regional efforts to limit the flow of arms into the Palestinian territories.

—Recognize that Hamas's power stems from genuine support among a significant segment of the Palestinian public and that Hamas will likely remain a spoiler as long as it is outside of Palestinian governing institutions. Although there is no guarantee that the organization will play a more constructive role within a national unity government, Washington should support conciliation between Fatah and Hamas as a way to diminish the Islamists' incentive to undermine negotiations, forcing Hamas to either accept a peace agreement that addresses Palestinian rights or lose the support of the Palestinian public. The aim should be less to "reform" Hamas than to put in place political arrangements that are conducive to successful negotiations and that limit Hamas's incentives to be a spoiler.

—Encourage Egypt, Saudi Arabia, and other Arab actors to pressure Hamas to police the cease-fire agreement with Israel and to convince the Hamas leadership to accept the April 2002 Arab League Peace Initiative, especially as Israeli leaders are voicing renewed interest in that plan. In this context, the United States should be willing to drop its insistence that Hamas accept the Quartet's criteria—recognition of Israel, renunciation of armed struggle, and adherence to previous Israel-Palestinian Authority agreements.

—Recognize that no one can predict election outcomes in Palestine, as the Bush administration discovered, that elections are unlikely to resolve the current Palestinian divisions, and that they cannot be a substitute for efforts of political reconciliation, although such elections should be supported.

—Hold Israel to its commitment to freeze new construction of Jewish settlements in the West Bank and in the Jerusalem area. Critically, this freeze should halt the construction of new communities, outposts, and "thickening" of existing settlements, which often entails expropriation of additional Palestinian land. In addition, Washington must urge Israel to allow Palestinians greater freedom of movement throughout the West Bank. In Gaza, provided the cease-fire between Israel and Hamas holds, the Israelis must permit a greater flow of goods in and out of the territory.

—Appoint a special peace envoy to pursue actively a final-status agreement between Israel and the Palestinians, while coordinating with other tracks of negotiations. A special envoy, however, cannot be a substitute for the direct involvement of the president or the secretary of state, who must be engaged to sustain an effective diplomatic effort.

—Put forth American ideas on final status in the Palestinian-Israeli track at the appropriate moment. To keep the hope of a two-state solution alive, this should be done sooner rather than later.

—Work to bolster and train Palestinian forces to police effectively the West Bank and lay the ground for capable unified Palestinian security forces after an agreement is reached.

—Support Turkish mediation in the Syrian-Israeli negotiations and become more actively engaged in these negotiations as both sides have indicated a strong desire for an American role. The United States should also return its ambassador to Damascus.

—Encourage the continuation of a Lebanese national unity government and its participation in negotiations with Israel.

—Activate two new multilateral tracks: one addressing regional economic cooperation, especially in a postpeace environment, the other addressing regional security cooperation.

—Develop a plan for the deployment of international forces in the West Bank and Gaza once a peace agreement is in place; these forces will be essential in the implementation phase for building a unified Palestinian police force and beginning the effective separation of Israelis and

Palestinians. Their deployment must commence immediately following an agreement to help coordinate the peaceful withdrawal of Israeli forces.

AN OPPORTUNITY TO BE SEIZED

The next president of the United States may be the last to have the option of seriously pursuing a two-state solution to the Palestinian-Israeli conflict. Dynamics on the ground in Israel and the Palestinian territories are dangerously close to a situation in which the parties may no longer be amenable to that outcome. For the United States, there are no practical alternatives to the two-state solution, and its diminishing prospects will likely result in another generation of conflict and instability, further complicating American policies in the Middle East.

Yet the new administration will almost certainly have an opportunity: the number of people in the Middle East who are prepared to accept the idea that Israel and a Palestinian state can coexist peacefully based on the 1967 boundaries is now larger than ever. In public opinion polls conducted in 2008, more than two-thirds of Arabs surveyed indicated an acceptance of this solution, while majorities of Israelis and Palestinians continue to hope for it.[2] Israeli and Arab leaders have defined the two-state solution as a foreign policy objective, and Arab governments have reiterated their support for the 2002 Arab Peace Initiative aimed at establishing a Palestinian state, ending the conflict, and making peace with Israel.[3] Increasingly, Israeli leaders have expressed renewed interest in the Arab Peace Initiative and in the idea of a comprehensive peace. At the same time, most governments and elites in the region see the American role as indispensable, and most view the American elections as a new opportunity for peace diplomacy.

Nevertheless, these promising trends are increasingly overtaken by a sense of disbelief in the possibility of a peaceful agreement. In the Arab world, 55 percent of the public does not believe this outcome will ever be achieved, and only 13 percent believe that it is achievable in the next five years. More troubling, an increasing number of Palestinian and Arab intellectuals are abandoning the idea of a two-state solution and are now advocating a one-state solution in which Jews and Arabs coexist in a binational state. In Israel some mainstream voices are now arguing that the two-state solution is unachievable and that Israel must consider alternatives.

These trends are the result of changes on the ground that may become insurmountable. On the Israeli side, continued expansion of Israeli settlements, especially around Jerusalem, and changes in supporting infrastructure, particularly in the West Bank, make it increasingly difficult to envision the kind of settlement evacuation that will be necessary for a Palestinian state that meets the minimal aspirations of most Palestinians. On the Palestinian side, the increasing power of Hamas and the popularity of militant methods have undermined the Israeli public's faith in the viability of a peaceful settlement.

Given the improbability that the majority of Israelis will accept a single state in which Jews will be a minority, the consequence of the collapse of the two-state solution will likely be protracted conflict for the foreseeable future, with each side trying to defeat, rather than compromise with, the other. Palestinian frustrations and despair and increasing Israeli insecurity will inevitably affect Arab-Jewish relations within Israel itself and Israeli relations with neighboring states, especially Egypt and Jordan.

THE CONTINUED IMPORTANCE OF THE ARAB-ISRAELI CONFLICT FOR AMERICAN INTERESTS

The Arab-Israeli conflict is not the source of all the challenges the United States faces in the Middle East. Yet, this conflict remains important to the configuration of forces in the region, to Arab public opinion, and to Washington's ability to achieve its regional interests. Resolving this conflict remains an important American interest.

The importance of the Arab-Israeli conflict has been recognized by successive American administrations at least since the 1973 Arab-Israeli war, when it became clear that the tension between American interests in the Arab world, especially those concerning oil, and the American commitment to Israeli security could be effectively resolved only if the conflict between Israel and the Arabs were reduced. Moreover, the conflict is of high importance to a number of players in the region. It is central to Lebanon, which witnessed a devastating war with Israel in 2006 and could face another one as the tension between Israel and Hezbollah remains high. In addition, the presence of several hundreds of thousands of Palestinian refugees on Lebanese soil remains not only a pressing humanitarian issue but a complicating factor in Lebanon's confessional political system. The conflict is central to Syria, whose Golan Heights Israel has occupied since the 1967 war. For Jordan, the issue is critical because a majority of its population is Palestinian and any instability resulting from a collapse of the two-state solution might spill over into Jordan. For Egypt, Gaza's isolation ultimately will lead to instability along the Gaza-Sinai border, and Cairo may find itself responsible for the Palestinians there. Cairo is especially concerned that radicalization and militancy in Gaza would spread to Egypt.

While many Arab governments, especially the small states in the Gulf Cooperation Council, are concerned about the Iraq war and the rise of Iranian power, they view the Arab-Israeli conflict as critical to the stability of the region and as the most exploitable of all issues facing the Arab world. They believe that Iran will use it to empower militancy and radicalization, which in turn threatens to undermine their stability.

The Arab-Israeli conflict has turned into a theater in which extremist leaders play for support throughout the Arab world. Hezbollah leader Hassan Nasrallah and Iranian president Mahmoud Ahmadinejad have gained widespread public support for their defiance of Israel and the United States.[4] Similarly, the absence of serious progress in the Palestinian-Israeli negotiations coupled with continued bloodshed and suffering has increased Arab public support for militant groups, with more people sympathizing with Hamas than with the government of Palestinian president Mahmoud Abbas.

These trends suggest that the Arab-Israeli issue, especially the Palestinian-Israeli conflict, remains important to other regional challenges such as Iran, Iraq, and the war on al Qaeda and its allies. It will be difficult for the new American administration to mobilize support within the Arab world for American-led pressure on or confrontation with Iran when Arab publics see the United States as a bigger threat than Iran. Similarly, Arabs may want to support the emergence of Iraq as a stable and powerful Arab state, but they fear American dominance and believe that the United States is in Iraq not only to control oil supplies but also to help Israel.

This environment makes it harder to fight militant groups, even al Qaeda. Among those who favor any aspect of al Qaeda's ideology, the largest segment sympathizes not with al Qaeda's agenda but with the perception that it stands up to the United States. As this attitude becomes pervasive, it inevitably spills over into the rank and file of government bureaucracies and potentially even the security and military services of Arab governments.

There are also compelling humanitarian reasons to act. In the sixty years since the establishment of the state of Israel, Israelis have never known real peace. Until the June 2008 cease-fire, which remains fragile, Israelis had been subject to daily rocket attacks from Gaza, while the threat of terrorism, the prospect of more war in Lebanon, and talk of annihilation from Iran's president Ahmadinejad continue. Many Palestinians have remained stateless refugees for the past sixty years, and the conditions of hundreds of thousands, especially in Gaza and Lebanon, have actually worsened. Occupation for the vast majority of those living in the West Bank and Gaza has been anything but a temporary condition; it has been a state of affairs that has spanned their entire lives. Thousands have been killed or wounded, and thousands more remain in Israeli prisons. The degree of daily humiliation and basic struggle to survive, especially after the imposition of a blockade on Gaza, should not be ignored.

WANING PROSPECTS FOR REACHING A TWO-STATE SOLUTION

Changing perceptions among Palestinian elites, fragmentation of the Palestinian territories, and a strengthening Israeli hold on the West Bank are creating a situation in which the viability of a Palestinian state existing alongside a secure Israel is becoming an impossibility. At the same time, rocket fire from the Gaza Strip into southern Israel, largely halted by a delicate cease-fire in 2008, makes it less likely that the Israeli electorate will support a withdrawal from West Bank territory if it fears that major population centers along the Mediterranean coast will be targeted.

Changing Elite Perceptions

In the 1990s Israeli and Palestinian political elites began to see the two-state solution not only as an acceptable compromise to the conflict but also as inevitable. Since the collapse of the Camp David negotiations in

July 2000, however, there has been a discernible transformation. First, many Israelis and Palestinians began to doubt that the other was committed to peace, and the degree of pessimism grew even as majorities remained supportive of reconciliation in principle. Second, religious framing of the conflict began to compete aggressively with the previous nationalist narrative that had given rise to openness toward a two-state solution.

It had taken Palestinian secular elites at least two decades after the creation of Israel to begin defining the conflict in nationalist Palestinian terms and two more decades before they formally accepted the notion of peace with Israel. On the Israeli side, it took the political elite more than four decades to accommodate itself to a Palestinian state in the West Bank and Gaza. The trends are now moving in another direction.

Even separate from the position of Hamas and other Islamist groups, Palestinian secular nationalist elites are now debating among themselves whether the nationalist project has failed, with many believing that a viable Palestinian state is no longer possible and that pretending that it is still viable is costly to the Palestinians. Some early advocates of the two-state solution have already abandoned it publicly. Many within the Palestinian Authority (PA) openly debate their current course.

Without a peace settlement, more and more people among the moderate secular elites will abandon the notion of a Palestinian state in the West Bank and Gaza. The intellectual alternative to Hamas by the secular nationalists will likely become the one-state solution, a single state encompassing Israel, Gaza, and the West Bank, in which Arabs and Jews are equal. This is a prospect that the vast majority of Israelis will continue to reject.

Social, Economic, and Territorial Fragmentation of the Palestinian Territories

The continuation of the conflict and occupation has had dire consequences for the Palestinian population of the West Bank and Gaza Strip—and for the prospects of a viable Palestinian state. The West Bank and Gaza Strip have become politically fragmented from each other, while both territories have become economically fragmented from the rest of the region.

Hamas in Gaza is under international sanctions for its unwillingness to accept Israel's right to exist, give up armed struggle, and uphold agreements between Israel and the PA. Israel, the United States, and other countries regard the PA (West Bank) under the leadership of President Abbas and Prime Minister Salam Fayyad as the legitimate Palestinian government that seeks a peaceful solution to the conflict through negotiations with Israel. Fearing a Hamas takeover of the West Bank, Washington has sponsored negotiations between Abbas and the Israeli government. Despite international recognition, the PA (West Bank) is politically weak and has limited ability to control its own territory—the relative quiet of the West Bank is in general the result of the Israel Defense Forces' presence in the area. It is important to note, however, that Prime Minister Fayyad has deployed Palestinian security forces to the major cities of the West Bank, where they have helped establish order.

The dire humanitarian consequences of the blockade of Gaza and restrictions on movement within the West Bank have fragmented the Palestinian territories from the region. Whereas the Palestinians' overall economic development, health care, and education once equaled or compared favorably with their Jordanian, Egyptian, Syrian, and Lebanese neighbors, that is no longer the case. In the decade between 1998 and 2008, almost every socioeconomic indicator for the Palestinian population of the West Bank and Gaza Strip declined, some precipitously. In 1998 and 1999, the Palestinian economy grew at 3.9 and 3.0 percent per capita respectively. But with the outbreak of the al-Aqsa intifada in late 2000 and the subsequent years of conflict and closures, the overall Palestinian economy contracted sharply. Per capita GDP fell 5 percent in 2000, an additional 20 percent in 2001, and a further 23 percent in 2002. The Palestinian economy has never recovered because most of the 146,000 Palestinian laborers in the Israeli agricultural and construction sectors—remittances from Israel represented 21 percent of Palestinians' disposable income at the start of the intifada—were replaced with foreign workers. Israel's closures and military incursions greatly reduced job opportunities in the West Bank and Gaza Strip while destroying agricultural fields, small businesses, modest manufacturing facilities, roads, and power plants there, all of which were critical components of the Palestinian economy.[5]

Given the sharp reduction in GDP and employment, it is not surprising that the number of Palestinians who now live at or below the poverty line has increased substantially. Poverty rates in the West Bank and Gaza Strip were generally high before 2002, averaging around 20 percent of the population, but by 2002 the World Bank found that 60 percent of the Palestinian population was living on less than $2 a day (the Bank's measure of poverty) and by 2003, 72 percent of the Palestinian population was living in poverty, with a single breadwinner for every seven Palestinians. The suspension of international aid after Hamas's electoral victory in January 2006 has only accentuated the deterioration of economic conditions for the Palestinian population. Hardship has become widespread in the West Bank and Gaza Strip. Relatively wealthier cities like Jerusalem, Ramallah, and Nablus have experienced moderate increases in poverty rates, whereas previously poor places like Khan Yunis, Gaza City, and Hebron have seen poverty rates explode. The difficult conditions in the West Bank and Gaza Strip since 2000 have also had a negative impact on the Palestinian health and educational systems.[6]

Continued Israeli Settlement

The decline in Palestinian socioeconomic conditions has occurred against the backdrop of Israel's continued investment in the infrastructure of its occupation in the West Bank. Although the conventional view of the Oslo period—September 1993 to December 2000—is one of great hope, during this time the number of Israeli settlers in the West Bank grew from 110,900 to 187,600. Overall population growth of settlers in the West Bank slowed after the outbreak of the al-Aqsa intifada in 2000, but by 2006 (the last year for which statistics are available), the Jewish population in the West Bank was 255,600, among 2.5 million Palestinians, an overall increase of 130 percent from the early 1990s.[7] Demographic studies of the Arab and Jewish populations in the territory between the Jordan River and the Mediterranean Sea indicate that within ten to fifteen years the number of Israeli Jews and Palestinians (including those who are citizens of Israel) will be roughly equal. Within another decade, the total number of Arabs will exceed all the Jews of the area that includes Israel, the West Bank, and the Gaza Strip.

Since the November 2007 Annapolis meeting aimed at restarting peace talks, the government of Israel has announced its intention to construct over 2,000 new homes in Har Homa, Betar Illit, and Pisgat Zeev, which the Palestinians and the international community consider occupied territory, although Israel regards them as neighborhoods in "expanded Jerusalem." Commitments made to the United States to dismantle "illegal outposts"—protosettlements that do not enjoy government sanction—have not been met.

Beginning in 2002 Israel began constructing a 460-mile-long security barrier (composed of both fencing and, in heavily populated areas like Jerusalem and Bethlehem, concrete walls) separating Israel and many of its larger settlements from the Palestinian population of the West Bank. The current route of the barrier traces the 1949 armistice line—the Green Line—in places, but at other points it cuts deep into Palestinian territory.[8] While Israel's supreme court has ordered the Israel Defense Forces to change the barrier's route, particularly in places where it bisects or even surrounds Palestinian villages, these decisions have proven to be the exception to the rule. The barrier incorporates only 8 percent of the West Bank, but that figure does not provide a full picture of the extent of Israel's territorial control. When one takes into account nature preserves, military bases, settlements, outposts, bypass roads, tunnels, and an array of physical barriers hindering or preventing Palestinian movement, the amount of territory that the Israelis control is far greater than the territory behind the wall. The barrier has, despite Israeli protests to the contrary, taken on a sense of permanency. Taken together, the proposed path of the barrier and the government's master plan for the expansion of existing settlements strongly indicate that Israel plans to hold onto West Bank territory well beyond the amounts it currently controls.

In addition to the barrier, Israel has significantly expanded additional security measures within the West Bank. This new infrastructure includes checkpoints—some of which are actually designed as large border-crossing installations—earth mounds and other physical obstructions that prevent access to roads, and the development of a network of bypass roads, tunnels, and highways for the exclusive use of Israelis. The practical effect of these measures has been profound for both Israelis and Palestinians. A precipitous drop in terrorist attacks originating in the West Bank has allowed Israelis to enjoy greater security. At the same time, how-

Occupied Palestinian Territory

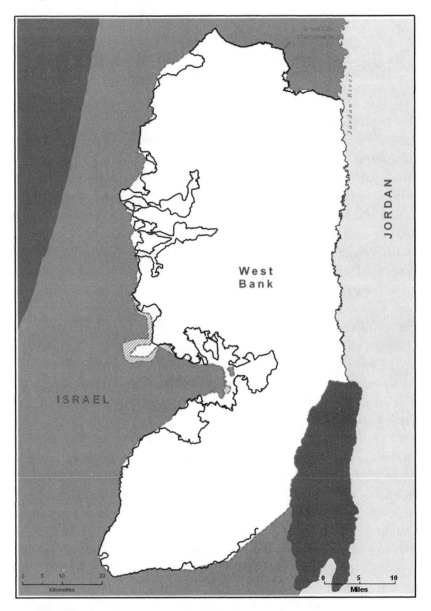

Note: The Green Line is 199 miles; the barrier route, shown by the heavy line, is 449 miles.

Source: United Nations Office for the Coordination of Humanitarian Affairs.

ever, the expanded security regime has made communication and normal life for Palestinians within the West Bank very difficult and is, in part, responsible for increased Palestinian social and economic dislocation.

CONSEQUENCES OF THE COLLAPSE OF THE TWO-STATE SOLUTION

Resolving the Israeli-Palestinian conflict is important for treating other branches of the Arab-Israeli conflict. If Palestinian-Israeli peace is deemed improbable, the prospects for stable Syrian-Israeli peace and Lebanese-Israeli peace diminish, even if Syria is prepared to conclude its own separate peace with Israel. The degree to which Arab states will move to normalize relations with Israel is partly dependent on the Palestinian track; even the two states that have peace agreements with Israel—Egypt and Jordan—maintain a relatively "cold" peace; their publics remain angry with Israel, largely because of the Palestinian-Israeli conflict. Therefore, even if peace is achieved between Israel and Syria, the United States will likely continue to be viewed negatively and thus have a more difficult time garnering support for other important policies, including fighting al Qaeda, stabilizing Iraq, and limiting the power of Iran.

The potential collapse of the two-state solution presents a variety of policy challenges. From the perspective of both parties, the status quo is untenable. The likelihood is remote that Israelis would willingly forgo the Jewish character of Israel in favor of a binational arrangement with the Palestinians. Given demographic realities, it is improbable that the Palestinians will accept permanent occupation. Instead, they are likely once again to take up arms against Israel in a destabilizing conflict that will surely harm American interests and prestige. Some Israelis may welcome the battle, confident that Israel would prevail. Some Palestinians and other Arabs may also welcome such a conflict because they believe that time is on their side. These attitudes will only ensure the continuation of the struggle.

Without a viable two-state solution, Israel would likely seek to consolidate its settlements in the West Bank and carve out borders that are maximally secure not only for its citizens inside the pre-1967 borders but also for the settlers; it is possible that settlement consolidation would be primarily aimed at settlement blocs behind the barrier, with Israeli military policing of the rest of the West Bank. The net result would likely be further fragmentation of the Palestinian territories. Under these circumstances, Palestinian militancy would likely increase, threatening Israeli security and deepening the humanitarian crisis in the West Bank. These developments would put new pressures on Jordan to provide relief, services, and refuge for Palestinians. In time, the enormous demands on Jordan's infrastructure, society, and political system resulting from a new crisis in the Palestinian areas could ultimately threaten the stability of the Hashemite Kingdom.

In addition, Israel's unilateral actions would also likely include isolating Gaza as worry mounts about Hamas's arms buildup there. Egyptian officials are deeply concerned that as the establishment of a Palestinian state becomes increasingly improbable, Egypt will have to contend with ever-larger numbers of Gazans in Sinai. This influx would create a highly inflammable environment with severe humanitarian consequences and increasing pressure on Egypt to provide Gaza with services. Cairo is concerned that this situation would lead to coordination between Palestinian and Egyptian extremists, jeopardizing Egyptian security and disrupting Sinai—an engine of Egypt's lucrative tourism industry. Moreover, the Egyptians fear that these groups could launch attacks on Israel directly from Sinai or retreat into Sinai from Gaza. How, they ask, would the Israeli military respond and how would the Egyptian security forces respond? In such a scenario there are many gray areas that could undermine the Israel-Egypt peace treaty. Inevitably, Gaza's relationship with Egypt will affect the domestic environment in Egypt, particularly as an issue that mobilizes Egypt's opposition across the political spectrum. If the conflict between Israelis and Palestinians remains unresolved, the situation in Gaza may ultimately test Egyptian-Israeli relations, which have been the anchor of the American Middle East peace strategy since the Camp David Accords. These accords have remarkably withstood a variety of challenges over the last three decades, but voices challenging them will likely increase, especially as Egypt grapples with the post-Mubarak era.

Iran, Hamas, and Hezbollah would be the winners should the current trends foreclose the possibility of a Palestinian state. They could argue with greater credibility that Israel and the United States never had any intention of dealing with the Palestinian problem in good faith. Once more, they could claim that the Egyptian, Saudi, Jordanian, and even Palestinian leaderships were either complicit or too weak to oppose Israel's American-supported predatory policies in Palestine. This narrative, which is already widely accepted in the Arab world, coupled with the failure of the two-state solution, would only boost the popularity of advocates of militancy in the region.

RECENT AMERICAN POLICY

The overall approach taken by George W. Bush's administration toward the Arab-Israeli conflict was one of conflict management rather than conflict resolution. American initiatives lacked the backing of or serious engagement by the president and often resulted in the opposite of the intended outcome, as in the case of the election of Hamas and its subsequent takeover of Gaza. Although the Bush administration came to recognize in its last year in office the need for active American diplomacy and worked with Israel and the Palestinians to narrow the gap on final-status issues, there was little indication that this effort was a priority for the president.

To be sure, the Bush administration inherited a difficult environment following the collapse of Palestinian-Israeli and Syrian-Israeli negotiations (on President Bill Clinton's watch) as well as the outbreak of the al-Aqsa intifada in the fall of 2000, which resulted in Israeli military operations in the West Bank and Gaza. The 9/11 terrorist attacks inevitably reshaped American priorities, downgrading the Arab-Israeli conflict on the president's agenda. Yet following those attacks, the president was well positioned to devote diplomatic energy to the Arab-Israeli issue, as he commanded overwhelming American public support and significant international sympathy, at a time of bloody confrontation between Israel and the Palestinians. Once the Iraq war decision was made, the Arab-Israeli issue became even less of a priority for the United States. Public posturing was never backed by real follow-through. From the road map for peace that President Bush proposed in 2003 to the Annapolis conference in November 2007; from the appointment of special envoy for Middle East peace Anthony Zinni, to the establishment of the Quartet (the United States, European Union, Russia, and the United Nations) and its envoys James Wolfensohn and Tony Blair to mediate the conflict, the

Bush administration engaged in visible diplomacy. But no diplomacy is effective, no matter what form it takes, if the issue is not a priority for the administration.

The subordination of the Arab-Israeli conflict to the "war on terrorism" and to the war in Iraq manifested itself in Washington's approach to Syria, Hezbollah, and Hamas. The United States sought to isolate, rather than engage, important parties in the conflict. The White House actively discouraged Israel from renewing negotiations with Syria in 2006 and 2007 (although some Israelis believed that such talks would serve their interests) because the administration classified Syria as a state sponsor of terrorism (given its support for Hezbollah and Hamas and its role in Iraq). The Israelis ultimately renewed peace negotiations with Syria through Turkish mediation in 2008. Similarly, the administration apparently encouraged Israel to wage war on Hezbollah in 2006 and may have discouraged it from ending its military strikes early, even though the ultimate result was more harmful to promoting peace talks because it empowered radicals in the region. Finally, after the unexpected victory of Hamas in the Palestinian parliamentary elections in 2006, the administration pursued a policy of isolating Hamas, seeking to reverse the outcome by strengthening Fatah. That only managed to produce internecine Palestinian violence that resulted in the surprising Hamas takeover of Gaza.

By punishing Hamas, the president hoped that Gazans would blame the Islamist group for their suffering. It was believed that by helping Abbas through improvements on the ground, the Palestinians would rally behind his leadership.

There are few indications that that policy has worked and some indications that it has produced the opposite results, especially given limited tangible progress in the negotiations and little improvement in people's lives in the West Bank. Neither the Palestinian public nor Arabs more broadly seem to blame Hamas for the Gaza blockade. Some opinion polls in the summer of 2008 showed a drop in support for Hamas among Palestinians (ironically after the Gaza cease-fire agreement between Hamas and Israel), but the polls showed no matching increase in the popularity of Abbas's party, Fatah. Moreover, Hamas has full control of Gaza—Abbas has minimal abilities to affect events there, while the Palestinian Authority's control in the West Bank is still highly dependent on Israel's security role in the area.

THE SYRIAN-ISRAELI AND THE LEBANESE-ISRAELI TRACKS

It has become clear that the unintended consequences of U.S. policy on the Israeli-Palestinian track have been matched by similar consequences on the Lebanese and Syrian fronts. On the Syrian track, the administration's early opposition to Syrian-Israeli negotiations has given way to tepid support for Turkish mediation. On the Lebanese front, one must recognize the dynamic effect that Syrian-Israeli negotiations can have on relations between Lebanon and Israel. In general, talks between Damascus and Jerusalem should make negotiations between Israelis and Lebanese possible. Progress between Syria and Israel would, in turn, likely produce results on the Lebanese track, holding out the possibility of effecting significant political change in Lebanon. If, for example, there were sufficient progress between the Israelis, Syrians, and Lebanese, the Israel Defense Forces would be able to withdraw from the Shebaa Farms—a small strip of territory along the Syrian-Lebanese border, which Beirut insists is Lebanese, but that the United Nations recognizes as Syrian. If the Israelis redeployed from the area, it would undermine a last remaining rationale for Hezbollah's militia in Lebanon. A withdrawal is unlikely to lead to Hezbollah's disarmament because its goals are in part domestic. But given Hezbollah's sensitivity to Lebanese and Arab public opinion, Israel's redeployment from Shebaa would likely place enormous political pressure on Hezbollah regionally and within Lebanon and would diminish the likelihood of its initiating military attacks against Israeli targets.

More broadly, Israeli-Syrian peace is central for regional stability and for a number of U.S. interests in the region. Syria is the only Arab state with a strong strategic relationship with Iran, it hosts and supports Hamas's leadership, and it is an essential supporter and arms supplier of Hezbollah in Lebanon. Bordering Iraq and hosting hundreds of thousands of Iraqi refugees, Syria is critical to the stabilization of Iraq. As a result, Syrian-Israeli peace would undoubtedly improve the prospects for regional stability, isolate Iran, weaken other militant forces in the region, and transform the psychological environment in Israel and the Arab world.

The Palestinians are no longer worried that Israeli-Syrian negotiations will compete with the Palestinian-Israeli track. Historically, Palestinians feared that Israel would play one track against the other to extract max- imal concessions from both, that Israeli-Syrian negotiations would delay a Palestinian-Israeli agreement, and that Israeli-Syrian peace would diminish Israel's incentives to reach an agreement with the Palestinians. In recent months, however, Palestinian thinking has changed, with the leadership welcoming the revival of Israeli-Syrian talks and seeing them as an asset.

The contours of an agreement between Syria and Israel are clear given the previous negotiations during the Clinton administration and other contacts since: full Israeli withdrawal from the territories occupied in the 1967 war in exchange for full peace; normal relations; and security arrangements, such as demilitarized zones, observation stations, and the possible deployment of international forces or monitors. In many ways the negotiations are less about details (although some, such as Syrian access to the Sea of Galilee, remain critical) and more about strategic decisions by both sides. Given the significant ramifications of a potential Syrian-Israeli agreement, the next American president should encourage both sides to move in that direction. A good place to start is the ongoing Turkish mediation efforts.[9]

In the end, peace between Israel and all its neighbors will be essential for regional stability and for advancing American interests in the region. But the Palestinian-Israeli conflict remains central and the most pressing. In the context of a new American strategy for the Middle East, both Syr- ian and Palestinian tracks should be pursued simultaneously but without concern about the sequencing of agreements. When one side sees possi- ble benefits in a serious process, the chance that it will work to under- mine an agreement on the other track becomes smaller and the prospect that it will reinforce progress there becomes greater.

A NEW WAY FORWARD

Appealing as it may seem for the next administration to relegate Arab- Israeli peacemaking to a second-tier issue, a hands-off approach to this difficult and complex problem is likely to make the situation on the ground a good deal worse and more dangerous. While some analysts— both in Israel and the United States—have begun thinking about a so- called regional solution to the Palestinian-Israeli problem through an elaborate set of land-swaps among Israel, Egypt, Jordan, and the Palestinians, there is little reason to believe that the Arab side would accept these types of agreements. The Egyptians, for example, reject the idea of ceding land in the Sinai to enhance the viability of the Gaza Strip. To decisionmakers in Cairo, Gaza is a problem of Israel's making and the resolution of the problem is the establishment of a Palestinian state in Gaza and the West Bank. The Palestinians themselves would never accept proposals that further fragment the West Bank even if they were offered other territory as compensation. The next administration needs to revive the idea of Palestine and Israel existing side by side peacefully and should actively seek to end the conflict. Merely managing the conflict at this stage will make it less solvable in the future.

A Framework for Security and Peace in the Middle East

Aggressive American diplomacy to address the Arab-Israeli conflict can succeed only if it is coordinated with other American priorities. Many of the important issues facing the United States today are directly linked to the Middle East: the Iraq war, the war on al Qaeda and its allies, Iran's nuclear program, and the supply and cost of energy. These issues will remain priorities for the new administration, regardless of what it does on the Arab-Israeli front. Therefore, policy toward the Arab-Israeli conflict can be most effective if it is formulated in the context of a broad vision, articulated in a framework for security and peace in the Middle East, where Arab-Israeli diplomacy does not compete with the other priorities.

Such a regional initiative must be designed to reduce the number of potential spoilers and create incentives for most of the players to cooperate. One of the attractive features of the Madrid Conference of 1991, for example, was the way it created incentives for Israelis, Syrians, Palestinians, and Jordanians to support bilateral peace negotiations, and for Saudi Arabia, Morocco, and other Arab countries to engage multilaterally on economic development, arms control, water resources, and refugees. While the issues have changed somewhat since then, the idea of a broader framework for negotiations on regional issues, even if they do not all move at the same pace, is essential. In particular, this framework should include two multilateral tracks: one addressing regional economic cooperation, especially in an environment of peace; the other addressing regional security cooperation, to which all states in the region should be invited, including Iran. Those who choose not to participate risk being further isolated.

Arab-Israeli peacemaking must be a presidential priority. The president's influence and prestige are critical in building the domestic and congressional coalitions necessary for creating incentives that will encourage Arabs and Israelis to move toward a compromise solution. As long as American diplomacy is a priority for the administration, the mechanism of American engagement is less central. A special envoy can be useful to sustain the mediation effort, but such an envoy cannot be a substitute for the direct involvement of the president or the secretary of state.

An Arab-Israeli Peace Initiative

In designing a diplomatic initiative to resolve the Arab-Israeli conflict, one must begin with a few key observations.

First, there is little trust of the other side among Palestinians and Israelis and little faith in signed agreements that do not quickly lead to tangible change. American credibility is especially low among Palestinians and Arabs more broadly. Yet, there will inevitably be a time gap between reaching an agreement, marketing it to a skeptical public, and implementing it. This time lag provides a perfect opportunity for spoilers to act. As witnessed even during the more optimistic times of the Oslo agreements in the 1990s, the incremental process that was supposed to be conducive to confidence building turned out to be more suited for opponents of the process on both sides.

Next, the time for incremental agreements has passed. Besides the absence of trust, one central flaw in the incremental approach that postponed agreement on the final-status issues in the past is that any intermediate compromise was seen as undermining each party's leverage for the more important round of future negotiations on final-status issues. For more than a year Israelis and Palestinians have been engaged in final-status negotiations; it therefore makes little sense to abandon them for interim agreements whose dubious value has already been established. Conversely, partial agreements—such as defining the borders of the Palestinian state before resolving the issues of Jerusalem and refugees— may have utility in demonstrating that substantive progress is possible.

In addition, negotiations between Israel and Syria, Lebanon, and the Palestinians are interconnected, in part because of the presence of large Palestinian refugee populations in Lebanon and Syria, and in part because of the influence that Syria can wield with the opponents of a Palestinian deal such as Hamas, Palestine Islamic Jihad, and Hezbollah.

One of the incentives for Israel in negotiating peace with its neighbors is the potential normalization of political and economic relations with other Arab countries. This has been more evident recently as Israeli leaders, cognizant of the benefits that would come from normal political and economic relations with Arab states such as Saudi Arabia, have increasingly become open to the idea of a comprehensive peace. That incentive, which is even more appealing given the growing economic vibrancy of the Arab oil states, must be built into the negotiations. Multilateral negotiations on these issues provide one mechanism for achieving this goal.

And last, although it has historically been a controversial issue, the United States and its allies should support a robust multilateral force in the West Bank and Gaza Strip—but only after an agreement between Israel and a unified Palestinian partner is reached. For such a force to be effective, it must be credible and acceptable to both sides—Israeli and Palestinian—in the context of their own commitments to peace. In such an environment, a contingent of capable international forces would reassure both sides and allow the Palestinians to build national institutions in a secure environment. Moreover, an international force would serve an important symbolic function, indicating that the international community considers peace between Israelis and Palestinians of particular importance.

Bearing these points in mind, the new president will need to build into his initiative a range of tactical approaches that will help generate an environment conducive to reaching and implementing an agreement:

Help rebuild Palestinian capabilities. The president should continue efforts, begun under President Bush, to rebuild Palestinian security capabilities. Without effective Palestinian security forces, any agreement between Israel and the Palestinian Authority would be vulnerable to groups opposed to peace. At the same time, the building of such capabilities cannot succeed if it is perceived as an instrument for creating Palestinian unity through force, especially given Hamas control of Gaza.

Moreover, absent an agreement, Israelis will remain wary of creating too powerful a Palestinian force, in case the negotiations fail.

Press Israel to freeze settlement construction. The next administration should hold Israel accountable to its commitment to freeze new construction of Jewish settlements in the West Bank, including in the Jerusalem area. There should be no exceptions to this halt in construction, covering the establishment of new communities, outposts, and importantly, thickening of existing settlements, which often entails expropriation of additional Palestinian territory. Both public criticism of Israeli settlement policy as well as conditioning portions of aid to a settlement freeze can be effective in eliciting Israeli compliance. Along with continued Palestinian violence, this is the single most important issue undermining confidence in the negotiations. Halting construction in the West Bank will provide an opportunity to prove Hamas wrong by clearly demonstrating that negotiation, not militancy, is the best path to realizing Palestinian goals. Hamas's popularity is derived, in part, from a persuasive narrative that Israel has no intention of ceding land to the Palestinians and that negotiations only provide more opportunity for the Israelis to expropriate Palestinian land. Conversely they point to Israel's unilateral withdrawal from southern Lebanon and Gaza as proof that violence is the only effective way to liberate Arab land. As settlement construction continues and the stalemate between the sides drags on, the Palestinian population can only conclude that the logic of Hamas's claims is accurate.

Bring Hamas into the fold. The next administration should support the emergence of a Palestinian unity government, one that includes Hamas, to negotiate with Israel. So long as the Palestinians are divided, a final-status agreement is highly unlikely to be reached, and if it is reached, it is unlikely to be successfully marketed and implemented. If Hamas is not included in the negotiations, it will have every incentive to bring the process down. Given that it controls Gaza and has significant assets in the West Bank, it would probably succeed. Washington should eschew the Quartet's conditions on Hamas and encourage Egypt, Jordan, Saudi Arabia, and other regional allies to convince the Hamas leadership to accept the April 2002 Arab Initiative, which promises peace, an end to the conflict, and normal relations between the Arab world and Israel in exchange for Israeli withdrawal from occupied lands. A critical component is to convince Hamas to accept an effective cease-fire, without which both a national unity government and fruitful negotiations with Israel cannot be sustained. This element will no doubt be challenging, but Hamas has proven itself highly attuned to public opinion. If the administration can show progress on the ground, such as pressing Israel to halt settlement construction, and thus strengthening the Palestinian public's support for movements toward peace, Hamas will find itself under pressure to acquiesce.

Refrain from imposing a solution but offer ideas. The next administration should not impose a solution on the parties but put forth ideas on final-status issues in the Palestinian-Israeli track as appropriate. Domestic Palestinian and Israeli politics are so fragmented and the issues so consequential that it is hard to envision that the parties will on their own produce a mutually acceptable draft. An American proposal on final-status issues will likely need to include the following elements:

—Borders should be negotiated on the basis of the 1967 lines, with the smallest possible land swaps to accommodate the largest number of settlers adjacent to the 1967 lines while assuring maximum contiguity for the Palestinian state.

—The "right of return" and refugee issues must be settled in a manner that simultaneously acknowledges Palestinian rights and finalizes all claims associated with these rights in a fashion consistent with maintaining Israel as a state with a Jewish majority and maintaining the sovereign right of both Israel and Palestine to determine who can enter their respective territories. Refugees should have the right to settle in the Palestinian state or be offered a choice of other countries for resettlement, and, if agreed by Israel and the Palestinians, a specified number (that does not alter the Jewish majority) could be settled in Israel itself. Compensation should also be part of the settlement.[10]

—The status of Jerusalem is central to both sides, partly because of its religious significance to Jews, Muslims, and Christians. Jerusalem was the principal issue of contention during the failed Camp David summit in July 2000, but before those talks collapsed, Palestinian officials had accepted the incorporation of Jewish suburbs of east Jerusalem into Israel and Israeli officials had accepted the incorporation of Arab suburbs into the Palestinian state. A way must be found for Jerusalem to serve as the capital of both Israel and Palestine that will preserve the religious status quo within the walled city and in which each community controls its respective holy sites. There is a history of proposing a special status for Jerusalem—in the 1947 UN partition plan, its status was imagined differently from the rest of the partitioned territories, and many countries, including the United States, have considered Jerusalem as a special case throughout the conflict.

Offer constructive interim ideas. As soon as the parties commence negotiations, the United States could propose two consequential steps that have both humanitarian and psychological implications and that will set the stage for permanent-status negotiations. First, simultaneous with a freeze on the construction of Jewish settlements, the international community should work with the Israeli government to put on the table financial incentives for settlers prepared to move inside Israel's pre-1967 borders. In particular, Israel should be encouraged to pass a bill that has already been introduced in the Knesset, which would compensate settlers who choose to vacate West Bank settlements. Second, there is a need to address the most pressing Palestinian refugee problem outside of the West Bank and Gaza: the refugees in Lebanon. Over 400,000 Palestinian refugees are in Lebanon, where they constitute about 10 percent of the entire population. Most remain stateless, limited to residency in twelve densely populated camps, with high unemployment and limited access to educational and health services. They present a humanitarian challenge as well as a political challenge. It is highly unlikely that most would be permanently settled in Lebanon (given Lebanon's problematic demographic issues) or in Israel. To the extent that the United States, European countries, and others may want to offer citizenship to some refugees in the context of a final-status agreement, it is important that such offers come forth as the negotiations start. However, such an initiative must not be seen to come at the expense of any claims these refugees may have in the context of a final-status agreement.

CONCLUSION

Left on its current trajectory, the Arab-Israeli conflict is on the verge of moving into a potentially disastrous phase, in which Israelis and Arabs broadly come to believe that the two-state solution is no longer viable.

The consequences of such a development would be grave for Israel, the Palestinians, and all of their neighbors including the two states with which Israel has peace treaties, Egypt and Jordan. Regionally, this state of affairs would help fuel militancy and embolden those opposed to American foreign policy in the region. Some of the possible consequences could include a new Israeli unilateral policy in the West Bank, the onset of a new Palestinian intifada, a unilateral Palestinian declaration of independence, the collapse or dissolution of the Palestinian Authority, and further empowerment of Hamas in the West Bank. While the United States must prepare for such scenarios, all would have a detrimental impact on American interests and would further destabilize the region, not only in the short term but also in the coming decade. The immediate choice for American foreign policy is whether to embrace or abandon the two-state solution. Given the grave consequences associated with a collapse of the two-state solution, the choice should be clear. But the president must know that achieving the two-state solution, or even preventing its collapse, would require elevating American peace diplomacy in the new administration's priorities.

It is unlikely that the parties can resolve final-status issues without an active American role. Unlike the negotiations between Israel and the Palestine Liberation Organization in Oslo, where the parties were negotiating directly for the first time and the issues were merely interim, both the Palestinians and Syrians have been engaged in detailed negotiations with the Israelis that have fully defined the issues of contention and substantially narrowed the gap. It is highly unlikely that final agreements can be clinched without an active American role that includes the submission of bridging American ideas. The new administration should initiate sustained diplomatic efforts in the context of a broader regional initiative that connects the Arab-Israeli issue to other American priorities in the Middle East in a determined effort to achieve lasting peace agreements.

NOTES

1. Daniel C. Kurtzer and Scott B. Lasensky, with William B. Quandt, Steven L. Spiegel, and Shibley Z. Telhami, *Negotiating Arab-Israeli Peace: American Leadership in the Middle East* (Washington: U.S. Institute of Peace Press, 2008).

2. Shibley Telhami conducted this survey in conjunction with Zogby International in March 2008; 4,046 participants were interviewed in six countries: Egypt, Jordan, Lebanon, Morocco, Saudi Arabia, and the United Arab Emirates.

3. The Arab Peace Initiative was first floated in February 2002 by then–Crown Prince Abdullah of Saudi Arabia to *New York Times* columnist Thomas L. Friedman. In March 2002, at its Beirut summit, the Arab League formally endorsed Abdullah's proposal. For Friedman's column, see Thomas L. Freidman, "An Intriguing Signal from the Saudi Crown Prince," *New York Times,* February 17, 2002. For the text of the initiative, see "The Beirut Declaration," www.saudiembassy.net/2002News/Statements/StateDetail.asp?cIndex=142.

4. When asked to name the two states that are most threatening to them, more than 80 percent surveyed in 2008 opinion polls named Israel and the United States; only about 10 percent named Iran. As for the source of anger with the United States, it is clear that the central issue is the Arab-Israeli conflict, followed by the U.S. military presence in Iraq and the Persian Gulf. When asked what step the United States could take to improve their view of the United States most, a majority cited American diplomacy to resolve the Arab-Israeli conflict as the single most important issue. For six years in a row, two-thirds to three-quarters of Arabs identified the Palestinian issue as the single most important issue or among the three most important issues (over 80 percent in the 2008 opinion polls).

5. The peak of Palestinian joblessness came in 2002, when 31 percent of the Palestinian labor force was out of work. The public sector picked up some of the slack, which widened the Palestinian Authority's budget deficit but was never able to reduce unemployment by more than 6 percent. Since 2003 Palestinian unemployment has ranged from 25 to 29 percent.

6. Historically, Palestinians have enjoyed high levels of school enrollment and achievement in comparison with their neighbors. The second intifada and the Israeli response severely disrupted attendance. In 2002, for example, 226,000 pupils and 9,300 teachers were at various times throughout the school year unable to reach their classrooms and 580 schools were shut down for varying lengths of time. The situation improved somewhat for primary and secondary schools in 2003–04, but universities have been frequently closed since 2000. By 2006 the ending of international donor support had led to the virtual collapse of the Palestinian higher education sector.

7. Currently, an estimated 3.76 million Palestinians live in the West Bank, Gaza Strip, and East Jerusalem. In the four years between 1994 and 1998, the Israelis broke ground on 11,320 housing units in both the West Bank and Gaza Strip (primary sources such as the authoritative *Statistical Abstract of Israel* do not differentiate between construction in the two areas) and the Israeli government issued 3,741 tenders for construction in 1999, though it is unclear how many of those tenders actually resulted in construction. Between 2000 and 2004, 5,216 housing units were either completed or were under active construction in the occupied territories. After Israel's withdrawal from the Gaza Strip, beginning in 2005, construction was limited to the

West Bank, where the Israelis planned 1,358 homes of which 510 were complete by the end of 2006. *Statistical Abstract of Israel, 2007* (table 2.7).

8. The intellectual origins of the barrier lie with the left-of-center Labor Party and the deep sense of hopelessness after the failure of peace negotiations at Camp David in July 2000 and the beginning of the second intifada. The specific goal of the wall was to separate the Israeli population from the Palestinians. Israel's political right initially opposed the barrier, fearing the consequences of the establishment of a de facto international boundary and thus the emergence of a Palestinian state. Yet, after a wave of suicide bombings during the spring of 2002, which killed 167 Israelis, the Likud government and its supporters embraced the idea of a barrier, but with an important twist. By insisting on calling it a security barrier, the government implied that the path of the barrier was not permanent and thus Israel would not be institutionalizing a border.

9. The talks have the potential to open a gap between Damascus and Tehran. As talks continue and even progress, this opening is likely to grow wider. It is here where Turkey's role is most important. Ankara, by dint of its now close political and economic ties with Damascus as well as the long history of mutual distrust between Turks and Persians, is a natural and positive counterweight to Iranian influence in Syria. Turkish prime minister Recep Tayyip Erdogan has been criticized in Washington for his ties to Syrian president Bashar al-Asad, yet Israeli officials acknowledge their abiding trust in the Turkish prime minister on the Syrian track specifically and would like the Turks to continue to play a constructive role in the talks. Washington's efforts to construct a regional coalition to contain Iranian influence are likely to improve as talks between Israelis, Turks, and Syrians continue. (Yet one has to be careful to keep in mind that isolating Iran cannot be an end in itself because isolation may increase Iranian incentives to acquire nuclear weapons. Clear incentives for Iranian cooperation must be provided in the context of the framework for security and peace in the Middle East initiative.)

10. For a full articulation of this proposal, see Shibley Telhami's congressional testimony to the Sub-Committee on the Middle East and South Asia of the House Committee on Foreign Affairs, "Addressing the Palestinian Refugee Problem," May 8, 2007, www.bsos.umd.edu/sadat/Telhami.Testimony.May06.htm.

ISOBEL COLEMAN

TAMARA COFMAN WITTES

6

Economic and Political Development in the Middle East
Managing Change, Building a New Kind of Partnership

U.S.-ARAB STRATEGIC COOPERATION in coming years will be crucial to confronting common regional challenges, but to be effective it will need to overcome the tensions of the past eight years. These tensions arose not merely from differences between the United States and its major regional Arab partners over the war in Iraq, U.S. counterterrorism policies, American neglect of the Arab-Israeli conflict, and its approach to Iran, but also from the Bush administration's start-and-stop attempts to encourage democracy. Bush's Freedom Agenda produced slim gains, while creating cynicism about American interest in democracy among regional activists, as well as tensions with Arab leaders. In the face of heightened public resentment of the United States in the region, U.S.-Arab strategic cooperation now faces greater scrutiny, and its underlying logic is less compelling and clear—to the publics both here and in the region and to some policymakers—than in the past. U.S. relations with Egypt, rooted in cooperation on Arab-Israeli peacemaking for over thirty years, have suffered as the peace process has faltered and domestic governance and human rights issues in Egypt have become a more prominent bone of contention. U.S.-Saudi relations have improved in recent years after the deep strains imposed by 9/11 and differences over the priority given to the Palestinian issue, but in the minds of many on both sides, the issues that divide outweigh those that bind.

As tempting as it may be, the next U.S. president cannot simply set aside concerns over democracy and development in favor of securing other interests. The challenges of domestic reform are increasingly the primary focus of many regional actors. They are a major topic of public and private conversation both in countries that are modernizing and prospering, and in those that are not. Demands for improved government and economic performance are pressed by international lenders and investors, as well as by local elites and hungry or angry publics. These heightened demands for reform are conditioning the environment within which the United States must operate to secure its interests in the Middle East in coming years.

The United States no longer faces a choice between supporting democratization and economic liberalization or protecting a mythic status quo. The region is already in the midst of transition. America has a clear stake in helping its key Arab partners, notably Egypt and Saudi Arabia, achieve smooth transitions on several levels:

—from closely controlled economies to ones that are open to vibrant local and global competition;

—from political systems that force their citizens to choose between supporting autocratic regimes and joining (illiberal and often autocratic) Islamist movements to a more diverse and open political marketplace; and

—from an aging political leadership to a new generation that may— or may not—prove more enlightened.

Disengagement from the domestic problems of the Arab world is a tempting policy option for the next U.S. president. However, with heavy investments and interests throughout the region, the United States cannot afford to walk away from its role in shaping the region's future.

America's long-term interests are still best served by encouraging its authoritarian allies to move along a path of liberalizing political and economic reforms. The United States should use its economic and political leverage to help build a more stable and prosperous Middle East that gives a vast and rising young generation hope for the future and reason to resist the dark visions purveyed by regional radicals. Only through more open and transparent political and economic systems will the region be able to accommodate the demands of its unprecedented youth bulge; only through expanding participation in politics will Arab leaders be able to develop their political legitimacy with this new generation and build public support for key policies, including both painful economic reforms and strategic cooperation with the United States.

Building a sustainable and effective policy to encourage Arab political and economic development will require a more honest balancing of America's strategic priorities. The mismatch between the Bush administration's lofty freedom and democracy rhetoric and the roller-coaster inconsistency of its actions has seriously eroded U.S. credibility. In particular, the Bush administration's conflation of democracy with elections produced illiberal results and undermined support for the deeper social and cultural changes and institution building that underpin real democratic progress. It is important for the next president to stake out clearly the values America stands for and will actively encourage and to make a case for democratic reform that speaks to the needs and aspirations of Arab citizens. But he must also acknowledge that political evolution takes time, and that the United States, while retaining significant influence over many of the region's authoritarian rulers, cannot dictate terms to them. Moreover, any American role in encouraging liberal change in the Middle East must acknowledge the inevitable tensions between promoting reform and securing other strategic goals. America's role is to provide a framework that incentivizes reform for local leaders and to support efforts by local reformers, while placing democracy and development into the context of broader U.S.-Arab strategic cooperation.

It is also time to institute in-depth reviews of U.S. relations with Saudi Arabia and Egypt, in order to place American policy on political and economic reform in a coherent context that anticipates and resolves necessary trade-offs between reform and other strategic goals. This process must take place before the soon-expected leadership transitions in Egypt and Saudi Arabia.

A REGION IN FLUX

After decades of economic underperformance, the Middle East is finally beginning to experience growth rates well above its historic averages. But economic progress is not keeping pace with population growth or with the demands of international markets. Meanwhile, political ferment has raised public expectations and has brought forward new public demands. Regime responses to these demands have not always been positive, especially with regard to the American objective of long-term democratization.

If the political and economic order in the region does not evolve in a more liberal direction, it is likely to go down a path that will make it harder for the United States to secure its interests and protect its important strategic partnerships. The next president therefore should not think that he can choose between preserving stability and promoting democratic development in the Middle East. If he does not promote change prudently, the situation will become even more unstable.

The Imbalance between Economic and Demographic Growth

While growth for the Middle East and North Africa region averaged less than 4 percent in the 1990s (up from barely 2 percent in the 1980s), in recent years it has been above 6 percent.[1] Strong oil prices are clearly an important part of the economic picture, but several of the larger economies are also beginning to experience the benefits of trade and financial liberalization. Still, the region's demography—relatively young and rapidly growing populations—creates a situation in which sustained growth in excess of 6 percent is necessary to address the high unemployment rate.

The Middle East's youth bulge is a well-known phenomenon. With 65 percent of the region's population under the age of twenty-five, the Middle East has the fastest-growing working-age population of any part of the world. As a consequence, just to keep pace with population growth, the region must create 80 million new jobs over the next fifteen years. If it hopes to put a dent in its already high unemployment rate (averaging 15 percent regionwide), it must create 100 million new jobs by 2020—a staggering requirement nearly doubling today's total employment. Moreover, it must achieve these employment gains in an increasingly globalized environment increasingly dominated by highly competitive and fast-rising India and China. Without making deep structural reforms, Middle East governments will never be able to meet the employment needs of their increasingly disaffected youth—a stark fact that, left unaddressed, leaves an entire generation ripe for alienation and radicalization.

Unemployment is most acutely a youth issue. Fifty percent of those unemployed are between the ages of fifteen and twenty-four. Unemployment is also highest among those who have some formal education. In the past, these college graduates could expect employment in the public sector, but as formal education has significantly expanded over the past generation and government coffers have come under increasing pressure, the public sector can no longer absorb what public school systems produce. The private sector is hard-pressed to pick up the slack. Beyond the other structural barriers to private sector growth, the region's rigid labor environment, which saddles the private sector with numerous restrictions, makes companies reluctant to hire.

Education policies are also part of the problem. Higher education is still largely geared to turning out paper-pushing bureaucrats, not to meeting the needs of private industry. There is a profound gap between the skill sets most regional secondary schools and colleges are developing and what companies are seeking. The result is an explosive combination of millions of young people with high expectations and little hope of fulfilling their dreams. Without jobs, and the accompanying financial independence, young men are not able to marry, a deeply frustrating situation in conservative societies where dating is not socially acceptable. In contrast to a generation ago, when marriage was both early and universal, today nearly 50 percent of men between the ages of twenty-five and twenty-nine are unmarried due to economic hardship and lack of affordable housing.[2]

Glaring income disparities—with super-wealthy elites garnering an ever larger share of the gains while large majorities live in poverty—are also cause for concern. With the price of oil significantly higher in recent years, luxury cars clog city streets while construction crews race to finish the latest upscale mall, luxury hotel, and high-end gated community. But at the same time, bread riots occur in Cairo, and concern is growing in Saudi Arabia over the rapidly rising cost of food, which now accounts for the largest share of an average Saudi family's spending. (Food prices in Saudi Arabia are set to rise by more than 30 percent in 2008, a result of tight global supplies and the weak dollar.) In both countries, rising core inflation and global spikes in the prices of basic commodities are making life tougher for the average person.

As economic liberalization creates clear winners and losers and oil windfalls relieve some of the pressure on government budgets, Arab leaders must do more to spread the gains and losses. But across the region there is little trust in government to make the right decisions, and widespread concern about corruption. Arab publics grumble that government contracts and bank loans only go to those who are already wealthy or to the corrupt (and there seems to be a good deal of overlap between these categories). These attitudes combine with the hardship experienced by the poor to produce widespread and deep-seated cynicism among citizens about their governments. Meanwhile, economic and political elites use their influence to gain preferential policies enabling them to maximize profits from the current growth. Major reform programs are difficult to implement in an environment with such deeply vested interests.

The United States has encouraged economic and trade liberalization in the region, through support of Saudi Arabia's accession to the World Trade Organization (WTO), the creation and expansion of Qualified Industrial Zones in Egypt and Jordan,[3] and the expansion and deepening of economic ties through several bilateral free trade agreements (FTAs). For decades, the United States enjoyed a privileged economic position in the Middle East, but today that is being challenged. Many countries in the Middle East and North Africa view China, Russia, and Europe as increasingly important trade and technology partners who have little of the political baggage of the United States.

The tremendous oil surpluses of recent years are taking some of the urgency out of reform agendas. Conscious of the vast waste and corruption that defined previous petro-booms, the oil-rich Gulf states are eager to avoid those same mistakes. They are investing in massive—and in many cases much-needed—infrastructure projects and have hired sophisticated financial managers. Only time will tell whether these investments will significantly improve the productive capacity of the region. Over the longer term, oil income unaccompanied by policy change is insufficient to address the growing and pressing social and employment needs of the region's people, especially the young. In the less wealthy and more populous states of the region, the imbalance is more severe and the need for policy change more urgent.

The huge oil surpluses also make it harder for the United States to wield economic leverage in the region. Today, the Gulf states are again positioned as critical creditors to the rest of the world, particularly the United States, which relies heavily on foreign capital inflows. The sovereign wealth funds of the United Arab Emirates (UAE), Kuwait, and Saudi Arabia have more than $1.5 trillion in assets and are heavily courted by U.S. hedge fund managers and Wall Street firms. In this environment of economic turmoil, the United States simply has fewer economic carrots and sticks to wield. The buying power of America's vast market, though, still remains an attractive magnet for those Middle Eastern economies that produce goods for export.

Political Evolution or Revolution

The aborted elections in Algeria in 1991–92, and the ten-year civil war that followed, chilled the regional discussion of democracy. In the last five years, however, demands for political reform have accelerated. While some governments have rewritten constitutions (Bahrain), opened up political competition (Yemen), held first-time elections (UAE), extended the franchise to women (Kuwait), and overhauled legal codes (Morocco), no Arab leader has made either an unqualified commitment to or any significant progress toward full-fledged electoral democracy. Yet, public pressures for greater political accountability and greater political participation are not likely to fade, especially given the growing imbalances described above.

In some of the region's recent elections, Islamist movements have fared well, raising fears of Islamist takeovers through the ballot box—a scenario threatening not only to rulers but also to the region's liberals, reformers, and minority populations. In the Palestinian Authority, the electoral victory of Hamas in 2006 would have been a test for this concern, had violence not trumped peaceful politics for both Hamas and its Fatah rivals. But across today's authoritarian regimes, which constitute most of the region and America's most important Arab allies, Islamist takeovers are largely a hypothetical concern: Islamists, like other opposition groups, are competing for representation in parliaments with very limited authority relative to the region's powerful executives. Moreover, while the democratic commitments of some Islamist parties can be questioned, others have now developed sustained records of working according to the rules of the political game laid down by ruling regimes. Finally, it is not clear that Islamists would in fact win majorities in more open and diverse political systems.

The Islamists' dominant position among the political opposition today is at least in part the result of the tightly controlled political sphere in most Arab countries, where secular alternatives can organize and grow only at the sufferance of the nervous state while Islamists can use religious "cover" to organize. Even in the two oft-cited cases of Islamist victories (Hamas in 2006 and the Algerian Islamic Salvation Front [FIS] in 1991), voters in fact gave the Islamists only small pluralities of support, which electoral rules translated into parliamentary majorities. And Hamas's victory was at least in part a reaction to years of corrupt and often brutal Fatah rule.

Some reformers argue that the best way to limit the Islamists' appeal is to open up the political sphere, producing more diversity, competition, and choice. However, governments are, by and large, unwilling to take that gamble, pointing to Iran (1979) or Algeria (1991) as the inevitable result of allowing religious voices greater space in politics. Government officials constantly repeat the "one man, one vote, one time" warning to justify their containment of Islamist politics. It is also a self-serving argument, since it is their political repression that helps to ensure that Islamists remain the bogeyman of political opposition.

Some Arab leaders have been willing to experiment with reforms that allow greater freedom of expression while producing little impact on political power. This is generating citizen impatience and cynicism. The question is whether, as economic imbalances become more extreme and more prevalent, Arab regimes have sufficient resources (beyond pure coercion, which they certainly have in abundance) to maintain their authority.

While the regional trends described above affect them differently, both Egypt and Saudi Arabia face significant domestic challenges right now—and those challenges are not divorced from their relations with Washington. U.S.-Egyptian and U.S.-Saudi cooperation are more necessary than ever to stabilize the region, but that cooperation is now heavily burdened by the fact that our Arab partners must bear their publics' resentment of America's regional policies, while we feel the sting of the Arab public's resentment of their governmants' domestic failures.

In the current environment, this resentment strengthens the arguments of regional radicals that oppose American interests, notably Sheik Hassan Nasrallah, the leader of Hezbollah, and Iran's Mahmoud Ahmadinejad. Arab leaders are aware of this dynamic but prefer not to recognize the role that their own governance deficits play in contributing to it.

American inconsistency and hesitancy on political reform issues has harmed the credibility of its efforts in this area and created a higher bar for such efforts to clear in the future. Moreover, American policy in the region has raised public anti-American sentiment to unprecedented heights. Thus, any vocal American intervention on behalf of political reform carries a high risk of backlash, with that risk increasing the more the United States is viewed as making unilateral demands. At the same time, regional activists credit American attention to democracy and human rights for creating an umbrella under which they can better press their own demands for change. Given the overshadowing presence of the United States in the region, there is no way for the next U.S. president to avoid a situation in which America is held at least partly responsible for regional political dynamics, whether they are regressive or progressive.

To sustain and defend U.S.-Arab strategic cooperation in these challenging times—when regional radicals are gaining, local demands for change are pressing, and the governments of both Egypt and Saudi Arabia will face major leadership transitions—American policy must shift toward building relationships rooted in formal understandings and partnerships that benefit Arab citizens as evidently as they benefit their leaders. Such a policy demands an American commitment to both resolving regional conflicts and liberalizing economic and political reforms. The drift in U.S.-Arab relations needs to be replaced by a coherent vision of America's role in building the region's future.

Before the next president articulates a commitment to reform and builds new partnerships, though, he needs to rebuild strategic understandings with key regional partners. American leverage lies mainly with the governments in the region, not with their repressed and resentful populations. Bush administration efforts to build links to Arab civil society had limited payoffs, and the Bush rollback of democracy promotion after 2006 left a very bitter legacy with that audience. Moreover, the United States requires sustained cooperation with Arab governments on key regional security issues and must determine how to anchor proreform efforts in the context of sustained bilateral relations. Arab leaders are aware of the challenges they face, but do not currently acknowledge the extent to which their domestic failings help fuel regional radicalism; a strategic dialogue could help clarify for them the costs of the current stagnation, and the benefits of moving forward with necessary changes.

Dialogue can also help identify American incentives that could help Arab governments reduce the risks of reform. For example, easing the dislocation costs of economic privatization and liberalization could reduce the risk of wide-scale public discontent and thus encourage governments to ease political controls too. American effort to promote reform must begin with renewed engagement and dialogue with Arab regimes to determine where common interests and common ground on a reform agenda can be found.

The next administration should take the opportunity early in its term to review relations with both Egypt and Saudi Arabia to determine ways to help these two important countries address their internal challenges while building a solid foundation for long-term cooperation with the United States. This review should encompass all aspects of bilateral relations, from trade to arms sales to foreign assistance, public diplomacy, and cultural affairs. At the same time, the new American president should immediately engage in his own personal conversations with the Egyptian and Saudi leaders about the relationship between political and economic reform, domestic stability, and regional extremism. It will be much easier and more fruitful to have these conversations with Hosni Mubarak and King Abdullah al-Saud than with their successors, who will be more concerned with regime consolidation than with revising or renovating bilateral relations. The next sections of this chapter provide context and recommendations for a comprehensive dialogue with each of these two key American partners.

EGYPT

Egypt is in a period of prolonged economic and political transition. The government is partway through a challenging process of economic reform, which has already caused some social unrest. Politically, however, the country has stagnated. After nearly three decades of rule by President Mubarak, what comes next is on everyone's mind. Most Egyptians—including many within the government—say they want and need change in their society. The question urgently facing Washington and Cairo is over how much economic dislocation and political instability each is willing to tolerate to achieve that change.

Hosni Mubarak, president for the last twenty-seven years, is now eighty years old. Speculation about his health is rife in Cairo, and anxiety over the coming leadership transition pervades Egypt. There is a widespread feeling of resignation that his son, Gamal Mubarak, will inevitably succeed his father. There is reason for concern that a badly prepared or badly managed political transition could result in chaos or increased repression as the new leader seeks to consolidate control. In addition, if Gamal is a weak president politically, he might rely on military backing to a greater extent, setting Egypt's political trajectory backward. Of course, if support from the military and security services is not forthcoming, Gamal may not be able to take control at all or to hold onto power if he does. A military-led coup in Egypt would be a very regressive outcome for the country.

Economic Change

The Egyptian economy has experienced strong growth in recent years—7 percent in 2007, more than double the rate of five years earlier. Foreign direct investment ($11 billion in 2007) is up tenfold since 2001. People in the business community give credit to the government's economic reforms, launched in 2004, which have reduced taxes, streamlined bureaucracy, and created a more favorable investment climate. The government is also slowly moving away from costly subsidies for basic goods. The business community largely credits the so-called "dream team" of reform-minded economic ministers for the country's economic progress, but the fact remains that the entire region is currently enjoying similar levels of economic growth. As the second largest economy in the Arab world after Saudi Arabia, Egypt is an attractive investment option for Gulf oil wealth, and for European Union and U.S. investors seeking to capitalize on the booming region.

Egyptian government officials openly express their hope that Egypt can follow China's model of promoting economic liberalization without the destabilizing costs of political reform. Many in the Egyptian government assert that people want "bread before freedom"—in other words, that citizens place their economic well-being above political rights and that American pressure for democracy is therefore misplaced or presumptuous. Supporting this rationale is the fact that Egypt is in dire need of continued and robust economic growth. The International Monetary Fund estimates that Egypt needs to sustain its current growth rate of 7 percent for at least the next five years if it hopes to see a significant reduction in poverty rates and unemployment.[4] Currently, 40 percent of the population lives on less than $2 a day, and 20 percent of the population lives on less than $1 a day. Poverty is particularly acute in rural areas. Broad-based economic development is not happening nearly fast enough in Egypt to meet public expectations.

Segments of the business community and some politicians are skeptical that Egypt is capable of delivering sustained economic growth without political reform. Many of the industries that are now flourishing— such as high-end real-estate development and information technology services—are not creating enough jobs at a fast enough pace to make a dent in the country's high unemployment rates, particularly for the large youth population (nearly one-fourth of the population is between fifteen and twenty-four, and 30 percent of them are unemployed).

Political Change

Clearly the Mubarak regime has prioritized economic reform over political reform. In fact, there is a strong sense that political reform has not only stalled but moved backward in recent years. The 2005 presidential and parliamentary elections and the rise of the Kefaya ("Enough") movement the same year offered some hope that political reform could take root in Egypt. Since then, the government has cracked down on all opposition groups and has, through a series of constitutional amendments and other legislative changes, tightened its grip on power. Those within the ruling regime—and many within the middle class who are fearful of an Islamist takeover—argue that the need for stability justifies this tight political control.

The economic situation, however, could have serious political repercussions. When ordinary citizens become frustrated by their inability to meet pocketbook demands, as they have in recent months, they have few legitimate channels to seek redress from their government. Local strikes are frequent in different regions of Egypt today and could potentially coalesce into broader protest. The government, for its part, has no coherent response to the economic and social problems currently burdening Egyptians, and the ruling party is increasingly divided over policy choices that affect the power bases of different factions.

The Muslim Brotherhood continues to represent the most organized and popular political opposition. After years of promoting social welfare programs for the poor and riding the tide of religious conservatism in the country, the Brotherhood has a strong grassroots following. In the 2005 parliamentary elections, running as independent candidates, the Brotherhood turned its grassroots popularity into a political reality. Even after limiting the number of candidates it put forward (a tactical move to appease the government), the Brotherhood still won 22 percent of the seats.

Among Cairo's political elite, the Muslim Brotherhood is variously described as one of the truest forces for democracy today in Egypt or as an oppressive movement intent on Iranian-style theocracy. Because it is officially banned as a political party and faces no real competition from the other opposition movements, it has been little tested. Under heavy pressure from its members and critics in the media, the Brotherhood released a draft of its political platform in September 2007—the first of its kind—that lays out the group's political positions. The platform, particularly with respect to the Brotherhood's stance on women and Copts, has been seized upon by the group's critics as evidence of its exclusionary and intolerant practices.

Within the organization, there is a wide range of views on politics, from the conservative attitudes reflected in the 2007 draft party platform to more progressive attitudes toward women, minorities, Israel, and the West. The attitudinal breaks are largely along generational lines, and the movement now contains at least three generations of constituents. The older generation of traditionalists is still firmly in the driver's seat of the organization, while younger, more progressive members are restless. Some believe that, in a more open political environment, progressives within the movement either would be able to use the group's claim of internal democracy to replace older leaders or would split from the traditionalists entirely. The chicken-or-egg nature of this debate, however, leaves a major issue in Egyptian politics unresolved for now.

The government's political crackdown since 2005 has not been restricted to the Brotherhood; the secular opposition also struggles to maintain unity and relevance in the face of this repression. The Kefaya movement in 2005 and 2006 was an important focal point for secular, liberal Egyptians concerned with the future of their state. Through it they were able to demand competitive elections and constitutional reform. They were supported in their efforts by liberal-minded judges and encouraged by the U.S. government. However, after the Muslim Brotherhood won a sizable portion of the seats in parliament and U.S. pressure for greater political openness dissipated, the Kefaya movement lost much of its momentum. Today, its leaders languish on the sidelines or in prison.

Current public dissent is manifested through sporadic labor actions and an emerging youth mobilization taking shape through community websites like Facebook. (The Facebook group supporting the labor strikes in the Nile Delta city of Mahalla, in April 2008, had more than 70,000 members at the time, and is still active). However, neither the labor nor youth movements has a clearly defined platform, viable organizational structure, or even solid leadership. Thus, there is potential for more coherent and organized political action arising from these sectors, but it is so far unrealized. With few political options, many activists are focusing their energies on promoting the building blocks of democracy and civil society—a freer press, basic human rights, judicial independence and integrity, and economic transparency—as they bide their time for a better environment. An upswing in government repression has dimmed their hopes for near-term change.

The United States has taken a series of contradictory, expedient positions on political reform in Egypt, which has left both the Egyptian government and its secular and Islamic opposition frustrated with U.S. policy. Those inside the government feel the United States does not sufficiently recognize the strategic importance of Egypt in the region as a stable ally and that Washington downplays the risks of change. They question why the United States would push for political reforms that could cause instability and "hand Egypt over to the Islamists." Opposition leaders feel betrayed by Washington's half-hearted encouragement of political reform. They question America's political and financial support for a regime that is highly unpopular with its own people and warn that the United States must press for greater openness before the situation becomes explosive. Both sides question what America's goals and intentions are not only in Egypt but in the region as a whole. Frustration with Washington is compounded by the widespread belief in American omnipotence: that the superpower could, if it chose, resolve festering problems through decisive *diktat* (this belief extends beyond domestic politics to the Arab-Israeli issue).

In Egypt, perhaps more than in any other Arab country (except Iraq), America is held accountable for just about everything that occurs domestically and regionally, whether there is a clear cause-and-effect relationship or not. Egyptians certainly blame the United States for their own government's repressive domestic policies, arguing that the Mubarak regime would not be able to sustain its autocratic rule without U.S. political and financial support. The provision of substantial military aid, particularly as the corresponding U.S. economic assistance has dropped, reinforces this view among average Egyptians and activists alike. Thus, the United States is directly implicated in the Egyptian regime's failure to deliver effective governance or to make good on the promises of liberalization and enhanced political participation that Mubarak embraced during his 2005 reelection campaign.

At the same time, American economic aid has declined to a level where it does not greatly affect the Egyptian economy, and as progress has been made on basic health and education, American assistance has increasingly been directed to less-visible projects with longer-term objectives. U.S. military aid exclusively supports Egyptian procurement of American equipment and training. While this aid offsets other Egyptian military expenditures, it is also relatively invisible to and distant from the lives of average Egyptians.

Policy Recommendations

To build a stronger foundation for U.S.-Egypt relations that will help foster economic and political reform, we urge the next American president to take the following steps:

Engage in a strategic dialogue. In the 1990s, the U.S.-Egypt Partnership for Economic Growth and Development (also known as the Gore-Mubarak Partnership) provided high-level opportunities for ongoing dialogue on economic reform and development issues. A renewed dialogue must be broader, encompassing constituencies in the Egyptian government to include the military and security services, and creating standing working groups on issues ranging from counterterrorism cooperation to human rights. A key American goal for this dialogue should be to determine whether common ground can be found on additional goals and benchmarks in both economic and political reform. If a package of reforms can be mutually agreed upon that includes both economic and political steps, then upgraded levels of economic assistance could be offered, tied to achievement of clear benchmarks as spelled out in new understandings modeled on the 2004 financial sector memorandum of understanding that both Egyptian and American policymakers cite as a success. If a package of reforms cannot be agreed upon, minimal economic assistance should be maintained at the fiscal 2009 budget request level of $200 million.

Condition new economic assistance on reform and governance. Imposing new behavioral conditions on existing U.S. assistance—both economic and military aid—is one of the most contentious issues between Washington and Cairo. While some in Washington have seen withholding aid as an effective way of influencing the Egyptian government, that stance creates enormous tensions with a key U.S. ally. Moreover, it is doubtful that such an approach can be effective, as the Mubarak regime is unlikely to loosen its grip on power to appease the United States. Conditionality also stirs up strong feelings of nationalism that the Egyptian government can use to mobilize public support and thus strengthen its grip on power. As one official stated, "An Egyptian would rather starve than have his food conditioned."[5]

On the other hand, positive conditionality and a priori conditionality on new assistance can be effective tools.[6] *The next president, therefore, should tie new economic assistance to political reform but should not add more conditions to the existing, minimal levels of economic aid.* Benchmarks for reform that might be targeted with this type of approach should include those focused on improving political liberty—for example, removing seditious libel laws used to prosecute journalists who criticize the president, easing the path for new political parties to organize and get on the ballot, and ensuring that new antiterrorism laws include safeguards for civil liberties and end the practice of trying Egyptian citizens in military courts.

Some have argued that Egypt is more in need of American investment than it is of U.S. development aid. In the long term, this is true. Right now, however, the gaping inequalities in Egyptian society and the rising social costs of economic reform mean that economic assistance can play a valuable role in maintaining the Egyptian commitment to a liberalizing economic agenda. After a ten-year negotiated reduction to $415 million in fiscal 2008, the Bush administration proposed a minimal level of $200 million in economic aid for fiscal 2009, of which $50 million was designated for democracy assistance. Increasing assistance above this minimal level should be contingent on finding a mutually agreed agenda for reform in both political and economic sectors that America can support.

Reiterate the importance of democratic legitimacy for Egypt's next leader. By receiving Gamal Mubarak in the White House in May 2006, and remaining otherwise silent on the question of Egypt's upcoming leadership transition, the Bush administration appeared to give its blessing to dynastic succession. U.S. support for Gamal is now widely perceived as a fait accompli in Egypt. Although a father-to-son succession is still not inevitable, the likeliest alternative would hail from the military or intelligence services. The United States should reiterate publicly its desire to see a democratic transition in Egypt and should make explicit its expectation that a new Egyptian president, whatever his identity, will only acquire legitimacy through a truly open, free, and competitive election. This stance should be coordinated with (and ideally vocally supported by) European states and the European Union.

Maintain military aid, with caution. America's military assistance to Egypt serves important symbolic and strategic purposes. For the United States, the aid is a demonstration of commitment and validates the logistical support Egypt provides to U.S. naval and air forces operating within the Central Command. For the Egyptian military, the main advantages of the assistance are prestige and the ability to shift more local budget resources to other military needs, including subsidizing the continued significant military role in the productive economy. Reducing or conditioning military assistance to Egypt on human rights grounds does catch the attention of the Egyptian political elite—but if this threat had to be carried out, it might undermine the relatively quiescent stance the military has so far taken toward political questions. American investment in Egyptian military assistance is worth maintaining as an insurance policy against military meddling in politics during the coming leadership transition. The Egyptian military's stance toward reform can be an important lever of influence, precisely because it both values its relationship with the United States and acts as a mainstay of the regime. In making the case for reform, Washington must address military as well as political leaders and must make clear its interest in moving the Egyptian military toward greater professionalism and a depoliticized role within the state. In particular, the International Military Education and Training assistance program is an important means to achieving this goal.

Broaden political contacts with peaceful opposition groups. The United States should meet with the leaders not only of the secular opposition but also of the Muslim Brotherhood. Unlike Hamas, the Brotherhood has long disavowed the use of violence and confirmed its commitment to the political process. Since it now makes up more than one-fifth of the Egyptian parliament, U.S. officials should have greater exposure to the group's leadership and begin to cultivate relationships with the leaders of the Brotherhood's next generation. The occasional, somewhat furtive meetings that have occurred between U.S. officials and the Brotherhood's parliamentary representatives are not sufficient for developing a deeper understanding of this important political constituency in Egypt. Dialogue is not the same thing as endorsement; questions remain about the Brotherhood's commitment to democracy and coexistence with Israel. U.S.-Brotherhood contacts should be presented as only one part of broader U.S. engagement with the political opposition in Egypt. The United States government should not allow the Egyptian government to wield a veto over discussions with Egyptian citizens from any peaceful political stream.

Maintain independent democracy assistance funding. In an effort to contain the independence of Egypt's civil society, the Egyptian government has begun to challenge American funding of some local civic groups. The next president should insist on the principle that the U.S. government must be the one to determine the recipients of its democracy and governance funding. The freedom of civic groups to apply for and accept international funding is a clear element of their basic freedom of association, but efforts to restrict this right are accelerating among autocratic governments around the world. The United States should work with other developed democracies (such as the United Kingdom and Germany) that fund projects in Egypt to insist on respect for this basic right. Democracy assistance programming should also take account of renewed activism within the labor unions. In keeping with long-standing commitments to Congress, the administration should incorporate labor rights into all its trade diplomacy with Egypt.

Pursue a free trade agreement. Egypt's export-oriented business sector is pro-reform and is slowly gaining strength relative to the traditional government-dependent domestic business sector. To boost the leverage of the export-oriented sector, as well as to help grow a productive sector of the economy that produces new jobs, the United States should follow up more actively on the Trade and Investment Framework Agreement with Egypt, with an eye to opening free trade agreement negotiations by 2010. FTA negotiations are a powerful incentive for additional governmental economic reform and will mobilize key pro-reform constituencies within the ruling party and economic elite. Other cases in the region (Bahrain and Morocco) demonstrate that free trade agreements can provide an entry point for more intensive engagement over regulatory reform and improvements in both legal frameworks and the rule of law.

While it is appropriate for the next president to consider human rights criteria in determining whether to open FTA talks, this conditionality should not come at the expense of a free trade agenda that would strengthen local reformers—that would be cutting off one's nose to spite one's face. FTA negotiators should also place emphasis on those elements of an agreement that would give local activists tools to hold government accountable, including transparency and labor rights provisions.

SAUDI ARABIA

Saudi Arabia today is emerging from the turbulence of the post-9/11 period. Having acknowledged the challenge of domestic radicalism, it has used military and social tools to combat it and seems to be achieving some degree of success. The country still faces a range of pressing social and political issues, however. At the same time, King Abdullah appears committed to steering his country on a course of change. His—and his successor's—challenge is to find the right pace of change that can accommodate the needs of Saudi Arabia's burgeoning youth while not alienating the country's conservative population.

While King Abdullah himself is widely viewed as a reformer con-strained by more conservative elements in the ruling establishment, other drivers of change include the dynamism of neighboring Gulf societies and external pressure, especially from the United States and particularly with regard to religious freedom. In recent years, Saudi Arabia has expe-rienced a more relaxed and open environment on a number of fronts, from women's dress to public discussions of domestic social and politi-cal issues. In addition, there is more vigorous reporting in the newspapers of abuses of state power, there is freer religious observance by Shi'ah and non-Muslims,[7] and the first, albeit small, steps toward political participa-tion were taken in 2005 with elections for a number of municipal coun-cil seats. But this environment of increased social freedom remains unpredictable and even arbitrary, with continued cases of blatant abuse by the *mutawwa* (religious police).

The need for economic and social reforms becomes urgent because of the country's youth bulge. While the whole region is experiencing a "youth-quake," demographics in the kingdom are particularly skewed toward young people. According to the World Bank, 37 percent of the Saudi population was under age fifteen in 2005, the most recent year for which data were available. It is not clear how the country's less-well-educated youth will fare in this time of economic and social transition. Nor is it obvious that the new "post-oil" economy the kingdom is attempting to build will offer more opportunity for upward mobility to young people who are not already privileged with private school educa-tions and university study abroad.

Economic Challenges

Today, Saudi Arabia is awash in oil revenues. While this windfall can help alleviate the youth-bulge challenge and smooth transitions, it does not eliminate the country's core problems. With its growing wealth, the Saudi government is investing in infrastructure, including the building of whole new cities and the launching of ambitious higher educational ini-tiatives in the form of overseas scholarships and the creation of King Abdullah University for Science and Technology, a coeducational institu-tion launched with a $10 billion endowment.

Many of the projects, however, are seen as "white elephants," or elite-focused projects that will contribute only marginally to the country's long-term employment and productivity needs. Large-scale government spending is one of the few ways to redistribute income in a country that has no income tax. However, the lack of budgetary transparency, the privileged role of members of the royal family, and rampant corruption make efficient redistribution difficult and leave much of the population wondering where all the money is going.

Inflation is currently a problem, in part because of the combination of high oil prices and the linkage of the Saudi riyal to the U.S. dollar. Inflation exacerbates the underlying inequalities. Although GDP per capita is growing, income inequality is growing faster.

Saudi youth will enter a fully saturated labor market unless significant structural reforms are made. Official unemployment figures are notoriously unreliable, but a figure of 25 percent is often cited. Expanding the service sector in Saudi Arabia is one much-discussed route to employment, but it would require social changes, such as increasing opportunities for tourism and leisure, that the country's conservative society will likely resist (allowing movie theaters has been rumored for years but has still not happened). Also, too few Saudi graduates have the requisite skills to succeed in service industries.

Political Change

Under pressure from Washington, the Saudi government has moved hesitantly toward limited political reforms, the centerpiece of which was partial municipal council elections in 2005. Election euphoria soon faded into a more sober recognition of the obstacles to and opportunities for reform. Liberals realized that they are more divided and disorganized than the conservative social forces they oppose and also clearly a minority within society. They are now more focused on civil liberties, community organizing, and local politics—including lobbying and mobilizing around the new municipal councils. They recognize that the appointed members of the municipal councils and the Shura Council, the national consultative council that advises the king, as well as the king himself, are their allies in the struggle for greater reform. But they mistrust the motives of these actors and are impatient with the pace of change.

Even with the king acting on behalf of reform, the pace and prospects for change are real concerns. King Abdullah is now in his eighties, and his reign might not be long enough to consolidate the changes that reformers would like to see. The royal family encompasses divergent views on the core questions of reform, and policy still requires consensus to succeed. This makes the stakes high for Saudi Arabia in the upcoming royal succession(s).[8] The new succession law and the recently established Allegiance Commission (a body of royal family members who will approve the king's selection of a new crown prince), may be significant if they can improve the predictability of future governance and ensure that divisions within the royal family do not hijack the reform process. Since the new law of succession clarifies who is eligible to rule in the future, it might also provide incentives for those candidates' constructive behavior. Government corruption and royal expenditures are publicly discussed issues now, but the desire for the royal family to be held more accountable for its actions is widespread.

Democracy is a concept many Saudis still view with ambivalence, and the elite consensus is for small steps that begin a political process that can mature and gain momentum over time. The Shura Council, for example, is quietly beginning to play a more active role than in the past—reviewing legislation and incorporating more diverse viewpoints in its membership. However, outright dissent and open criticism of the government are still not tolerated. Religious intolerance, including of other streams within Islam, remains widespread. Ongoing attempts to reform Saudi schools' curriculum remain very much focused on trying to introduce greater tolerance as well as on teaching civic responsibilities.

Saudi Arabia's accession to the World Trade Organization was an important driver behind some limited legal reforms and greater transparency in business. But Saudi follow-through has been slow and inconsistent. International norms and practices with regard to human rights issues continue to be useful levers for engagement with the kingdom's rulers on reform.

Recommendations for the United States Regarding Saudi Arabia

To strengthen U.S.-Saudi cooperation, broaden American engagement with Saudi society, and encourage further reform, we urge the next American president to take the following steps:

Sustain high-level discussions. The strategic dialogue under way in recent years has already produced greater common understanding on the importance of some human rights issues and some substantive progress on religious freedoms and rule of law. The dialogue should continue to include a "human development" working group that ensures regular exchange between American and Saudi officials on issues of political and social freedom and basic human rights.

Foster economic dynamism. The United States should offer a menu of programs—wherever possible, with private sector participation—to foster greater economic dynamism and increased opportunities for younger Saudis to join the private sector. Such programs could include training and entrepreneurship programs for young Saudis, new credit mechanisms to provide small business loans, and credit insurance, training, and other steps to try to cultivate a more venture-capital-oriented lending culture among Saudi banks.

Expand commercial contacts. The next administration should plan high-profile trade missions to the kingdom. This would go a long way to repairing the sense of abandonment by the United States that has pervaded the kingdom's business elite since 9/11. The investment opportunities in Saudi Arabia are significant, and the United States is already losing some of its potential market to other countries that are currently taking advantage of a weak U.S. presence. While reluctance to engage exists on both sides, it is largely because of exaggerated Saudi perceptions about U.S. government scrutiny of Saudi-origin transactions and U.S. visa and travel restrictions. To counter this misperception, the U.S. government and business community should capitalize on the improvements made in the Saudi business environment in the wake of WTO accession. In addition, increasing business contacts will help to expand social contacts as well and will give Saudi Arabia further incentive to loosen its travel restrictions and open the kingdom more to external influences.

Pursue democracy programming. In recent years, American democracy-oriented programming in Saudi Arabia has been sidetracked to "safe" subjects like breast cancer awareness, or engaging individual Saudi participants in larger, regionwide programs. But Saudi civic activism is gaining vitality and the ranks of activists are growing. More concrete forms of support for their work should be explored, including capacity building, small grants from the embassy, or country-specific Middle East Partnership Initiative programs.[9] While there is a potential for backlash against U.S. involvement, reformers within the kingdom are best placed to judge, and they still view U.S. support as important to maintain momentum behind reform initiatives.

Continue to press on human rights issues. Gross human rights violations still occur frequently in the kingdom. While public statements from Washington can sometimes have perverse effects, the United States should not remain silent. Instead, it should use private pressure—and at times public persuasion—to steer its Saudi partners toward behavior more congruent with international human rights norms. These norms include freedom of speech, women's equality, and religious toleration—all of which underpin successful democracy as well.

Expand relations with Saudi Arabia's next generation of leaders. The United States has little influence on succession in the kingdom and might lose ground if it is perceived as picking favorites. But, keeping in mind that policy change in the kingdom depends on consensus among senior family members, the United States should broaden its dialogue with the next generation within the al-Saud family, who over the coming years will inevitably take on greater prominence in decisionmaking. The case for reform should be made as widely as possible.

Regionwide Recommendations

In addition to these country-specific recommendations, other U.S. government policies can help foster economic and political development across the region:

Maintain U.S. assistance to Arab reformers. The United States should continue official financial and public support for reformers across the region, despite concerns that support from the U.S. government creates a backlash. Reformers are generally sophisticated enough to weigh the costs and benefits of accepting support from the U.S. government, and many continue to view that support as a net positive. The value of programs like the Middle East Partnership Initiative (MEPI) should not be discounted just because they are a legacy of the Bush administration. MEPI programming has been a relatively low-cost way for the United States to build links with and encourage reformers throughout the region, and has served as an important outreach mechanism for the U.S. State Department, expanding and improving American understanding of political trends in the region. In the end, American support—both direct (through the U.S. government) and indirect (through the National Endowment for Democracy and regional foundations)—should be offered to Arab activists, leaving them to decide whether they can afford to accept it.

Focus on human rights. America can best support domestic Arab reformers by helping them gain the space within which to raise their own demands on their governments. American advocacy of basic human rights such as free speech and free association will help ensure that our support for democracy in Arab countries never outstrips internal demands for change. These basic rights are essential ingredients for democratic progress.

Prioritize state building in weak states. The weak governments of Iraq, Lebanon, and the Palestinian Authority, suffused with conflict, have been unable to enforce the basic principle of the state's monopoly on the use of force. Under such conditions, the Bush administration's pressure for elections produced electoral legitimacy for armed militias, instead of progress toward stable democracy. In Iraq, the hopefulness of Election Day faded into the reality of a fractured parliament that exacerbated sectarian divisions. In Lebanon today, internal and regional conflicts undermine—and perhaps for now doom—prospects for more meaningful democratization. The May 2008 deal between the U.S.-backed March 14 movement and the Hezbollah-led opposition is clear evidence of the weakness of state institutions in the face of social conflict.[10] The United States should prioritize the strengthening of government institutions in Lebanon over electoral reform or other procedural advances in democratic practice. Until the Lebanese government can demonstrate sovereignty and capacity sufficient to protect and serve the interests of the Lebanese people, electoral mechanisms will only serve to calcify existing sectarian divisions in the country. Similarly, in the Palestinian Authority, internal political conflict and the conflict with Israel reinforce one another—conflict resolution and building an effective, responsive Palestinian Authority are key requisites for a functional Palestinian democracy. Rebuilding the Palestinian Authority is beyond the scope of this chapter but is addressed in chapter 5. At a minimum, it is clear that Palestinians who are more politically acceptable to the United States than Hamas will not be able to acquire public support without the prospect of substantive progress in Palestinian-Israeli relations.

Sustain and build momentum for reform in moderate countries. Morocco and Jordan have both made important commitments and steps toward domestic reform, and in 2004 Jordan in particular played an important role in goading other Arab League members to take political reform seriously and make some new commitments. Yet both Morocco and Jordan now face decisions about how much further to go and how quickly. Jordan, in particular, has experienced some backsliding in the face of security concerns. American incentives, like the Millennium Challenge Corporation compacts and additional trade and aid incentives, are important to build momentum for additional economic, social, and political reforms in these two countries and elsewhere in the region. The demonstration effects might not be overwhelming, but they are still significant and should be wielded to increase pressure on larger states like Egypt to make additional moves toward democracy.

Encourage the process of Gulf Cooperation Council (GCC) integration. The United States has welcomed in principle economic integration among Gulf states, but bilateral American trade agreements with Gulf countries have occasionally created tension within the GCC, which includes Bahrain, Kuwait, Oman, Qatar, Saudi Arabia, and the United Arab Emirates. The process of regional integration produces progressive changes in local regulation, helps inculcate norms associated with economic liberalization and government transparency, and should strengthen and stabilize regional economies against oil price shocks and other potential sources of disruption. As the Gulf region moves closer to monetary union and harmonization of trading rules, the United States should support these changes. Since the smaller Gulf states have demonstrated more dynamism in recent years, strengthening economic integration might also heighten their impact, and perhaps help to move more recalcitrant member states toward greater openness.

Revitalize public diplomacy. The next president will enjoy a window of opportunity to reintroduce America to Arab societies. But this window will be very narrow, both because the problems in the region are so pressing and because the new president will be relatively constrained in changing America's approach on the core issues of Iraq, the Arab-Israeli conflict, and relations with Iran. While public diplomacy is beyond the scope of this paper, there is both opportunity and demand for a revitalized American public outreach to the Middle East, especially to younger people and especially in Saudi Arabia. Many Saudis and other Gulf Arabs have a desire for a more multidimensional relationship with the United States, one that engages society and culture, not just economics. The educational sector is a critical field in which U.S.-Arab ties could be rebuilt, as well as an arena in which more liberal and pro-American modes of thought could be consolidated within the Arab public. Expanded student and other social exchanges and cultural programming could help to begin to reverse the long slide in pro-American attitudes in the region.

CONCLUSION

In implementing an American policy that roots U.S.-Arab cooperation in a commitment to reform, the next president must still weigh conditions within individual countries and the strategic trade-offs involved in pressure for changes in domestic governance. America has powerful incentives to offer, and there is a yearning in the region for renewed American engagement that touches wide swaths of Arab society. But American engagement must be wielded in a coherent manner, directed toward goals about which the American government speaks and acts with transparency. A new president will inevitably face difficult choices among competing policy priorities. Accusations of double standards are inevitable, but clear language and individualized attention is responsive to this concern, while defending the United States from charges of imposing a one-size-fits-all model of reform. Wherever possible, reform should be encouraged by supporting the demands of indigenous activists and by using international norms, positive incentives, and societal and cultural exchange and learning.

NOTES

1. In 2005–06, the region's growth rate of 6.1 percent outperformed both Latin America (4.75 percent) and sub-Saharan Africa (5.3 percent), although it trailed behind East Asia (9 percent) and South Asia (8.1 percent).

2. Interview with Navtej Dhillon, senior fellow at the Middle East Youth Initiative, Wolfensohn Center for Development, Global Economy and Development, Brookings Institution. See also "The Middle Eastern Marriage Crisis," *NOW*, Public Broadcasting Service, July 11, 2008 (transcript of interview reprinted at www.brookings.edu/ interviews/2008/0711_middle_east_dhillon.aspx).

3. Qualified Industrial Zones (QIZs) allow goods manufactured in these areas to enter the U.S. duty-free and quota-free. They are designed to stimulate investment and employment in those regions.

4. See "IMF Economic Survey," August 2006 (www.imf.org/EXTERNAL/ PUBS/FT/SURVEY/2006/082106.pdf).

5. In fiscal year 2008, Congressional appropriators mandated a cut to Egypt's aid package if Cairo failed to take steps toward greater political freedom and toward improved border security with the Gaza Strip. Secretary of State Condoleezza Rice waived these restrictions on national security grounds in March 2008, but the episode caused diplomatic tensions and gave Egypt's Foreign Minister an opportunity to lambaste the United States publicly for its paternalism.

6. The Millennium Challenge Corporation (MCC) has formed compacts with several Middle Eastern countries that desire higher levels of American assistance, and the prospect of MCC eligibility was a powerful lever for U.S. officials in requesting specific improvements in democracy and human rights.

7. See U.S. Department of State, "Country Reports on Religious Freedom, 2007" (www.state.gov/g/drl/rls/irf/2007/90220.htm).

8. Given the age of those next in line, it is not unlikely that several successions will occur in quick order before the torch is passed to the next generation.

9. The Middle East Partnership Initiative (MEPI), launched in December 2002, is a State Department program to encourage reform in the Middle East. Its grants go primarily to civil society partners such as nongovernmental organizations and universities. MEPI's focus has been on political reform, economic development, education, and women's empowerment.

10. A stalemate between the pro-Western Lebanese government (headed by a coalition known as the "March 14 movement") and the pro-Syrian, Hezbollah-led opposition prevented election of a new Lebanese president for seven months, beginning in late November, 2007. The dispute was settled in a deal brokered in May, 2008, by the Gulf state of Qatar, whereby Hezbollah would rejoin the cabinet, efforts to disarm Lebanese militias (primarily Hezbollah) would be set aside, and General Michel Suleiman would become Lebanon's new president.

DANIEL BYMAN

STEVEN SIMON

7

Counterterrorism and U.S. Policy toward the Middle East

THE NEXT PRESIDENT should make counterterrorism an integral part of his approach to the Middle East but not the only driver of his regional policy. Terrorist attacks can derail, at times dramatically, an administration's regional objectives and in extreme circumstances can cause tremendous loss of innocent life and reduced public confidence in government.[1] The radicalization that underpins terrorism stemming from the Middle East will make it harder for the new administration to pursue political reform in the region and to enlist regional governments in cooperative endeavors. In addition to these threats to U.S. regional interests, a successful attack carried out on U.S. soil or against American civilians abroad could lead to a significant loss of life and may create domestic political pressures for actions that would be difficult to resist even though this might prove counterproductive. Counterterrorism, therefore, should be seen as a significant policy concern but weighed among many interests. Moreover, counterterrorism does not occur in a vacuum: for it to succeed other U.S. interests must also advance.

The next administration can reduce the threat posed by terrorism by implementing the following policies:

Strengthen local capacities to counter violent extremism. Terrorism is best fought by governments in the region, but the United States can play a key role in bolstering their intelligence, police, financial, and other capabilities.

Help local states apply best practices for deradicalization. Regional states, particularly Saudi Arabia, have tried to develop effective means to fight radicalization and stop the rise of militancy. However, regional programs are of uneven quality and some are in their early stages. The United States should encourage use of the most successful methods.

Avoid, to the extent possible, reinforcing perceptions that the United States is at war with Islam. Although it is difficult for the United States to send a consistent message, a presidential priority should be to make clear that the U.S. struggle is focused on a relatively small group of violent radicals out of touch with the mainstream of their religion.

Help ensure that Iraqi refugee camps in Jordan and Syria do not become sources of militancy. Refugee aid programs and greater government capacity are necessary to reduce the risk that the 2 million Iraqi refugees could over time support violence back in Iraq and become a source of unrest in their host countries.

If a decision is made to pull out from Iraq, retain U.S. military and intelligence capacity in the country that is sufficient to disrupt al Qaeda activities. Al Qaeda of Iraq (AQI) is down but not out, and if there is a U.S. drawdown, the president needs to ensure that the capacity remains to operate effectively against AQI.

Continue to fund the Sunni Awakening in Iraq and press the government of Iraq to bring as many Sunni volunteers into the security forces as possible so that members do not restore ties to al Qaeda.

Counter Hamas and Hezbollah by working with regional allies to strengthen their security-related institutions rather than by directly challenging these deeply rooted movements.

Recognize the danger of failed or failing states in the region as incubators of and magnets for terrorist groups. U.S. programs designed to strengthen law enforcement, the judiciary, the police and security services, and other institutions of governance in such states must be augmented.

CURRENT THREATS

One of the most difficult Middle Eastern counterterrorism challenges is the transnational nature of many of the threats arising from this region, involving not only states in the Middle East and the United States but increasingly other countries around the world. Preachers in the United Kingdom, recruiters in continental Europe, planners in Pakistan, and non-Arab Muslim extremists all must be factored into the counterterrorism policies of the United States and its partners in the Middle East. The threat can be broken down into four overlapping components:

Direct attacks on the U.S. homeland emanating from the Middle East. Terrorist attacks from the Middle East against the U.S. homeland have been rare. Many of the attempted attacks since 9/11 were hatched in al Qaeda bases in Pakistan and launched from Europe rather than from the Middle East.[2] Nevertheless, the 9/11 plot showed the importance of the Middle East as a fundraising and recruitment center for al Qaeda, whose core leadership and support is still largely derived from the region.

Attacks on U.S. personnel abroad. Far more common than attacks on the U.S. homeland have been attacks on U.S. personnel overseas. Before 9/11 al Qaeda struck devastating blows at U.S. embassies in Africa and the USS *Cole* in Yemen. Even excluding war zones like Iraq and Afghanistan, U.S. personnel stationed throughout the Middle East are at risk from terrorist attacks. The 2002 killing of a U.S. Agency for International Development official in Jordan, the bombings of U.S. facilities in Saudi Arabia in 2003, and plots against U.S. embassies in Singapore and France suggest the range of American targets.

Attacks that threaten the stability of U.S. allies and the lives of their citizens. U.S. allies in the Middle East have borne the brunt of the attacks since 9/11. In Iraq attacks on U.S., Jordanian, UN, and Iraqi targets snowballed into a civil war. Saudi Arabia has battled a low-grade insurgency involving international terrorists since 2003. Algeria appears to have weakened Islamist insurgents to the point that the survival of the regime is not in question, but terrorism remains a problem, and violence has spread to Jordan, Lebanon, Morocco, Tunisia, and Yemen. So too have U.S. allies outside the Middle East suffered attacks, particularly in Europe, South Asia, and Southeast Asia.

Attacks that threaten U.S. interests. Even when casualties are few, terrorism can endanger social cohesion, as in Europe, or impose a "terror premium" on the price of energy. From a U.S. counterterrorism perspective, global and regional groups are obstacles to the preservation of U.S. interests.

In addition to differentiating the various targets of terrorism, the incoming administration should differentiate between those groups behind the threats. Al Qaeda, its affiliates, and those it inspires—a collection that this chapter refers to as the global jihad—pose the greatest and most immediate danger to the United States. Yet regional terrorist groups such as Hezbollah and Hamas (the Islamic Resistance Movement) also threaten U.S. interests and countering them should be an important part of U.S. counterterrorism policy. Finally, the United States must recognize the danger of failed or failing states, which often enable the generation of new terrorist groups and provide a haven for established ones, as well as the emergence of new state sponsors of and havens for terrorism in the region. The following are the groups of greatest threat to the United States and its interests in the Middle East.

THE GLOBAL JIHAD

The al Qaeda core around Osama bin Laden suffered reverses after 9/11 but has steadily reestablished itself. Although it is not as strong as it was before 9/11, it is far stronger than it was in the organization's dark days of 2002. The Iraq war gave it new life, validating its narrative and boosting recruitment and fundraising. The movement has reestablished itself in tribal areas of Pakistan, where it enjoys considerable freedom of maneuver.

A central uncertainty for the new administration will be whether al Qaeda and its allies return to their roots and focus on local targets rather than on the United States. U.S. strategy has sought "disaggregation," that is, prying local components of the jihad from the global center's influence and resources and defeating them one by one.[3] However, the enhancement of al Qaeda's haven in Pakistan and the movement of several local groups in North Africa, Yemen, and elsewhere toward the al Qaeda center have slowed or perhaps reversed this emphasis on local targets for now. From Pakistan, bin Laden and his lieutenants have directed plots in Europe, fostered links to fighters in Iraq, trained would-be jihadists from around the world, and wreaked havoc in Pakistan itself. In Iraq, Saudi Arabia, and Algeria, local movements have assumed the al Qaeda label to highlight their global ambitions and garner credibility among local supporters of bin Laden. It is conceivable that a relocalization will follow once the large numbers of Saudis, Libyans, and others return to their home countries from Iraq. Local governments are concerned about this possibility and, in the case of Egypt, have coerced imprisoned jihadist preachers to declare that attacks on local rulers are sacrilegious.

At an operational level, the global jihad appears to be in a strategic pause. Over the past year, the number of conspiracies and successful attacks has declined. Among the reasons for this are better police work, international coordination, the expenditure of jihadist energy in Iraq, and possibly jihadist fatigue. Some prominent jihadist theoreticians now argue that the jihad has done more harm than good to Muslim interests, while several local affiliates appear to be questioning their ties to the al Qaeda core. This trend toward reexamination, under way since 2003, might be harming recruitment to the jihad.

However, senior police and intelligence officials in Denmark, France, Germany, Italy, the Netherlands, Spain, and the United Kingdom have expressed considerable worry about the consolidation of an al Qaeda infrastructure within their jurisdictions.[4] These concerns are compounded by difficulties that governments in western Europe have encountered in integrating Muslim residents. Officials believe that the alienation of migrants as well as second- and third-generation Muslims is creating conditions that favor violent extremism. Yet, although Iraq has been a mobilizing factor for European Muslim militants, relatively few have actually gone to Iraq to fight. Fears that large numbers of veteran fighters would return to Europe to wreak havoc so far appear to be unfounded.

Elsewhere, cooperation between the United States and its allies Indonesia and Malaysia to counter jihadist networks has worked well. No major attacks have taken place in those countries since the Bali and Jakarta bombings in the wake of 9/11. Africa, in contrast, is an area of active expansion for the global jihad. Outside the Maghreb, Somalia, Kenya, and Mauritania constitute problems, as attacks in these countries and the presence of an al Qaeda infrastructure suggest. Links between the jihad in this theater and the Middle East are thin, but the exceptions are serious, as when jihadists attempted to shoot down an Israeli airliner in Kenya in 2002.

Al Qaeda in Iraq is small and weak, with the best current estimate of fighters at 850. The vast majority of these are indigenous Iraqis, but the leadership tends to be of foreign origin. That this is an uncomfortable situation for al Qaeda is obvious from its effort to tag its leaders misleadingly with ostentatiously Iraqi names. Overall, AQI is probably responsible for 10 to 15 percent of attacks against Iraqi security forces and Shi'i civilians; AQI attacks against U.S. forces are thought to be about 7 to 10 percent of the total. (The AQI leadership takes credit in the media for an average of 10 percent of recorded attacks.) Despite its small numbers, however, AQI served as a catalyst of violence, especially from 2003 to 2007, through its audacious and costly attacks against a range of targets considered taboo by other parties, including children and UN representatives. The group also experimented with combinations of toxic chemicals and high explosives. Perhaps most important, AQI consciously sought to foment a sectarian civil war in Iraq, both as a means of undermining the U.S. presence and because of AQI's fierce hatred of the Shi'ah, whom it regards as apostates.

AQI's current weakness stems from overreach as well as from U.S. action on the ground. More or less simultaneously, the group alienated unaffiliated Iraqis by brutally enforcing conservative, Wahhabi-style mores in neighborhoods under its control, usurping tribal smuggling routes, and attempting to assert control over the Sunni insurgency. These missteps impelled more mainstream Sunni leaders, whose forces had been badly beaten by the Jaish al-Mahdi, often referred to as the Mahdi army, in the 2006 battle of Baghdad, to forge a tactical alliance with local U.S. forces—an alliance the United States was far more willing to accept in the desperate days of 2006 than in the heady aftermath of the invasion itself. The combined efforts of the former insurgents (known as the Sunni Awakening movement) and the firepower of U.S. forces inflicted serious damage on AQI.

In October 2007 the U.S. ambassador to Iraq declared that al Qaeda "simply is gone" in much of Iraq—a judgment shared by military and intelligence officials.[5] It still can attack, but its operatives have less time to plan, train, and recruit.

How will this turn of events affect al Qaeda's fortunes? Whether the United States stays or goes, global jihadists and their supporters will claim that they have already won twice over: first, by virtue of the intervention, which they use to confirm their narrative of a United States bent on global occupation, and second, by creating the appearance of having thwarted Washington's allegedly imperial designs. A U.S. decision to disengage militarily from Iraq will likely be pointed to as reaffirmation of these beliefs. On a propaganda level, al Qaeda will claim that it drove the United States from Iraq, regardless of the reality. In addition, a U.S. withdrawal would reinforce the broader jihadist argument that the United States, if hit hard, will fold. However, given the size of the propaganda victory the United States has already conferred on Islamic extremists, and the way that U.S. military operations continue to confirm the jihadist worldview, a decision to remain in Iraq solely to avoid emboldening radicals would be unproductive.

Al Qaeda's challenge is to lock in the perception of victory despite a very real setback. The degree to which it succeeds will depend on the successful absorption of the Sunni Awakening movement into the Iraqi security forces, the manner in which the United States withdraws, and the overall stability of Iraq after the United States draws down. The blow to al Qaeda's credibility is potentially large but contingent on U.S. actions.

REGIONAL GROUPS OF CONCERN

Although al Qaeda and its local affiliates have strong bonds and share an agenda that focuses on the Middle East and the U.S. role there, the region is plagued by other terrorist groups unaffiliated with, and even opposed to, al Qaeda. The Lebanese group Hezbollah and the Palestinian group Hamas are both formidable terrorist organizations; however, their interests in the United States are primarily indirect. The threats they pose, their goals, and their organizational structures differ considerably from al Qaeda and its allies. Neither organization directly targets Americans. Rather, they attack the forces of U.S. allies (particularly Israel, but also pro-Western voices in Lebanon) and thus pose a threat to U.S. interests in the region.[6]

Hezbollah is among the most skilled terrorist groups worldwide, a sponsor of terrorism, and a formidable guerrilla organization that has clawed at Israel repeatedly since the Israel Defense Forces (IDF) withdrew from Lebanon in 2000. Hezbollah's sponsorship of terrorism includes backing Palestinian groups (since 2000, Hezbollah has increased training, funding, and logistical support for Hamas, Palestine Islamic Jihad, and other anti-Israel groups) and working with militant factions in Iraq. Even though Hezbollah is not a government as such, its armed forces and control of territory suggest enough sovereignty to warrant the title state sponsor of terrorism. Hezbollah, which exhibits many of the trappings of a regime that runs a state, also has a truly comprehensive media presence, supports a mammoth social services network, and constitutes the largest political force in Lebanon.

Hamas and several other Palestinian terrorist groups (including Palestine Islamic Jihad and the Fatah-affiliated al-Aqsa Martyrs' Brigade) do not target U.S. forces and are hostile to al Qaeda. However, they do conduct terrorist attacks on Israel that kill Israeli civilians, some of whom are also American citizens, and undermine the chances for Middle East peace. Like Hezbollah, Hamas is a social services provider and a political movement as well as a terrorist group. Hamas, which runs the Gaza Strip, has grown considerably stronger since seizing power there in 2007. Israeli and Jordanian officials interviewed agreed that Hamas now dominates Gaza in a way that Fatah and the Palestinian Authority never did. Hamas, inspired by Hezbollah, is turning its fighters into a more formal military organization (officials in the Middle East also claim that Iran has stepped up its military training of Hamas). Hamas's political success has sent a message that Israel and the United States are best opposed through violence, and interviews suggest that the credibility of this claim has disheartened many pro-U.S. voices in the Arab world.

Countries within the European Union have been talking to Hamas, and the United States and Israel both do so as well, albeit through intermediaries. Hezbollah has been legitimized as well by outside players, particularly Qatar, a U.S. ally, which has facilitated Hezbollah's objective of gaining veto power over Lebanese government decisions. The difficulty with the current situation is that this tacit recognition runs counter to efforts to delegitimize organizations that use terrorism to advance their interests. The new administration will have to confront how best to deal with this awkward reality.

FAILED AND FAILING STATES AND STATE SPONSORS OF TERRORISM

A look at where terrorist groups are active in the Middle East illustrates the dangers posed by failed or weak states. In Saudi Arabia and Jordan, al Qaeda's ambitions are strong, but entrenched regimes with effective security services have contained the threat. In Lebanon, Iraq, and Gaza, in contrast, the weakness of the state has allowed groups that use terrorism to play a major role by coupling violence with delivery of social services, which exploits the government's incapacities. As these groups take root, the state becomes even weaker and progressively unable to command popular legitimacy.

The United States needs to improve greatly its ability to manage the problem of failing and failed states. Such states allow terrorists operational space in which to recruit, train, and plan attacks. In addition, the strife generated in these states leads local young men to join violent organizations and opens the door to foreign fighters. In some cases, as in Lebanon, the local government becomes too weak or lacks the legitimacy to stop a potent terrorist organization like Hezbollah from effectively conducting its own foreign policy while paralyzing that of the state.

Washington's current approach toward state sponsorship of terrorism rests on a flawed understanding of the problem and a correspondingly flawed policy response. The Department of State in its formal list of state sponsors of terror lists the following countries: Cuba, Iran, Sudan, and Syria. Of those on the list, Iran and Syria pose the biggest problems, and in both cases, their involvement in traditional international terrorism is down considerably from the peak of their involvement in the 1980s.

The United States should revise its list of state sponsorship of terrorism. A new list would point out the true sponsors as well as describe countries whose passivity, deliberate at times, allows terrorists to flourish. It would also have gradations that would allow the executive branch considerable flexibility to reward improvements and punish increases in support. Perhaps most important, states that no longer use terrorism should be able to get off the list, even if they remain adversaries of the United States in other contexts.

This shift is particularly necessary today, since much of the problem of state sponsorship of terrorism involves actors that are not on the list, such as Pakistan, Lebanon, Yemen, and the Palestinian territories. Some are informal allies of terrorist groups, while sponsorship for others is in part explained by incapacity. Yet these new state sponsors are actually more dangerous to the United States and its interests than are the remaining traditional state sponsors, because some of these new sponsors are tied to Sunni jihadist groups such as al Qaeda—currently the greatest terrorist threat facing the United States. The nightmare of a terrorist group acquiring nuclear weapons is far more likely to involve Pakistan than it is Iran or North Korea. Iran is often willing to provoke the United States, but it has also demonstrated respect for U.S. military power and caution in its relationship with terrorist groups. Tehran has had chemical weapons for more than twenty years and yet has not transferred them to terrorist groups. In addition, Iran's closest proxy, Hezbollah, has evinced little interest in nuclear weapons. Iran's caution in this area is likely to continue but could end should it believe that the United States is poised to try to overthrow the clerical regime by force.

The emergence of the al Qaeda sanctuary in tribal parts of Pakistan—a country outside the scope of this chapter, yet one whose actions greatly affect security in the Middle East—is perhaps the most dangerous development in the war on terror since 9/11. Yet Pakistan is not the only haven terrorists enjoy, particularly if one looks beyond al Qaeda. The following countries or entities in the Middle East deliberately or inadvertently allow terrorists operational freedom. Some of these have already been classified as state sponsors of terrorism—Iran and Syria—but others have not.

Iran

Iran has been one of the world's most persistent and proactive state sponsors of terrorism since its Islamic revolution in 1979. It debuted on the Department of State's list of such sponsors in 1984, where it has since remained. Iran has supported an array of Shi'i militant groups—usually through the Islamic Revolutionary Guard Corps—and is particularly close to Hezbollah, which it arms, trains, and funds on a massive scale.

Iran also maintains ties with several Palestinian groups. Relations with Palestine Islamic Jihad are particularly close, but Tehran also has regular contact with Hamas and provides it with limited funding and training. Israeli officials claim that Iran's training of Hamas has increased considerably since Hamas's takeover of Gaza. Much of Iran's outreach to the Palestinian groups is done through Hezbollah, which gives Iran a veneer of deniability.

Since 2003 Iran has deployed hundreds of intelligence and paramilitary personnel to Iraq. Iran's closest ties may be to the Islamic Supreme Council of Iraq (ISCI), formerly known as the Supreme Council for the Islamic Revolution of Iraq (SCIRI), but Tehran has also sought out many other relationships, even at the price of weakening ISCI. Iran's ties to Jaish al-Mahdi have matured substantially. Tehran has provided safe haven for its leader, Moqtada al-Sadr, while the Revolutionary Guard reportedly has trained groups of Iraqis in camps near Tehran, instructing them in the use of shaped charges, mortars, rockets, sniper and kidnapping operations, and intelligence. All of these attack options could be brought to bear against U.S. regional allies while continuing to pose a problem for U.S. forces in Iraq.[7] In addition to Iraq's Shi'i community, Iran has long-standing ties to the Patriotic Union of Kurdistan, which is now one of two major partners in the Kurdish regional government, as well as with an array of local Kurdish leaders.

Although it is an overstatement to say that Iran controls those groups, Iran's influence is often considerable, particularly with Hezbollah and some Iraqi Shi'i groups. In exchange for its money and training, recipients serve Iran's interest in disrupting the peace process and weakening pro-U.S. governments.

Syria

Though Damascus is less supportive of terrorism than it had been in the past, its current support spans the gamut from active backing of some groups to relatively passive support for other causes.

Syria has long backed an array of Palestinian groups, including the Popular Front for the Liberation of Palestine General Command, Palestine Islamic Jihad, Hamas, and the Popular Front for the Liberation of Palestine. These groups have an official presence in Syria, and with Syrian support, some of their fighters have trained in Lebanon. Syria also has worked closely with Hezbollah, using the group to put pressure on Israel and to maintain influence in Lebanon, a priority after Syrian forces departed Lebanon in 2005. Syria has at times armed the group directly. More important, it has used its influence in Lebanon to bolster Hezbollah's freedom of action, and Damascus has deliberately facilitated the flow of weapons from Iran across the Syrian-Lebanese border.

Syria also is linked to a number of assassinations in Lebanon. A UN investigation found that Syrian officials were involved in the assassination of former Lebanese prime minister Rafiq Hariri. As the 2005 report noted, there is "probable cause" to think that the assassination could not have happened without the approval of top-ranked Syrian security officials.[8] Although the perpetrators are unknown, many rumors tie Syria to a string of assassinations of Lebanese figures linked to the anti-Syrian March 14 movement. If true, these allegations would be consistent with an established Syrian proclivity to kill its opponents in Lebanon.

Finally, U.S. officials have regularly criticized Syria for not policing its border with Iraq and for allowing various insurgent groups to enjoy a de facto haven in parts of the country. Many jihadists transit Syria en route to Iraq, and jihadist logisticians enjoy some freedom to organize this traffic. In addition, some insurgent leaders lived in Syria and even held meetings there, a degree of freedom that would be difficult to achieve without the complicity of the Asad regime. Regional officials argue that Syria has recently made it more difficult for fighters to go to Iraq, but it is still far from using all its capabilities to stop this cross-border traffic.

The Gaza Strip

Hamas has controlled the Gaza Strip since it eliminated the Fatah party presence there in 2007 after winning a victory in the 2006 legislative elections. If Hamas is viewed as a legitimate, albeit hostile, government, then many of the activities that have occurred on its watch (for example, mortar attacks on Israeli cities) are best viewed as acts of war rather than terrorism. However, if it is considered a substate group that is not part of the legitimate Palestinian Authority government because its 2007 seizure of power was undemocratic, then the same acts are terrorism, abetted in effect by the incapacity of the Palestinian Authority. The semantic difference matters: war and counterterrorism involve different norms and legal principles, and many among the international community would judge Israel's response in different ways depending on the framework used.[9] As of the writing of this chapter, the shelling has stopped and there is a tenuous cease-fire between Hamas and Israel.

Iraq

Various terrorist groups operate in Iraq, ranging from Iran-linked groups like Jaish al-Mahdi to Sunni groups that have ties to al Qaeda. Some, like Jaish al-Mahdi, maintain social service networks and focus on targets in Iraq while others, like al Qaeda in Iraq, disdain this approach and harbor ambitions beyond Iraq. These groups destabilize Iraq and inhibit a political settlement. Groups linked to AQI have sown unrest in Jordan, Lebanon, and Saudi Arabia.

In contrast to the Hamas government in Gaza, many of Iraq's problems stem from incapacity. The Iraqi government is strongly opposed to AQI, but its ability to act on its own against the group is limited at best: most of the successes have come from the support of Sunni tribal leaders who see AQI as a threat to their influence. However, deliberate toleration is also part of the problem. For example, the Kurdish regional government at times allows the Kurdistan Workers' Party (PKK), a terrorist group, to operate without significant interference.[10]

Lebanon

In Lebanon, Hezbollah holds several seats in the cabinet and is one of Lebanon's largest parliamentary blocs. However, Hezbollah is in direct opposition to the March 14 movement, an anti-Syrian and relatively pro-Western bloc that in theory controls the government and is sympathetic to the idea that Hezbollah should disarm—an idea Hezbollah vehemently rejects. The Lebanese army could not defeat Hezbollah if it confronted it, which may not be an issue since many of its members would disobey orders if asked to shut down the group, thus underscoring the weakness of state institutions.

Today, Iran and Hezbollah remain exceptionally close, but Iran's day-to-day control of Hezbollah is more limited than it once was. Although Iran and Hezbollah still coordinate key decisions, particularly outside of Lebanon, and Iranian weapons and particularly financial support still greatly benefit the group, the relationship is more partner than proxy. Hezbollah leaders still respect Ayatollah Ali Khamenei, Iran's supreme leader, but the veneration is not close to what the group felt for Khamenei's predecessor, the charismatic Ayatollah Khomeini. In addition, much of Hezbollah's rank and file looks first to the Lebanese leader Ayatollah Mohammad Hussein Fadlallah for religious guidance. Militarily, Hezbollah operatives have become highly skilled through Iranian training and now have hardened battlefield experience through years of warfare against the Israel Defense Forces. Finally, Hezbollah has developed its own fundraising capacity within Lebanon and among the Lebanese diaspora.

Hezbollah's shift toward independence is even more pronounced with regard to Syria, its other traditional sponsor. Before the Syrian withdrawal from Lebanon in 2005, Damascus used Hezbollah to put pressure on Israel: it would encourage Hezbollah to lie low or step up attacks depending on Syria's diplomatic needs. Since the withdrawal, however, the primary benefit of this relationship to Damascus is Hezbollah's influence in Lebanon. As the strongest and most organized political and military force in the country, Hezbollah has led the pro-Syrian forces opposed to the March 14 movement. Hezbollah has also opposed an international tribunal to investigate Syria's role in the Hariri assassination. As a result, Syria is dependent on Hezbollah to maintain its influence in Lebanon. In the past, the United States and Israel expected that a peace agreement with Syria would result in a Syrian crackdown on Hezbollah in Lebanon. However, the departure of Syrian forces and Syria's need for street power in Lebanon has diminished Syria's potential role as a peace enforcer.[11] In addition, Hezbollah leader Hassan Nasrallah's personal popularity and Hezbollah's prestige now help prop up Bashar al-Asad's legitimacy in Syria.

Yemen

While Yemeni security forces have at times made important arrests of al Qaeda members and like-minded groups, the government is often lenient toward violent jihadists, particularly those who direct their activities outside the country. Important terrorists have escaped Yemeni jails, often with the connivance of local security officials, and jihadists who went through the government's reeducation program reportedly later went to Iraq to fight against U.S. forces.[12] Sanaa seems to balance its crackdown on al Qaeda members with efforts to divert the jihadists' focus from Yemen to other countries—at this point, the Yemeni government and al Qaeda in Yemen have reached a "tacit nonaggression pact."[13]

U.S. diplomatic pressure on Sanaa to halt this accommodation will need to increase dramatically, and the United States should condition foreign aid in large part on Yemen's cooperation in counterterrorism efforts. In contrast to many other countries in the region, there are few American interests in Yemen to compete with counterterrorism.

A NEW WAY FORWARD: COUNTERTERRORISM TRADE-OFFS

As the new administration formulates a counterterrorism policy for the Middle East, it should consider two issues that are critical in framing counterterrorism policies: the consequences of a loss of U.S. international standing and the effect of democracy promotion on counterterrorism.

Regional Public Opinion

Personal testimonies and other evidence suggest that anger at U.S. policies has motivated many young men to take up arms to fight against U.S. interests. Perhaps more important, the unpopularity of U.S. policies has allowed terrorist organizations to portray themselves as heroic underdogs battling a cruel and brutal colossus. As a result, financial support for the organizations has remained strong, and regional counterterrorism efforts have attracted less popular cooperation.

The way in which the United States has framed the war on terrorism most likely has won more recruits to the jihadist cause. The focus on bin Laden, coupled with the inability to capture or kill him, has enhanced his stature among those attracted to militancy, helping al Qaeda recruit, raise money, and otherwise sustain the organization. In addition, the United States' frequent, explicit identification of terrorism with Islam has led many Muslims to believe that the war on terrorism is, in reality, a war against their faith. To some extent this is inescapable, since the jihadists are Muslim and they are the ones who cast their objectives in Islamic terms. Nonetheless, the language deployed by many U.S. opinion makers and the media makes it easier for Muslim populations abroad to see the United States as opposing Islam rather than terrorism. Therefore the incoming administration should continue the Bush administration's recent terminological shift in dropping the word *Islamic* before *terrorism*. In addition, presidential and other high-level statements should always make clear that U.S. counterterrorism efforts are focused on those who use violence, not those who simply dislike U.S. policies.

Pressure for Political Reform and Counterterrorism Cooperation

Perhaps surprisingly, according to senior U.S. counterterrorism officials, there was no lessening of cooperation with the United States in either Egypt or Saudi Arabia during the time that the Bush administration vocally deplored authoritarian governments and explicitly blamed the 9/11 attacks on the lack of regional political reform: rhetoric that in essence blamed allies for the deaths of Americans and painted their regimes as illegitimate. To the extent that Washington's criticism registered, Cairo and Riyadh probably concluded that cooperation with the United States in the effort to suppress violent extremism within their territories served their own interests. Cairo and Riyadh may have calculated that antiterrorism cooperation could help deflect U.S. criticism of their political systems or strengthen their argument that political reform would only help the terrorists.

For the most part, Arab regimes will continue to cooperate on counterterrorism efforts because it is in their interests to do so. However, the depth and scope of this cooperation could change if these regimes sour on their relationships with the United States. Regimes that sought to push back against U.S. pressure would have the option of confining intelligence liaison contacts to issues that solely serve their unilateral interests. For example, they might avoid arresting individuals who are a threat to the United States but not to the regimes themselves. They might also adopt a Yemeni-style approach of diverting local radicals to fight the United States in Iraq and elsewhere rather than confront them at home. Given U.S. reliance on liaison relationships to generate human intelligence for counterterrorism, a host government's decision to retaliate against serious pressure for reform by limiting the flow of information would put the U.S. administration in a difficult position.

A NEW WAY FORWARD: COUNTERTERRORISM POLICIES

Prioritization of counterterrorism is perhaps the most important issue for the incoming administration to consider. Since 9/11 the global war on terrorism has served as the United States' number one priority not only in the world in general but in the Middle East in particular. For the Middle East region, counterterrorism must remain an important factor in U.S. policy; however, it should not always drive that policy. In the struggle against al Qaeda and its allies—the most important counterterrorism concern for the United States—other issues, such as the security of Pakistan's nuclear program and energy security, must be taken into account as policy is shaped. Iran, a state sponsor of terrorism, is a menace more because of its nuclear program and subversion in Iraq than because of its support for groups like Hezbollah, however troubling that is. Since Israel is now negotiating peace with Syria, another state sponsor of terrorism, and an informal cease-fire with Hamas, an avowed enemy that embraces terrorism, the next president should recognize the advantages of alternative approaches to dealing with the terrorist threat.

The next president must focus on potential hot spots. As noted above, Iraqi refugees in Jordan and Syria could pose a problem to the two countries' stability. Strife in Syria could make the government more aggressive in its foreign policy if it seeks to divert attention from its failings. Massive unrest might destabilize yet another Arab state in the Middle East heartland, increasing the operational space in which terrorists and other radicals can operate on the borders of Jordan and Israel, America's allies. It therefore makes more sense, from a counterterrorism perspective, for the next president to support the Israeli-Turkish effort to put Syria out of the terrorism sponsorship business through peacemaking. In Jordan's case, the next administration needs to increase aid to help it handle its refugee challenge.

The next president should recognize the link between the deep anti-U.S. sentiment in the Arab and Muslim worlds and U.S. counterterrorism efforts. Changing America's image will be difficult but a new president (particularly one not associated with the Iraq war) is likely to get a positive reception in the region. This honeymoon, however, is likely to end quite quickly if U.S. regional policies on Iraq and the Palestine issue remain similar to what they have been. A new president could gain some goodwill by reenergizing Israeli-Palestinian negotiations, but compromise agreements could prove unpopular and any setback would also reduce the credibility of U.S. efforts to address popular grievances. Resolving or tamping down the Israeli-Palestinian dispute will not end terrorism, but it will diminish a potent grievance on which terrorists draw to recruit.

The next president also must consider programs designed not just to fight terrorists today but to prevent individuals from embracing terrorism in the future. Part of this challenge relates to issues of anti-Americanism or the lack of effective governance, as noted above. Yet the lack of freedom and economic opportunity in the Middle East can help generate terrorism as well. The president therefore should revitalize programs like the Middle East Partnership Initiative and push for economic reforms because both can aid the counterterrorism agenda.

Dealing with Regional Groups

The next administration will face a situation in which many U.S. allies are engaging with regional terrorist groups, such as Hamas and Hezbollah. As discussed, the main problem here is that engagement weakens any international pressure to delegitimize the use of political violence. At the same time, a U.S. military confrontation with these groups would only cause their popularity to rise; direct attacks would lead local populations to rally behind these groups and could lead them to retaliate by striking directly at Americans. Therefore, the next president should engage these groups only through allies rather than directly, refraining from implementing a military operation against them. Hamas is already being hit hard by Israel, and past Israeli attempts have often backfired when it pressed Hezbollah militarily. Because these groups are well integrated into their societies, only a massive on-the-ground effort would uproot them completely. And even then they would return if no credible replacement for them emerged. U.S. energies are best spent on discreetly supporting allied efforts to weaken these groups while helping build rivals for power that have local credibility. The track record, however, is not encouraging. The United States and Saudi Arabia unsuccessfully expended considerable effort to counter Hezbollah in Lebanon and put the elected government on a secure footing. U.S. Arab allies are likely to be weak reeds to lean on for this effort.

The next administration needs to understand that an Israeli-Syrian peace deal is no longer necessarily a guarantee that Hezbollah will not attack Israel or will otherwise be reined in. As noted above, Damascus's influence over Hezbollah is far less than it was in the 1990s, when Syrian-Israeli talks appeared close to success. As part of a peace deal, Damascus would have to stop allowing terrorist organizations to remain within Syria, but its ability (as well as its desire) to halt terrorist activities from Lebanon is questionable. As part of the deal, Damascus presumably would have to stop Iranian arms from transiting Syria. However, Hezbollah would still be able to smuggle in considerable quantities of weapons from other sources.

Dealing with Failed and Failing States

The problem of failing states has no simple answer, particularly in the Middle East. Directly deploying U.S. military forces (beyond intelligence and special operations forces) is likely to backfire, stirring up nationalistic resentment and further opening the door for al Qaeda and other hostile groups to gain a greater local presence and perhaps use this to attack U.S. forces as well as oppose U.S. allies. The United States should instead focus on several other measures, such as training police, improving local institutions, and developing local ties.

Building a strong police force is usually much more important than aiding conventional military forces. Police typically are far better suited to defeating small groups, as they often know the communities well and are trained to use force discriminately. Current U.S. programs to train foreign police forces suffer from several glaring weaknesses. The State Department's Antiterrorism Assistance Program has counterparts in the Treasury Department, the Department of Defense, and elsewhere, but all are underfunded and are not treated as part of the core mission of the host institution. The U.S. military often trains police as cheap light infantry rather than as a force whose role is vital in counterterrorism intelligence and local security.[14] The incoming administration should create a robust police-building program as well as ensure that it has a bureaucratic home.

U.S. programs to improve the rule of law, reduce corruption, encourage local economic development, and undertake other nonmilitary measures are often underfunded and understaffed. The problem of weak states is here to stay, and the United States has to augment its bureaucratic capabilities to deal with it. So far, no U.S. government agency has embraced these key missions. A new administration should assign these necessary missions directly to U.S. government agencies and provide them with the resources and coordination to carry out this task.

The next administration should set the building of local ties as a priority. As the United States discovered too late in Iraq, what happens at the national level often has little direct impact at the local level. Washington needs to forge political, military, and intelligence ties with a range of substate groups in areas where the central government is weak. This will involve building up more diplomatic, intelligence, and civil affairs assets in key regions and cities as well as with the national government.

Managing Iraq as a Counterterrorism Challenge

Recognizing that, to some degree, the conditions for AQI's resurgence are beyond U.S. control and that renewed civil war will have its own impenetrable logic, several steps can stack the deck against an AQI comeback.

The new administration therefore should continue to provide financial support for local parties opposing AQI because part of the tribes' motivations to fight AQI is financial, and cutting U.S. assistance reduces their incentive to remain opposed to AQI. Local U.S. commanders (or, in the event of a significant U.S. drawdown, U.S. intelligence officers), should have considerable flexibility in how to allocate money. The other part of the tribes' motivation is that they think fighting AQI will pave their way into the state apparatus—some even think that it will get them back their former status. If the tribes come to doubt these outcomes, their incentive to cooperate will evaporate, especially if the flow of money begins to wane. Pressing the Iraqi government to integrate Sunni leaders while suppressing the most extreme Shi'i forces reduces (though hardly eliminates) the chance that Iraq will again be sucked into the vortex of massive sectarian strife, which would make Sunni Iraqis more likely to work with Sunni extremists, such as those affiliated with AQI.

The next president should ensure that U.S. forces remaining in Iraq or in the region retain the ability to disrupt major AQI concentrations and back up tribal and government forces when necessary. Local fighters should be able to call on the United States for air support, and U.S. counterterrorism operations should focus on disrupting large-scale training camps or other major targets (smaller-scale disruptions should also be attempted, but the necessary intelligence is likely to be far more limited if the United States reduces its on-the-ground presence in Iraq). Such support will help tilt the playing field in favor of U.S. allies.

In addition to taking steps inside Iraq, the United States needs to recognize the potential for terrorism to spread. If AQI or similar groups reestablish themselves in Iraq, they could use the country as a launching pad for attacks on Iraq's neighbors and even beyond. The hotel bombings in Amman in 2005 are a potential model: the attack was largely planned and organized within Iraq, making it difficult for Jordan's competent security forces to stop it. Al Qaeda in Iraq or a similar group with a heavy foreign influence would surely be tempted to strike Saudi Arabia, given the long-held, lightly patrolled border between the two countries and bin Laden's long interest in destabilizing the Al Saud family. Ties are tight between Sunnis in Saudi Arabia and Iraq: resistance groups in Iraq have at times turned to Saudi religious scholars to validate their activities. As already mentioned, a great many of the Arabs fighting in Iraq are Saudis.

To minimize the spillover from Iraq, strengthening military and intelligence training programs for Iraq's neighbors is essential so that they can better manage any unrest that occurs in their countries. A diplomatic priority should be to discourage Iraq's neighbors from meddling in Iraq, particularly on behalf of the al Qaeda–linked groups or Salafi jihadist extremists whose ideology and goals are similar to those of al Qaeda.

The flow of refugees from Iraq is a serious counterterrorism concern. The Iraq conflict has generated more than 2 million refugees, and Syria and Jordan have taken in most of them. Refugees who are not assimilated or well policed often carry conflict back into their home state or into their new host country. Bored, uprooted young men in refugee camps are prime recruits for terrorist groups. Interviews in Jordan suggest that the country is not prepared for a long-term refugee presence. Services are at the breaking point, unemployment is high, and there is no long-term strategy for integrating the huge number of refugees. Increased aid for Iraqi refugees in Syria would also be an appropriate inducement for Damascus to behave responsibly in Iraq and Lebanon, and toward Israel.

Washington should assist Jordan, Kuwait, Saudi Arabia, and other allies in managing refugee flows and policing refugee communities. Dispersing Iraq's refugees will reduce dangerous pockets of concentrated refugees and reduce risks to Jordan in particular. Financial support is needed to reduce the strain on allied countries. The United States should also increase the number of refugees it accepts as a matter of moral responsibility and to provide leverage on other wealthy states that receive them too.

Working with Allies in the Region

The most important component of day-to-day counterterrorism is intelligence and police cooperation from allied governments.[15] This cooperation is a rare bit of good news in an otherwise dismal counterterrorism picture. In the Middle East in particular, the United States has long had strong counterterrorism relationships, and these have become even stronger since 9/11. The next president should take steps to ensure these partnerships remain robust. Equally important, the next president must make sure that improving these partnerships is well integrated into the overall relationships, ensuring that counterterrorism is taken into account when the overall bilateral relationships are evaluated and advanced.

SAUDI ARABIA

Saudi Arabia—a close ally of the United States—at times has functioned as a passive sponsor of terrorism. However, after the trauma of the 2003 attacks on the kingdom by Salafi jihadists, the regime turned decisively against al Qaeda and its local sympathizers, methodically arresting or killing radicals. Senior U.S. intelligence officers who were interviewed award generally good marks to Saudi counterparts for tenacity and willingness to share information with the U.S. government.

Nevertheless, many of the jihadists in Iraq come from Saudi Arabia, and wealthy Saudis still fund them as well as other insurgent groups tied to al Qaeda and radical religious schools in the West and the Muslim world.[16] The Saudi religious establishment still churns out anti-Shi'ah and anti-Western propaganda. The capacity of the Al Saud regime to stanch the flow is limited by the popularity of jihadist causes and the perceived political risks entailed in attempts to crack down on fundraising and recruitment. Moreover, the Al Saud regime relies on its ties to the religious establishment to bolster its domestic legitimacy. Thus it prefers to avoid alienating leading clerics or popular opinion on Islamist issues, even though both at times support violence that can ultimately harm the kingdom as well as neighboring states.

The Saudi government, however, has shown the ability to insist on clerical compliance on vital security issues. It has undertaken creative programs to suppress jihadist activity, combining better police work with a propaganda campaign that stigmatizes jihadists as sacrilegious. Saudi authorities also launched a new prisoner reeducation and rehabilitation program, which pairs prisoners with state-sanctioned religious leaders and counselors. Saudi officials maintain the program has an 80 to 90 percent success rate and a relatively low rate of recidivism.[17] This approach warrants close U.S. attention. The Saudi approach, in theory, offers a valuable nonmilitary means that has the potential to reduce terrorist recruitment and increase defections from terrorist groups. It also discredits the broader movement, as the disaffected and co-opted individuals are a powerful indictment of the group's message that it is following Islam's true teachings. These individuals' examples are particularly compelling for younger radicals, as they have street credibility, in contrast to the many other voices urging the rejection of violence. If the Saudi program proves to be effective, it should be a focus for global U.S. antiterrorism assistance and emulated in other countries after being adjusted to meet local conditions.

OTHER GULF COOPERATION COUNCIL STATES

Al Qaeda in Saudi Arabia, under increasing pressure there, is attempting to shift its attacks outside of the kingdom and to focus on neighboring Persian Gulf states instead. Since 2002 United Arab Emirate (UAE) authorities have arrested up to a dozen al Qaeda members whose countries of origin include Algeria, Iran, Saudi Arabia, Sudan, Syria, and Tunisia. A number of those arrested were planning major attacks or were key figures in the broader logistics and operations networks. There is a homegrown Sunni threat as well in the UAE, and some potential for radical activity among the 16 percent of the UAE's population that is Shi'ah.[18] A primary challenge is the UAE's weak banking laws, which enabled Dubai to serve as a hub for disguised jihadist financial dealings. As much as half of the $250,000 used to fund the 9/11 attacks is believed to have gone through Dubai. Although some banking laws have been strengthened, there is still a need for greater vigilance. The United States has a substantial investment in UAE security, yet, from an Emirati perspective, U.S. cooperation could be a lot closer, particularly information sharing. The next administration should recognize the vital role that the UAE plays in counterterrorism and step up cooperation in general as well as explore ways to improve information sharing.

JORDAN

The United States has long had an exceptionally strong counterterrorism relationship with Jordan. The Hashemite Kingdom has suffered from violence linked to al Qaeda and other Salafi jihadists, and in 2005, it experienced three near-simultaneous bombings of hotels in Amman that killed sixty people. In 1999 the Jordanian service disrupted a plot linked to millennium celebrations that would have been devastating. Jordanian officials are also concerned about Hamas and the growing prominence of Hezbollah, which they see as having the potential to radicalize Jordanian politics—a concern that, so far, seems unfounded, largely because King Abdullah has substantially reduced the space for dissent on this and other sensitive issues. In general, Islamist parties in Jordan opt for political participation, which necessarily entails acquiescence in U.S.-Israeli-Jordanian cooperation. There should be no mistaking this posture of submission for popular approval of the king's commitment to a security strategy that links Jordan closely to the United States and Israel.

For the new U.S. administration, that means bringing a fair degree of discretion to its partnership with the Jordanian court. Amman assists the United States with renditions and shares intelligence freely. Interviews with intelligence officials in Jordan suggested the keenness with which they view the relationship and their determination to keep it insulated from political controversy concerning Israel and Iraq. Israeli-Jordanian counterterrorism cooperation is close and effective, but the two partners have a strong incentive to keep the relationship under the radar.

ISRAEL

Israel has had to grow accustomed to terrorism, but during the second intifada, this concern alternated with the prospect of a nuclear Iran as the dominant security issue for the country. Since the height of violence in 2002, however, Israel has turned the tide, and deaths from terrorism are low, notwithstanding the implacability of Hamas, Hezbollah, and renegade Fatah elements. Despite their determination to attack Israel, Hamas and Hezbollah have competing priorities that might lead to tactical restraint. For Hamas, these include coping with Israeli operations against the group and the stranglehold Israel has on Gaza. Consequently, Hamas is now policing a temporary, informal cease-fire that has stopped most attacks from Gaza. Hezbollah, like Hamas, has local interests; hence its leaders' admission that the 2006 war resulted from Hezbollah's miscalculation, rather than a desire to spark a massive war. Nevertheless, Hezbollah has sworn revenge for the assassination of Imad Mugniyah, who led its terrorist wing—Hezbollah blames Israel for his death.

A significant risk for Israel is that it could become the target of the global jihadist movement. Al Qaeda and its allies have long opposed the Jewish state and at times have attacked Israeli and Jewish targets (in Kenya, Tunisia, and Turkey, among other places). Bin Laden and his deputy Ayman al-Zawahiri have also used the Palestine issue as a tool to win popularity among the Muslim masses. Although Israel's security services are vigilant against this threat—and Hamas's opposition to the Salafi jihadists has resulted in the closing down of the operational and inspirational space for them in the West Bank and Gaza—attacks on Israeli and Jewish targets outside Israel could grow.

U.S. counterterrorism relations with Israel are strong and involve a wide range of cooperation. Interviews conducted in Israel, however, suggest that government officials and analysts are far more concerned with Hamas and Hezbollah than they are with al Qaeda and other global jihadists. The latter are seen as a threat, but a secondary one. The next administration should continue the robust counterterrorism programs in place with Israel, with each side sharing information and otherwise cooperating on areas of mutual interest.

TURKEY

Although Turkey is neither Arab nor strictly a Middle Eastern state, it remains a regional transit hub for al Qaeda members and affiliated groups traveling between Europe, North Africa, and Iraq. Al Qaeda members have used the country as a haven. Indeed, Abd al-Hadi al-Iraqi, a senior member of the al Qaeda core sent by bin Laden to Iraq, was apprehended in Turkey in late 2006 and later transferred to Guantánamo.

More than half a dozen raids have been conducted, and hundreds of individuals have been rounded up, since November 2003. These cases involved Turkish militants' taking the initiative in trying to contact al Qaeda. However, al Qaeda is believed to have played a financial role in the plot by two Syrian nationals to bomb an Israeli cruise ship docked in the Mediterranean port of Antalya in the summer of 2005. One of the plotters is also known to have played a role in planning the November 2003 Istanbul bombings and to have fought in Iraq.[19]

The PKK use of Iraqi Kurdish areas as a safe haven from which to launch attacks into Turkey has led to Turkish incursions and provided the conditions for Iranian meddling in northern Iraq. The need to keep Iraqi Kurdistan from hosting the PKK and to keep Turkey from increasing its meddling in Iraq as a result has to be high on the new administration's agenda.

ALGERIA

Algeria is no longer plagued by the brutal civil war that brought the secular regime to the brink of collapse in the mid-1990s. As the regime bludgeoned its way to victory, it devastated the ranks of an exceptionally violent Islamist insurgency. Yet even as the threat to Algerian stability has diminished, Algerian terrorist groups appear to have broadened their ambitions and now are more focused on striking the United States and its allies throughout the Maghreb and Europe.

In late 2006 the most violent of the North African jihadist groups, the Salafist Group for Preaching and Combat (GSPC), merged with al Qaeda, under the banner of the al Qaeda Organization in the Islamic Maghreb (AQIM). (Al-Zawahiri himself approved the merger on the fifth anniversary of 9/11.) The rebranded group has shown remarkable regenerative capacity, despite the arrest or death of more than 1,000 members. AQIM recruits and attacks in neighboring Maghreb states. In 2007 AQIM plotted to bomb Western embassies in Tunisia. Additional plots have been uncovered in Morocco, and AQIM support cells have been discovered in Italy, Mali, Mauritania, and Spain.[20]

AQIM has also expanded northward and refocused its attention on Europe. AQIM is building on long-standing GSPC ties in Europe to plan future attacks. French officials have said that AQIM constitutes the biggest terrorist threat facing their country today. According to Europol, North Africans constitute the majority of terrorism arrests in Europe. Of these, Algerians make up the largest subset. Similarly, a joint intelligence report by the governments of France, Germany, Spain, and the United Kingdom from late 2006 found that of the roughly 200 Europeans who had undergone training and fought in Iraq, the majority were of North African descent. AQIM is reported to have formed a "regiment of emigrants" to carry out attacks in Europe.

U.S. ties to Algeria are not close, but they have improved considerably since 9/11, according to interviewed Algerian officials. Before then, the Algerian military regime was suspicious of Washington because of U.S. criticism over Algerian government brutalities during the height of the civil war with radical Islamists in the 1990s and skepticism over U.S. intentions in the region. After 9/11, and as more Algerian jihadists began to merge with al Qaeda, U.S. and Algerian perceptions of the threat began to align. Washington has now recognized Algeria as an important counterterrorism partner. This progress has been slow, however, as Algiers has often resisted a closer relationship. The next administration should try to steadily expand cooperation, recognizing that Algerian sensitivities and the lack of a robust bilateral relationship in general will make dramatic improvement difficult.

CONCLUSION

Even before the 9/11 attacks, it was clear that terrorism emanating from the Middle East posed a vital threat to the United States and its allies. In the years since 9/11, the United States has taken many important and overdue steps to improve its counterterrorism capabilities. At the same time, however, Washington has often failed to integrate counterterror-

214 DANIEL BYMAN and STEVEN SIMON

ism into its Middle East regional policy, to the detriment of both counterterrorism and other interests.

The next administration should continue to prioritize counterterrorism but not at the expense of other vital interests in the Middle East. Better counterterrorism will require more attention to the dynamics of the region and stronger coordination of the different U.S. departments and agencies involved in national security policy. The changes recommended above are designed to help move the United States in the right direction on counterterrorism without sacrificing, and indeed enhancing, other interests. Although such measures will not end the scourge of terrorism altogether, they will help make America and its friends safer than they are today.

NOTES

1. Dramatic terrorist attacks by militant groups have seriously undermined the reconstitution of Iraq, drove a wedge between the United States and Pakistan, destabilized Afghanistan, complicated U.S.-Saudi relations, and reduced the possibility of an Israeli-Palestinian accord. In Europe, terrorism stemming from the Middle East killed 191 people in Madrid in March 2004 and triggered the fall of Spain's pro-American government.

2. Bruce Hoffman, "The Myth of Grass-Roots Terrorism," *Foreign Affairs* 87, no. 3 (May-June 2008): 133–38; and Bruce Riedel, "Al Qaeda Strikes Back," *Foreign Affairs* 86, no. 3 (May-June 2007): 24.

3. David Kilcullen, "Countering Global Insurgency," *Journal of Strategic Studies* 28, no. 4 (August 2005): 597–617.

4. Author interviews of European security officials, May 2008.

5. Dan Murphy, "Al Qaeda Reveals Signs of Weakness," *Christian Science Monitor*, October 26, 2007 (www.csmonitor.com/2007/1026/p01s01-wome.html).

6. Hezbollah also is reportedly stepping up its direct role in training anti-U.S. groups in Iraq, but this is really part of a broader Iranian issue and should be dealt with in that context.

7. Hezbollah, with Iranian encouragement, has been active in training Iraqi Shi'i militants inside Iran and Iraq. In 2005 it sent a senior Lebanese commander to Iran to train Iraqi extremists.

8. See United Nations, *Report of the International Independent Investigation Commission Established Pursuant to Security Council Resolution 1595* (2005), p. 33 (www.un.org/News/dh/docs/mehlisreport/).

9. Author's interviews with Israeli officials in March 2008 and July 2008.

10. "Iraq's Kurdish Leader in a Bind," *Economist*, November 8, 2007, p. 78.

11. Emile el-Hokayem, "Hizballah and Syria: Outgrowing the Proxy Relationship," *Washington Quarterly* 30, no. 2 (Spring 2007): 35–52 (www.twq.com/07spring/docs/07spring_elhokayem.pdf).

12. Andrew McGregor, "Yemen and the U.S.: Different Approaches to the War on Terrorism," *Terrorism Monitor* 5, no. 9 (May 10, 2007): 5–8 (www.jamestown.org/terrorism/news/uploads/TM_005_009.pdf).

13. Brian O'Neill, "Yemen Attack Reveals Struggle among Al-Qaeda's Ranks," *Terrorism Focus* 4, no. 22 (July 10, 2007): 2 (www.jamestown.org/terrorism/news/uploads/tf_004_022.pdf).

14. William Rosenau, "'Little Soldiers': Police, Policing, and Counterinsurgency" (Santa Monica, Calif.: RAND, 2007).

15. Among others, see the chapters by Paul Pillar and Michael Sheehan in *Attacking Terrorism: Elements of a Grand Strategy*, edited by Audrey Kurth Cronin and James M. Ludes (Georgetown University Press, 2004).

16. One recent determination by U.S. military officials was that 41 percent of the foreign fighters in Iraq were Saudi nationals. See Richard A. Oppel Jr., "Foreign Fighters in Iraq Are Tied to Allies of U.S.," *New York Times*, November 22, 2007 (www.nytimes.com/2007/11/22/world/middleeast/22fighters.html).

17. An advisory committee of religious scholars, psychologists, and ex-militants meets with individual prisoners to discuss their background and experiences. The hope is that over time prisoners will recant. The ministry also runs six-week courses, described as "long study sessions," where prisoners interact with clerics and social scientists. The rehabilitation process includes the prisoners' families, who receive financial and other benefits. "Graduates" also receive help finding jobs. The dimensions of the problem are evident in the program's infrastructure, which includes five new specially designed prisons to house up to 6,000 inmates. As a practical indication of how Saudi authorities weigh the importance of winning hearts and minds, inmates get individual cells (unusual in Saudi jails where up to thirty individuals often are housed in a single communal cell) and lecture halls and classroom space. Roughly 2,000 prisoners are reported to have participated in the counseling program thus far, 700 of whom have been released. See Christopher Boucek, "Extremist Reeducation and Rehabilitation in Saudi Arabia," *Terrorism Monitor* 4, no. 16 (August 16, 2007): 1–4. (www.jamestown.org/terrorism/news/uploads/TM_005_016.pdf).

18. Radical preaching is overt in the city of Al Ain and the northern emirate of Ra's al Khaymah. (Chechen youths have attended a "training center for suicide bombers" in Al Ain.) Imams have periodically been arrested, particularly in Al Ain, and there have been reports of some mass arrests. Of the hundreds of mosques in Ra's al Khaymah, only a handful are under government supervision. Until recently the vast majority of the privatized mosques were funded and administered by foreigners. The United Arab Emirates is trying to get a grip on this situation by restricting the presence of foreign preachers, particularly South Asians, and requiring clerics to register with the Justice Ministry. These efforts, however, are likely to generate a backlash. Iranians constitute the largest expatriate group in the UAE after the South Asians. The UAE, especially Abu Dhabi, has long harbored fears that the large Iranian community in Dubai could pose a fifth-column threat to the UAE, and Iranian intelligence has established a substantial infrastructure in Dubai. Asked to name the more serious threat to security, senior UAE officials are more likely to name Hezbollah than al Qaeda. In the event of a U.S.-Iran confrontation, Iranian-sponsored terrorism against the UAE should be expected.

19. More recently, a German citizen was arrested on suspicion of involvement in a plot to bomb targets in Germany. His arrest in the town of Konya (where, incidentally, a number of arrests have been made) in November 2007 was tied to the arrest in Germany of three suspects, two German converts to Islam and an ethnic Turk, the previous month. In December 2007, Turkish authorities carried out raids in several cities, detaining nineteen members of an al Qaeda sleeper cell. In January 2008, a police officer was killed during a series of raids against al Qaeda militants in southeast Turkey. As recently as April 2008, police in Istanbul arrested forty-five people with suspected links to al Qaeda.

20. The Al Qaeda Organization in the Islamic Maghreb (AQIM) is suspected recently of two near-simultaneous car bombings of the UN and Constitutional Court in Algiers that killed dozens, including seventeen UN personnel; a suicide bombing outside the Algerian prime minister's office that killed twenty-five and wounded hundreds; a suicide bombing near the U.S. consulate and private American Language Center in Casablanca; and a suicide bombing of an Internet café in Casablanca.

About the Authors

STEPHEN BIDDLE is a senior fellow for Defense Policy at the Council on Foreign Relations. Before joining CFR he held the Elihu Root Chair of Military Studies at the U.S. Army War College Strategic Studies Institute. He has held teaching and research positions at the University of North Carolina, the Institute for Defense Analyses, and the Harvard University Belfer Center for Science and International Affairs. His book, *Military Power: Explaining Victory and Defeat in Modern Battle*, has won four prizes, including the Arthur Ross Award Silver Medal and the Olin Institute Huntington Prize.

DANIEL BYMAN is a senior fellow at the Saban Center for Middle East Policy at Brookings. He is director of the Center for Peace and Security Studies and an associate professor in the School of Foreign Service at Georgetown University. He has held positions with the National Commission on Terrorist Attacks on the United States (the "9/11 Commission"), the Joint 9/11 Inquiry and Senate Intelligence Committees, the RAND Corporation, and the U.S. government. He writes widely on issues related to U.S. national security, terrorism, and the Middle East. His latest books are *Deadly Connections: State Sponsorship of Terrorism* and *The Five Front War: The Better Way to Fight Global Jihad*.

ISOBEL COLEMAN is a senior fellow for U.S. foreign policy at the Council on Foreign Relations and director of CFR's Women and Foreign Policy program. She is the coauthor of *Strategic Foreign Assistance: Civil Society in International Security*. Her forthcoming book, *Paradise beneath Her Feet: Women and Reform in the Middle East*, will be published in 2009.

STEVEN A. COOK is a senior fellow for Middle Eastern Studies at the Council on Foreign Relations. He is the author of *Ruling but Not Governing: The Military and Political Development in Egypt, Algeria, and Turkey*. He has published widely on Arab and Turkist politics as well as U.S. policy in the Middle East. Before joining CFR, he was a research fellow at the Brookings Institution (2001–02) and a Soref Research Fellow at the Washington Institute for Near East Policy (1995–96).

RICHARD N. HAASS is president of the Council on Foreign Relations. Until June 2003 he was director of policy planning for the Department of State, where he was a principal adviser to Secretary of State Colin Powell on a broad range of foreign policy concerns. Previously, Haass was vice president and director of Foreign Policy Studies at the Brookings Institution. He was also special assistant to President George H. W. Bush and senior director for Near East and South Asian affairs on the staff of the National Security Council, 1989–93. He is the author or editor of ten books on American foreign policy, including *The Opportunity: America's Moment to Alter History's Course*.

MARTIN INDYK is the director of the Saban Center for Middle East Policy at Brookings. He served in several senior positions in the U.S. government, most recently as ambassador to Israel and before that as assistant secretary of state for Near East affairs and as special assistant to President Clinton and senior director for Near East and South Asian Affairs in the National Security Council. Before entering government service, Indyk served for eight years as founding executive director of the Washington Institute for Near East Policy. He has published widely on U.S. policy in the Middle East and the Arab-Israeli peace process. His book *Innocent Abroad: An Intimate Account of Peace Diplomacy in the Middle East* will be published in January 2009.

SUZANNE MALONEY is a senior fellow at the Saban Center for Middle East Policy at Brookings. She was responsible for Iran, Iraq, and the Gulf States and broader Middle East issues on the State Department's Policy Planning Staff. Before joining the government, she was the Middle East adviser at ExxonMobil Corporation and served as project director of the Task Force on U.S.-Iran Relations at the Council on Foreign Relations. She is the author of *Iran's Long Reach: Iran as a Pivotal State in the Muslim World* and a forthcoming book on Iran's political economy.

MICHAEL E. O'HANLON is a senior fellow of Foreign Policy Studies at the Brookings Institution. He is also director of research for the 21st Century Defense Initiative and senior author of the Brookings Iraq Index. A former defense budget analyst who advised members of Congress on military spending, he specializes in Iraq, North Korea, homeland security, the use of military force, and other defense issues. His latest books are *Hard Power: The New Politics of National Security* (with Kurt Campbell) and *A War Like No Other*, about the U.S.-China relationship and the Taiwan issue, with Richard Bush.

KENNETH M. POLLACK is director of research at the Saban Center for Middle East Policy at Brookings. He served as a Persian Gulf military analyst at the CIA, a senior research professor at National Defense University, and the director for Persian Gulf affairs at the National Security Council. His latest book is *A Path out of the Desert: A Grand Strategy for America in the Middle East*. He is also the author of *The Persian Puzzle: The Conflict between Iran and America*, *The Threatening Storm: The Case for Invading Iraq*, and *Arabs at War: Military Effectiveness, 1948–1991*.

BRUCE RIEDEL is a senior fellow for political transitions in the Middle East and South Asia at the Saban Center for Middle East Policy at Brookings. He retired in 2006 after thirty years' service at the Central Intelligence Agency, including postings overseas in the Middle East and Europe. He was a senior adviser on the region to the last three presidents of the United States as a staff member of the National Security Council at the White House. He was also deputy assistant secretary of defense for the Near East and South Asia at the Pentagon and a senior adviser at the

North Atlantic Treaty Organization in Brussels. Riedel was a member of President Clinton's peace team at the Camp David, Wye River, and Shepherdstown summits.

GARY SAMORE is vice president, director of studies, and Maurice R. Greenberg Chair at the Council on Foreign Relations. He is an expert on nuclear proliferation and arms control, especially in the Middle East and Asia. Samore has served as vice president for global security and sustainability at the John D. and Catherine T. MacArthur Foundation, director of studies and senior fellow for nonproliferation at the International Institute for Strategic Studies, and senior director for nonproliferation and export controls at the National Security Council from 1995 to 2001. He has written numerous works on proliferation, including three "strategic dossiers" published by the International Institute for Strategic Studies.

STEVEN SIMON is the Hasib J. Sabbagh Senior Fellow for Middle Eastern Studies at the Council on Foreign Relations. Before joining CFR, he was senior Middle East analyst at the RAND Corporation. He came to RAND from London, where he was the assistant director of the International Institute for Strategic Studies and Carol Deane Senior Fellow in U.S. Security Studies. From 1994 to 1999 Simon served at the White House on the National Security Council staff, following a career at the State Department where he specialized in regional security issues. He is the coauthor of *The Age of Sacred Terror*, winner of the Council on Foreign Relations's Arthur Ross Gold Award in 2004, and *The Next Attack*, which was shortlisted for the Lionel Gelber Prize for "best book on significant global issues" in 2006.

RAY TAKEYH is a senior fellow for Middle Eastern Studies at the Council on Foreign Relations. He is also a contributing editor of the *National Interest*. Takeyh was previously professor of national security studies at the National War College; professor and director of studies at the Near East and South Asia Center, National Defense University; fellow in international security studies at Yale University; fellow at the Washington Institute for Near East Policy; and fellow at the Center for Middle Eastern Studies, University of California–Berkeley. He is the author of the

Guardians of the Revolution: Iran and the World in the Age of Ayatollahs and *Hidden Iran: Paradox and Power in the Islamic Republic*.

SHIBLEY TELHAMI is a nonresident senior fellow at the Saban Center for Middle East Policy at Brookings. He is Anwar Sadat Professor at the University of Maryland and author of *The Stakes: America and the Middle East*. His many other publications on Middle East politics include *Power and Leadership in International Bargaining: The Path to the Camp David Accords*. His current research focuses on the media's role in shaping Middle Eastern political identity and the sources of ideas about U.S. policy in the region. He has served on a number of governmental commissions and as adviser to the United States Delegation to the United Nations.

TAMARA COFMAN WITTES is a senior fellow in the Saban Center for Middle East Policy at Brookings and directs the center's Project on Middle East Democracy and Development. Her most recent book is *Freedom's Unsteady March: America's Role in Building Arab Democracy*. Previously, she served as Middle East specialist at the U.S. Institute of Peace and director of programs at the Middle East Institute. Her work has addressed a wide range of topics, including the Israeli-Palestinian peace negotiations, Arab politics, and ethnic conflict. She edited *How Israelis and Palestinians Negotiate: A Cross-Cultural Analysis of the Oslo Peace Process*. She is also an adjunct professor of security studies at Georgetown University and a member of Women in International Security and the Council on Foreign Relations.

TOWARD A NEW U.S.–MIDDLE EAST STRATEGY:
PROJECT BOARD OF ADVISORS

The analysis and policy recommendations in these chapters represent the views of the authors of the papers alone. Board members critiqued drafts of each of the papers presented here, but they were not asked to endorse the views presented in any of the papers. In addition, neither the Council on Foreign Relations nor the Brookings Institution endorses the views presented in any of the papers.

Index

International Atomic Energy Agency
(IAEA): Additional Protocol, 108,
109; and Algeria, 96; and civilian
nuclear power program, 106; and
Iran nuclear program, 17, 78, 97,
99, 100, 101, 108
International Military Education and
Training assistance program, 176
International Monetary Fund (IMF),
170
Intifada, 140, 142, 146
Iran, 59–91; and counterterrorism,
80, 196–97, 203; current situation,
61–68; and democracy initiative,
84–86; diplomatic relations with,
68–72, 82–83; envoy for, 81–82;
mediators for, 84; negotiation
framework for, 76–81; nuclear
program of, 8, 65, 96–97, 100–03;
oil exports from, 5; recommendations for, 2, 8–9, 13–18, 72–88;
regional influence of, 5–6; as state
sponsor of terrorism, 52–53, 56,
64, 79–80, 109, 113–14, 195; timing of diplomacy with, 74–76
Iran-contra scandal, 68, 70, 72
Iran hostage crisis, 71
Iraq, 27–58; capacity improvement in,
183; and counterterrorism, 195,
198–99, 206–08; current situation,
31–41; ethnosectarian conflict in,
31–33; government of, 36–38; and
Iran policy, 63, 72, 78; Iran war
with, 64; Kirkuk, 30, 49, 51–52;
Ministry of Planning in, 46;
national military of, 33–36;
nuclear program of, 95; political
landscape of, 38–41, 49–51; recommendations for, 7–8, 41–54;
refugees from, 48–49, 207; and
regional actors, 52–54; second-
order problems in, 29–30, 46–54;
and Shi'i connections with Iran,
65; and Syria, 148; terrorism and

internecine violence, 46–48; U.S.
combat forces in, 1–2, 42–46,
54–57
Al-Iraqi, Abd al-Hadi, 211–12
Iraqi Army, 33
Iraqi security forces (ISF), 33–36; in
Anbar Province, 54; Badr cadres
in, 44; growth and capability of,
49–50; integration of, 47–48, 188,
206. *See also specific units*
Irbil, Iraq, 37
Islamic Salvation Front (ISF), 166
Islamic Supreme Council of Iraq
(ISCI), 39, 45, 197
Islamists, 165–67
Israel: and counterterrorism, 210–11;
and Hezbollah, 200; and Iran policy, 15–16, 63, 80; and NPT, 117;
nuclear capability of, 9, 95, 123;
and nuclear proliferation negotiations, 94, 113, 115–16, 125–26;
nuclear reactor strike on Iraq
(1981), 62; nuclear reactor strike
on Syria (2007), 96, 113, 122–23;
potential strike on Iranian nuclear
facilities, 113–15; U.S. mutual
defense treaty proposal, 116, 127.
See also Arab-Israeli conflict; Settlements; *specific peace negotiations and agreements*
Italy, 191

Al-Jaafari, Ibrahim, 40
Jaish al-Mahdi (JAM): and counterterrorism, 192, 199; and ethnosectarian violence, 32; and Iran, 197;
and Iraq elections, 44; and political
development in Iraq, 39, 40; status
of, 42, 47
Jalili, Saeed, 98
Japan, 73, 111
Jerusalem: and Arab-Israeli conflict,
154–55; poverty rates in, 141; settlements in, 134

80–81, 86; and Iran nuclear program, 116; nuclear deal with Pakistan, 96, 117, 126; oil wealth in, 165; policy recommendations, 181–82; political development in, 179–80; in WTO, 164, 180

Al-Saud, King Abdullah, 21, 168, 177–78, 180

Sectarian conflict. *See* Ethnosectarian conflict

Security barrier (Israel), 142–44

Serbia, 85

Settlements: and Arab-Israeli conflict, 142–44; expansion of, 142–44; freezing construction of, 21, 153; in Jerusalem, 134, 136; in West Bank, 134, 145

Shamir, Yitzhak, 115

Shanghai Communiqué (1972), 77

Shi'ah: and AQI, 192; and ethnosectarian violence, 32, 46–47; and Iran-Iraq relations, 65, 197; and Iran policy, 79; and Iraqi elections, 45; and political development in Iraq, 39–41; and U.S. military confrontation with Iran, 121

Shura Council, 179–80

Simon, Steven, 10, 187

Singapore, 189

Sky, Emma, 49

Small businesses in Iraq, 38

Solana, Javier, 98

Somalia, 191

Sons of Iraq (SoI): in Anbar Province, 54; and Maliki, 47, 48, 50; in security forces, 31, 52

South Africa, 84

Spain, 191, 213

State Department (U.S.): and counterterrorism, 205; and Iran diplomatic relations, 81, 82, 88; and MEPI programs, 183; state sponsors of terrorism list, 64, 195, 196

State sponsors of terrorism: and counterterrorism, 194–201; Iran as, 52–53, 56, 64, 79–80, 109, 113–14, 195

Status of Forces Agreement (Iraq-U.S.), 40

Succession law (Saudi Arabia), 180

Sudan, 195

Sunnis: and ethnosectarian violence, 32; insurgency by, 47; and Iran nuclear program, 116; and Iraqi elections, 45; in Iraqi National Police, 35, 188, 206; and political development in Iraq, 40–41, 50

Surge strategy: and ethnosectarian violence, 32; impact of, 29, 30; and local government capacity, 37

Syria: AQI in, 42; and Arab-Israeli conflict, 132, 137; and Bush (G. W.) administration, 147; and counterterrorism, 188, 197–98; and Hezbollah, 200; and Iran, 148; nuclear program of, 96, 113, 122–23; refugees in, 203, 207; as state sponsor of terrorism, 147, 195

Syrian-Israeli peace process: and Arab-Israeli conflict, 144, 148–49, 152, 203; and Bush (G. W.) administration, 147; and nuclear proliferation negotiations, 109; recommendations for, 2–3, 18–19; Turkey as mediator for, 134, 148, 149

Takeyh, Ray, 13, 14, 59

Telhami, Shibley, 19, 23, 131

Terrorist groups: as groups of concern, 193–94, 204–05; Iran support for, 52–53, 56, 64, 79–80, 109, 113–14, 195; in Iraq, 46–48. *See also* Counterterrorism

"Tooth-to-tail" ratio, 36

Trade and Investment Framework

THE BROOKINGS INSTITUTION

The Brookings Institution is an independent organization devoted to nonpartisan research, education, and publication in economics, government, foreign policy, and the social sciences generally. Its principal purposes are to aid in the development of sound public policies and to promote public understanding of issues of national importance. The general administration of the Institution is the responsibility of a Board of Trustees charged with safeguarding the independence of the staff and fostering the most favorable conditions for scientific research and publication.

In publishing a study, the Institution presents it as a competent treatment of a subject worthy of public consideration. The interpretations or conclusions in such publications are those of the author or authors and do not necessarily reflect the views of the other staff members, officers, or trustees of the Brookings Institution.

THE COUNCIL ON FOREIGN RELATIONS

The Council on Foreign Relations (CFR) is dedicated to increasing America's understanding of the world and contributing ideas to U.S. foreign policy. CFR accomplishes this mainly by promoting constructive debates and discussions, clarifying world issues, and publishing *Foreign Affairs*, the leading journal on global issues. CFR is host to the widest possible range of views, but an advocate of none, though its research fellows and Independent Task Forces do take policy positions. Please visit our website, CFR.org.

The Council on Foreign Relations takes no institutional position on policy issues and has no affiliation with the U.S. government. All statements of fact and expressions of opinion contained in all its publications are the sole responsibility of the author or authors.